MAD DOG

AN ENGLISHMAN

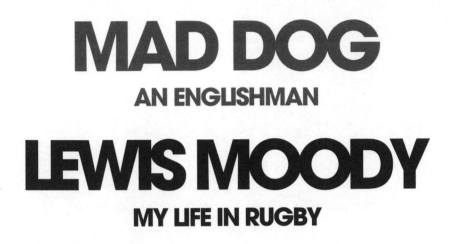

MAD DOG
AN ENGLISHMAN

LEWIS MOODY
MY LIFE IN RUGBY

with Ian Stafford

HODDER &
STOUGHTON

First published in Great Britain in 2011 by Hodder & Stoughton
An Hachette UK company

4

Copyright © LWM Sporting Consultants Limited 2011

A CIP catalogue record for this title is available from the British Library

Hardback ISBN 978 1 444 73433 1
Trade Paperback ISBN 978 1 444 73434 8
Ebook ISBN 978 1 444 73435 5

Typeset in Nexus Serif by Hewer Text UK Ltd, Edinburgh
Printed and bound by Clays Ltd, St Ives plc

Hodder & Stoughton policy is to use papers that are natural, renew-
able and recyclable products and made from wood grown in sustain-
able forests. The logging and manufacturing processes are expected to
conform to the environmental regulations of the country of origin.

Hodder & Stoughton Ltd
338 Euston Road
London NW1 3BH

www.hodder.co.uk

To my boys, Dylan and Ethan, who make me
smile through good and bad times

CONTENTS

ACKNOWLEDGEMENTS

I have been privileged to lead such a blessed life, and for this I am eternally indebted to my mum and dad, because their hard work gave me the many opportunities that have come my way. My dad taught me the true meaning of 'hard work' and I'd like to thank both my parents publicly for giving me the best start in life anyone could imagine. I love you guys.

I owe an enormous debt of gratitude to the many physios and medics who have helped me out of my gloom and back on to the rugby pitch. It is a cast of hundreds, maybe thousands – too many to name – but you know who you are and I can never thank you enough. They put in the hours to enable me to do the job I love with a passion, and without their hard work and dedication, and the surgeons who have rebuilt me over the many years, none of this would have been possible. Thank you so much.

Thanks also to Ian Stafford for his huge efforts in helping bring this book together. He is a journalist who has come through a pre-season training camp in rugby, a sport that is one of the toughest in the world, which more than qualifies him to write this book. Your work ethic is incredible, Ian, and I thank you for making this a truly enjoyable experience.

Many thanks also to my publishers, Hodder and Stoughton, in whom I have had total confidence from the very start. Roddy Bloomfield has given helpful advice at every stage and has always been encouraging and supportive. Sarah Hammond, his editorial colleague, has been full of sensible ideas and the model of efficiency, and Marion Paull, the copy editor, has been faultless. It has been a pleasure working with all of them.

I have benefitted from many sponsors over the years and I'd like to thank them all but, in particular, Guinness, who gave me the chance to make an everlasting record of my final days as a Leicester Tiger; Gilbert for supplying me with shoulder pads for the last ten years; and Nike for looking after the wellbeing of my feet for the last twelve years. Many, many thanks.

In Big Red Management I have the best management possible, headed up by my very good friends Mark Spoors and Louise Hewitt. Mark, I have enjoyed every moment of our time together. Your infectious enthusiasm is a joy to be around and never wears off. You are, as Jerry Maguire put it, my ambassador of quam. Louise, you have been my brain for the last few years. You have put up with my moaning and constantly had my best interests at heart. Your dedication to your work is exceptional and I could not have any more admiration for your professionalism. Thank you both so much.

I have to mention all my teammates for club and country, of course, whom I have had the great honour to play with and against over the years. From Bracknell minis to the British and Irish Lions, it has and always will be one of life's singular pleasures to have taken the field with you. The same is said to all my coaches, from Allan Gunner at Bracknell Under 10s to Sir Clive Woodward with England and the Lions, and to all the others from school to club and to country, who have all left their mark on the way I play the game.

Finally, and especially, I want to thank my wife, Annie, and my two boys, Dylan and Ethan, without whom my life would simply not function. I thank Annie for supporting me always, through the good times and the bad. I thank her for being my strength when I possessed none, and for putting up with all the crap while

I was away on tour or, as Annie called it, 'on holiday'. And I thank my boys for making me understand the true meaning of the word 'love'.

Lewis Moody, October 2011

Photographic Acknowledgements

The author and publisher would like to thank the following for permission to reproduce photographs:

Odd Andersen/AFP/Getty Images, Mark Baker/AP/PA Images, Henry Browne/Livepic/Action Images, Andrew Budd/Action Images, Lynne Cameron/PA Images, David Cannon/Getty Images, Paul Childs/Livepic/Action Images, Phil Cole/Getty Images, Andrew Cowie/Colorsport, David Davies/PA Images, Adam Davy/Empics/PA Images, Mike Egerton/Empics/PA Images, Kieran Galvin/Colorsport, John Gichigi/Getty Images, Paul Gilham/Getty Images, John Halas/Offside, Paul Harding/Livepic/Action Images, Richard Heathcote/Action Images, Eddie Keogh/Reuters/Action Images, Ross Kinnaird/Getty Images, Leicester Mercury, Matthew Lewis/ SWpix, Warren Little/Getty Images, Jamie McDonald/Getty Images, Brandon Malone/Livepic/Action Images, Phil Noble/PA Images, Steve Parsons/PA Images, Michael Regan/Action Images, Rex Features, David Rogers/Getty Images, Dan Rowley/Colorsport, Carl de Souza/AFP/Getty Images, Darren Staples/ Reuters/Action Images, Michael Steele/Getty Images, Paul Thomas/ Livepic/Action Images, Simon Watts/Offside, Haydn West/PA Images, David Wilkinson/Offside, Greg Wood/AFP/Getty Images.

All other photographs are from private collections.

GLOSSARY OF NICKNAMES

Alfie – Gareth Thomas, formerly of Cardiff and Wales, British and Irish Lions teammate, now playing rugby league.

Ashy – Chris Ashton, England teammate.

Backy – Neil Back, MBE, former Leicester and England teammate, until recently head coach at Leeds.

Balders – Adam Balding, former Leicester teammate.

Balsh – Iain Balshaw, former England teammate, now playing for Biarritz.

Banners – Matt Banahan, England teammate.

Borthers – Steve Borthwick, former England captain, Bath and England teammate.

Catty – Mike Catt, OBE, former England teammate.

Cockers – Richard Cockerill, former Leicester and England teammate, now Leicester's director of rugby.

Corbs – Alex Corbisiero, England teammate.

Cozza – Martin Corry, MBE, former Leicester and England teammate and captain.

Cuets – Mark Cueto, England teammate.

Daws – Matt Dawson, former England teammate, currently regular team captain on BBC's 'A Question of Sport'.

Deacs – Louis Deacon, England and former Leicester teammate.

Deano – Dean Richards, former Leicester teammate and head coach.

Dosser – Ian Smith, current Oakham School and former Leicester head coach.

Faz – Andy Farrell, OBE, former England teammate, now Saracens first-team coach.

Flats – David Flatman, Bath and England teammate.

Floody – Toby Flood, England teammate.

Fodes – Ben Foden, England teammate.

Garf – Darren Garforth, former Leicester and England teammate.

Geech – Sir Ian McGeechan, renowned coach of Scotland and the British and Irish Lions, currently performance director at Bath.

Geordie – Geordan Murphy, former Leicester teammate, Irish international and close friend.

Gomers – Andy Gomarsall, MBE, former England teammate.

Grewy – Danny Grewcock, MBE, former Bath and England teammate.

Gussy – Paul Gustard, former Leicester teammate.

Hask – James Haskell, current England teammate.

Hilly – Richard Hill, MBE, former England teammate.

Johnno – Martin Johnson, CBE, former Leicester and England teammate and captain, now England manager.

Kempy – Simon Kemp, England team doctor.

Lenny – Ben Youngs, England teammate.

Lloydy – Leon Lloyd, England and Leicester teammates.

Lol – Lawrence Dallaglio, OBE, former England teammate and captain.

Luges – Dan Luger, MBE, former England teammate.

Mearsy – Lee Mears, Bath and England teammate.

Minty – Nick Easter, England teammate.

Nobby – Dorian West, MBE, former Leicester and England teammate, now Northampton coach.

Noony – Jamie Noon, former England teammate.

Ossie – Austin Healey, former Leicester and England teammate.

Pasky – Phil Pask, England physio.

Pezza – Shaun Perry, former England teammate.

Potts – Stuart Potter, former Leicester teammate.

Robbo – Andy Robinson, former England coach, now head coach of Scotland.

Robbo – Jason Robinson, OBE, former England teammate.

Ronnie – Mark Regan, MBE, former England teammate.

Sammo – Paul Sampson, former England teammate.

Shaggy – Will Greenwood, MBE, former Leicester and England teammate, now Sky TV rugby commentator.

Shape – Shontayne Hape, England teammate.

Shawsy – Simon Shaw, MBE, England teammate.

Sheri – Andrew Sheridan, England teammate.

Sos – Matt Stevens, England teammate.

Stimmo – Tim Stimpson, former Leicester and England teammate.

Thommo – Steve Thompson, MBE, Wasps player and England teammate.

Tins – Mike Tindall, MBE, England teammate.

Topper – Scott Tindall, former Leicester physio.

Tweety – Dave Sylvester, England physio.

Vicks – Phil Vickery, MBE, former England teammate and captain.

Wellsy – John Wells, former Leicester teammate and head coach, now England forwards coach.

Whitey – Julian White, MBE, former Leicester and England teammate.

Wig – Graham Rowntree, former Leicester and England teammate, now England scrum coach.

Wiggy – Richard Wigglesworth, England teammate.

Wilko – Jonny Wilkinson, OBE, England teammate.

Woody – Tom Wood, England teammate.

Woody – Sir Clive Woodward, OBE, former England manager, now Performance Director of Elite Sports at the British Olympic Association and deputy chef de mission for Team GB at the 2012 London Olympics.

Worzel – Joe Worsley, MBE, England teammate.

Yog – Tom Croft, England and former Leicester teammate.

PREFACE

The sunshine of a New Zealand spring morning woke me three hours after I had fallen asleep. Annie, my wife, lay beside me in our hotel room, asleep and oblivious to my numb state of mind.

Had it really happened? Had we really lost to France the night before in the quarter-final? Were we really out of the World Cup?

It was all a little too much to take in. Like a child I lay there, hoping beyond hope that it had been a bad dream, and that this was the morning of the quarter-final, not the morning after. Try as I might, though, cold reality continued to numb my mind. There was absolutely nothing I could do to change what had happened twelve hours earlier in Eden Park. We had lost to France, an outcome that had never crossed my mind, not even when we were 16 points down at half-time.

It all felt so wrong in my head. Acceptance had not quite got the upper hand. My mind was blank. This really wasn't supposed to happen. I should have woken after leading my country to victory against our great rivals from across the Channel. The day ahead would have involved trips to the physios to patch up my battered body, handshakes and back slaps for a job well done, reviews of how we got the better of the French, and the first conversations with management and players, planning ahead to a World Cup semi-final against Wales.

Instead, there was nothing to do except start making preparations to leave Auckland and begin the journey home. Once we'd arrived at the knockout stage, this was always a possibility, but it was surprising how totally unprepared I was when the possibility became a reality.

Down in the hotel lobby, random people came up to me to say, 'Well done.' Well done? For what, exactly? We had just been knocked out of the Rugby World Cup at the quarter-final stage. They meant well. Of course they did. But there was nothing for which congratulations were due. England had played well below their potential for most of the tournament, and had clouded the issue further by off-field antics that gave the world's media a field day. And as captain, I had presided over this. It had been under my watch. I could not, and would not seek to, escape personal responsibility.

Back in my room I sat staring blankly at the walls. Annie had tidied up, taken a few cases down and met my mum and dad who, as always, were there for me. The telephone rang. The hotel wanted me out so that the next guests could move in. They rang again, and for a third time, because although I understood their request, I found it difficult to move. I was rooted to the chair, as if refusing to budge, reluctant to relinquish my World Cup hotel room.

Outside I could hear voices in French. Slipping my coat on and grabbing a suitcase I switched off the lights, opened the door and left the room for the last time. In the corridor, some of the French players whom I had faced in the quarter-final were moving in to the rooms vacated by the England players. You couldn't really make it up.

Worse, much worse, would follow. I entered the lift alone but, just as the doors were closing, a large hand forced them to open and in walked four of the French team, including Dimitri Yachvili. They looked at me, wearing my coat and holding my suitcase, nodded and each stuck out a hand to shake.

I have no particular problem with the French lads. They beat England fair and square on the night in Auckland, but did fate really have to decree that some of them would share a lift with me as I left the hotel, all packed and ready to walk away from a World Cup?

It was excruciating. I prayed for a hole to swallow me up. But I gritted my teeth, shook their hands, made some desperate small talk with Yachvili about training and said good luck to them all. I think they felt as uncomfortable as I did.

That's sport for you. For all the nuances, for all the adversity, for all the stories of heroes, emotion, valour and trauma, what it comes down to, always, is winners and losers. What happened in the Crowne Plaza in Auckland encapsulated this. Most of the people in the lift were joyous at their unexpected quarter-final victory over their fiercest rivals, but the remaining person had just been booted out of his room and indeed the World Cup by the very same people with whom he was now sharing that lift.

It was cruel, it was stark, it was almost funny, but it underlined the truth. We had lost, they had won, we were out, and they lived to fight another day.

Time, for me, had run out. I had already considered the prospect of retiring from international rugby even before the tournament had begun, no matter how England fared, and now my body pleaded for parole after an eleven-year sentence of being battered. The desire to play for England remained as strong as ever. I doubt it will ever fade. If I could turn out at Twickenham aged 70, I would, but my body would have given up on me three and half decades earlier. I yearned to spend so much more time with my understanding and long-suffering wife, and my two beautiful boys.

It would not be over completely. The thought of running out for my new club, Bath, in one of the most stunning cities in the country, on one of the most picturesque grounds in the world, was warming and consoling, but I knew, right then, that I had captained, and indeed played for, England for the very last time.

My Test career had ended in one of the greatest cauldrons in world rugby, Eden Park, Auckland. It had begun eleven years earlier in front of a small, slightly interested crowd on a North American tour, but in between I had won a World Cup and so much more for my country, let alone all the silverware with the Leicester Tigers, featuring some of the greatest players ever to have graced the professional scene.

It had been quite some journey, the highest of highs mingling with some desperate lows. So many injuries, so many operations, so many times premature retirement had crossed my mind. And then there was a demeaning illness that for a while dominated my life and made ordinary living practically impossible. Yet those summits so high that the clouds nestled way below had made every single moment of my time as an international rugby player worth it.

Never mind my misery that morning in Auckland. Never mind a lift full of those who had defeated me. It had been a quite wonderful, wonderful career and one, right then, which was difficult to fathom.

How could that skinny kid with poor eyesight and low self-esteem have managed to pull it off? How could that ridiculous student with little brains and even less common sense end up captaining his country on eleven proud occasions, including at a World Cup? How could that kid who displayed such total ineptitude when it came to the female race end up with a beautiful wife and two beautiful boys? How could any of it have happened?

Well, somehow it had, and as I waited in the hotel lobby before joining my family and heading out of Auckland, I began to piece it all together.

1
CLOSE SCRAPES
Tries and tribulations

To my family I am known as 'Little Lewy', which some people may think odd considering that, at 6ft 3in, I tower over everyone else, but it's because my father is also called Lewis, as was his grandfather. Dad must have won the argument with my mother, Heather, over my Christian name – when I suggested naming my first son Lewis as well, she, together with my wife Annie, were adamant that two living Lewis's were quite enough in the family. 'Every time I said the name Lewis both you and your dad would answer,' Mum explained, which must have been irritating.

Walton is my middle name, after great grandfather Lewis, and so another Lewis Walton Moody came into this world on 12 June 1978, at the Heatherwood Hospital in Ascot.

I had barely started with life before it was nearly over. Inside my first year a motorbike carrying a slab of concrete in a sidecar had smacked into the side of Mum's Volkswagen Beetle as she was driving around Binfield with me in the back in a baby seat on the passenger side. The motorcyclist ended up in intensive care, but recovered, and Mum, who jumped out of the Beetle screaming, suffered from whiplash. Luckily, I was unharmed but the car was a write-off.

In March 1980, I was in a great deal more trouble. I contracted croup, which is a respiratory condition that leads to swelling inside the throat and, in turn, a hacking, barking cough. One night it grew particularly acute and the doctors decided to hospitalise me the following morning. For the next few days I sat in a steam tent and then, with no signs of recovery, it was decided to perform a tracheotomy on me. After that, I was moved from Heatherwood to Wexham Park Hospital in Slough, where I was placed in intensive care.

My parents, who had followed the ambulance from Heatherwood to Wexham Park, kept a bedside vigil for the next few days. Eventually, my dad went home to sleep while Mum rested in a next-door room. One night I woke and reacted to the fact that I was in a strange room with a tube sticking out of my throat and my parents nowhere to be seen. I screamed, I cried and my face turned blue. The croup had turned into full-blown viral laryngitis.

The hospital tried to phone home to ask Dad to return as soon as possible – the doctors feared I would not be seeing the morning – but Dad was so tired he didn't hear the telephone ringing. It took the police throwing stones up at his window to wake him from his slumbers. It must have been horrific for him to have to follow the flashing blue lights of a police car as he raced to the hospital to discover whether his only child would live or die. Mum held me and managed to calm me down. For the next two weeks I remained in intensive care and to this day I bear the scar of the tracheotomy on my throat. Mum still gets upset talking about something that happened thirty years ago. She says it was the worst two weeks of her life!

This wasn't the end of my problems. As a child, whenever I contracted a cold or a cough, I would often be taken back to the same steam tent in hospital and have to sit there for days on end until my rasping breathing and hacking cough dispelled. The memories are hazy now, but I do recall waking up in the middle of the night at home on many occasions and freaking out because I lost the ability to breathe for long enough to scare me. I remember Dad sitting on my bed and calming me down, and I remember being in hospital when Valley Parade, Bradford City football club's ground, caught fire. I watched the news coverage on the hospital TV. That was on 11 May 1985. I was six years old.

By then, we had lived in Germany for a year and come back again. Dad was an engineer in the cement industry and, when I was three years old, he had been sent to Neubeckum, near Hamm, and the family went, too. This is a period of my life I cannot recall, except for being thrown under a fence once in the playground at the all-German kindergarten I attended! I was the only English-speaking kid there. By the time my family returned to Binfield I was speaking German as well as English. Unfortunately, this is no longer the case. I have barely uttered a single word since then and my bilingual talents are now long gone.

The ailments continued. In 1982 I was found to be allergic to chlorine in swimming pools. It produced a dry, barking cough and, with my history, nobody wanted to take any chances, hence the anti-histamines. To this day I cannot go too near horses because I have an allergic reaction that makes my face swell. It is just as well my lifelong ambition wasn't to become a jockey.

By the age of four my eyesight was so poor that I was forced to wear Milky Bar Kid glasses. Naturally, I became known as the Milky Bar Kid by all my little mates. Even worse, Windsor Hospital discovered an astigmatism in my left eye, which explained my short-sightedness. At home I had to wear a patch over my good eye to strengthen my bad eye. My parents tried to make out it was fun, and that I was a pirate. I'm not sure I quite saw it that way. I was switched to the type of spectacles you wear in the science lab at school and was stuck with them for quite a while until, much older, I realised it wasn't doing the trick with the ladies. So I turned back to my origi-nals and once again, this time in my teens, I was called the Milky Bar Kid. Eventually, I turned to contact lenses to help my rugby on the basis that it usually helps your game if you can see the ball. In the early days of contacts it felt like pouring acid into your eyes every time you put them in. Now I wear them all the time. Without them I would be rugby's answer to Mr Magoo!

Matthew Foster is the person who can be blamed for introducing rugby into my life. He was the son of my mum's friend Sue, and he came round to play one day while Mum and Sue had coffee. Matthew persuaded me to come with him to Bracknell Rugby Club, where they had a flourishing mini-rugby section. I was five years old and already loved nothing better than to run around, so to get the opportunity to do so with a ball, and to end up covered in mud having collected the odd bruise was my idea of heaven.

Even then the characteristics that are perhaps best known about me on a rugby field reared their head. While my new-found teammates enjoyed running and passing with the ball in hand, for me there was nothing better than to throw myself on the ball or run into people. Today, contact is discouraged for juniors playing the sport, which is probably right. Thank goodness that was not the case when I was five years old. It was love at first sight, and there is no doubt that contact was the main reason for this.

I remember once watching my dad play cricket for a local club. I was seven at the time. By the pitch a group of lads, aged 10 or 11, were playing rugby. I asked if I could join them and if we could tackle each other. The lads looked at me, some four years their junior, and quite sensibly suggested this would not be such a bright idea. In the first play I smashed one of them with a tackle and after that it was game on. Over the next thirty minutes or so they ran over me repeatedly, and I loved every single minute of it.

I was playing as a centre for my school team. I was bigger than most of my contemporaries and scoring loads of tries. Off the pitch, however, I continued to get into the kind of scrapes that would later litter my professional rugby career. Two instances stand out. First, when my friend Gareth Owen and I were playing golf in his back garden. Rather stupidly, I stood too close to Gareth, resulting in him impaling his driver into my forehead. I remember just standing there in a state of shock. His mother ran out into the garden just as my head exploded and blood shot out in all directions, which was the reason why I then started to cry.

Another time, Dad was on the end of a fearful bollocking from Mum after he allowed me to drive his sit-on lawn mower. On the face of it nothing should have gone wrong. All I had to do was sit on it, point it down the garden, and drive. Somehow I managed to hit the corner of the house. The heavy mower shot up the wall, I fell backwards on to the ground and the mower followed a split-second afterwards. Considering that it landed inches from my head, and the blades were still spinning round at a furious rate of knots, it was a near miss. Mum was not amused!

Will Carling was my hero at the time. He had just been made England's youngest ever captain aged 22 and, like me, was a centre. I was an only child so it often meant playing alone in the garden. I'd run about with a rugby ball, passing it to myself and shouting out the names of the England players of the time. Nobody got more mentions than Carling. I met him at a mini-rugby tournament held at Redingensians rugby club. Bracknell lost in the final to a much larger Welsh side, who beat us up. Meeting my hero, who looked resplendent in his purple England tracksuit, more than made up for the disappointment of losing the final. I persuaded him to sign a photo of himself that I had cut out of a newspaper and taken with me for the day. His simple 'To Lewis' message became my most prized possession and I have kept it to this day.

Nine years later Carling was responsible for my first serious mention in the national press. In one of my first senior games for Leicester, the Tigers were playing Harlequins at Welford Road and I managed to pull off a try-saving tackle on Carling. It was 1996, I was 18 and he was not too far off retiring from the game. The tackle merited me a few words in the national newspapers, which, at the time, I found very cool. To tackle my hero in a game was awesome but I wish I had said something to him, either after the tackle or after the game. The problem was that I was young and would not say much to anyone, even in the Leicester dressing room, mainly because most of the other players were icons of their day.

My other hero as a young kid was Daley Thompson. I liked the way he went about his business. He was obviously a tremendous character, whistling on the winner's podium, sporting suggestive T-shirts and performing somersaults on the pole-vault mat, but what I liked most about him was his all-round ability as an athlete.

At Eagle House I was the best at sport in my year, and by this I mean just about every sport – rugby, football, cricket, diving and most disciplines in track and field, ranging from the 100 and 200 metres to the high hurdles, the high jump and the long jump. At my final speech day before leaving for Oakham School and a new life, I was the recipient of five separate sports trophies. I was up and down to the stage like the proverbial yo-yo, and I found it faintly embarrassing. I was very proud, of course, to be praised as often as I was that day in front of all the parents and teachers, but I began wanting some other kid to win at least one sports trophy.

At Oakham I did not quite have it all my own way. Dad went to work at Ketton Cement, just outside Oakham, and the three of us moved to Rutland. Eagle House attempted to keep me on as a boarder, and even offered me a sports scholarship, but the Moodys left Berkshire for good. I was very sad to be leaving all my friends, but 10 year olds have little say in family matters.

At Eagle House, where there were 300 pupils, I had been the big fish in the pond. I was head and shoulders the best at sport, and I was also faring perfectly well in my academic studies. At Oakham, with 1,200 pupils, it was a different story. I remained the best in my year at rugby, and was pretty good at most other sports as well, but academically I was definitely lower than average, and found myself in the bottom sets for subjects such as Maths and English.

This was one of the reasons why my confidence became severely dented at Oakham for a good four to five years. I was reasonably popular, and it helped being the school rugby captain for my year, but I was neither cool nor a geek. I was your classic 'in-betweener' and therefore had a wide range of contrasting kids as my friends.

The advent of girls certainly challenged me. Eagle House had been all boys. Suddenly, at Oakham, I was surrounded by girls as well. It is fair to say I was clueless with the female section of the school. I did not understand them and never possessed the confidence to ask them out. I fell into the trap of becoming a girl's best friend. I was someone to talk to when, in reality, my motives were the same as every other boy. 'You're really good to talk to,' the girls would often say to me. 'Great!' I'd think, under my breath. It wasn't really the 'talking' bit that interested me. In all my time at Oakham, some eight years, I had two girlfriends, and that's if you count my first relationship with Clare Sullivan when we were aged 11 that lasted two days. I asked a friend of mine to end it for me – that's how good I was with girls. He failed to do so, she thought we were still going out, and it all became a little messy for a while. Then there was Chloe Knights, when I was 14 years old. She was the first girl I kissed, which makes me wonder what I did with Clare. She was very attractive and we managed to hold down a relationship for all of a month. There were the usual snogs and petting at village hall and on the tennis courts, but in terms of girlfriends that's your lot until, aged 20, I met Annie, who would become my wife and mother of my two children.

My late puberty hardly helped matters. I was the youngest looking 15 year old imaginable and I possessed a very high voice until well into my fifteenth year. The worst aspect of this was seeing everyone else changing in front of my eyes, while I stayed the same. Playing sport as often as I did resulted in taking loads of showers, where boys would obviously notice the stages of puberty. It really stressed me out. I remember checking my nuts every single day and saying to myself: 'Where's my fucking hair? Where's my fucking hair?' It was a day of sheer, unadulterated triumph when the first, short and curly sprig of pubic hair finally appeared like a snowdrop after winter.

Although my spiralling academic performances, my ridiculous National Health glasses and my complete inability with girls played their part, what really dented my self-esteem was the verbal bullying I was subjected to throughout my time at Oakham, but especially between the ages of 10 and 14, which, of course, are particularly formative years.

The crux of it was that a number of the boys in my year, and in the years above, would call me stupid, because I had a knack of speaking before engaging my brain – a trait that most people who know me in rugby would agree I still have. But when the 'stupid' tag came out, I reacted, which is a major error in any school playground or classroom or on any school playing field.

As a kid, I was very self-effacing and never wanted confrontation. But I hated being called stupid and made it known early on, which made me an easy target and, boys being boys, they honed in on me. In the greater sphere of life it may not seem such a big deal but, at the time, I found it very upsetting. Kids look for any chink in someone's armour and then pile in. Even though I was the rugby captain in my final year, which, at a school such as Oakham, was a significant badge of honour, a weak spot had been found and was exploited to the hilt. Often the cooler lads were the worst, especially the more intelligent ones. They clearly felt superior to someone who was not, academically, in their league. It did not help being one of the youngest in my year, either.

I was a day boy assigned to a boarding house, and this meant I lived at home but used the boarding-house facilities. Sometimes, when I was older, I'd stay overnight in the boarding house if it was my turn to take charge of the younger kids. I remember many nights sitting on my bed in the dorm, or back at home in my bedroom, disconsolate after another day's battering by my contemporaries. I think some of them truly believed it was harmless fun. Even my so-called friends were at it. I don't believe any of them had any idea just how wounding and belittling it was.

It caused me a great deal of stress. In 1990, for example, when I was 11 and 12 years old, I suffered from acute stomach pains, which, when finally diagnosed, proved to stem from a chronic form of colic brought on by the stress of school life. The stomach-aches would continue for much of my time at school.

I remember once when a friend discovered that I was sitting on the toilet. 'Is that you, Lewis?' he shouted. 'Yes,' I replied, with an obvious tone that said, 'Go away, I'm on the loo.' This prompted him to sing: 'Moody is moody, Moody is moody.' I reacted and the next minute there were half a dozen boys chanting the same phrase over and over again for over half an hour. I just sat there taking it in and refusing to leave the cubicle until they had gone. Looking back, having kids singing 'Moody is moody' hardly seems the worst thing to hit you in life, but at the time it was indicative of how I was treated by some at Oakham, and how insecure I became.

This affected my personality. I used to find summer holidays quite depressing because most of my friends were boarders who went back to their homes, which were dotted all over the country, leaving me with just a few kids to play with back in Ketton. I remember becoming friends with two village lads until a third boy joined us. Over the next few weeks he succeeded in turning the others against me until I was bombed out of the group. That absolutely devastated me and I cried my eyes out back home. I used to be on the receiving end of that kind of treatment at school. I never thought it would affect me away from school life as well.

I lost my temper just once. I was 17 at the time, and the first XV had just lost a game against Bedford Modern. I was distraught at the loss and when a friend started to take the mickey out of me, both for being cross about losing what he saw as a silly game, and also for being stupid, I pinned him up against a wall and told him, in no uncertain terms, never, ever to question rugby or my intelligence again. It seemed to do the trick. From that day onwards he never ventured into those evidently delicate areas again.

Rugby was my way to escape the bullying. It mattered an awful lot to me. I played for the school senior first XV in my final two years at Oakham, captaining the side in my final year. In truth, we were not the best team. I think we won nine and lost three that year. The better, Daily Mail Cup-winning sides that featured Tom Croft, Matt Smith and Alex Goode would come later. We had good times, though, none better than the traditional first XV drink after every game in the same Oakham pub, where we would sing songs, play games and feel very much part of a family. My own family used my rugby to force me to do my homework, go to bed, eat my vegetables and pretty much everything else as well. No homework, sleep or vegetables meant no rugby training at the weekend with my local club. It was what drove me and my parents knew it.

It also served its purpose away from the rugby field. I had been made to feel intellectually inferior and I began to use my ability as a rugby player as a defence mechanism. At 14 I became a Leicester Tigers colt, and then continued to play for the junior Tiger teams throughout the rest of my time at school. I also played for my county and for the Midlands. By 16 I had been selected for the England Under-18s. It was not something I rammed down people's throats. Far from it. I remained the self-effacing individual that I like to believe I am to this day. Yet there is no doubt that my progress in rugby provoked some jealousy within parts of the school, and motivation to pick on me whenever possible. Ironically, that helped my rugby career. I channelled all my anger and frustrations into my game. It was an area – the only area – in which I excelled, and I knew I was better than anyone else. When the boys teased me, I'd try to laugh it off to their faces, although not very convincingly. In truth, it was a huge, emotional challenge and one that, in time, forced me to deal with my character and figure out who and what I was.

If I have painted a picture of a desperately unhappy school life, this is only partly true. There were many good times, too, and many scrapes. Some were funny, others very concerning – the sort of adventures teenage boys often get up to and laugh about. Only now, at the age of 33, can I look back and realise how close to the line I came on so many occasions. Despite the unhappiness, mainly in the first four years at Oakham, when I recall my days there, the good times outweigh the bad. The memories are primarily happy. Not only that but it was and remains a very fine school that gave me the best opportunity academically, something I failed to fully grasp, and also on the sports field, where I feel I took my chance with both hands.

At 14 I got drunk for the first time in my life. It's not so much the getting drunk part that makes me shudder. That, after all, is one of a teenage boy's rites of passage. It was more the where and the how. Picture it – speech day, and parents and boys had gathered on the headmaster's lawn. Boys had a chance to sip a little wine, but it was probably not a good idea for me to sneak off with a bottle for myself and a friend. Four glasses later I could barely stand, the world was spinning in front of my bleary eyes and I had no idea what was about to hit me. For some reason, my parents did not recognise that their son was inebriated, even though I introduced them to a Spanish exchange student from whom, an hour earlier, I had managed to steal a few kisses, thanks to my temporary drunken boldness. Unfortunately, in front of my housemaster's wife, Mrs

Harvey, I tripped over my own, wobbling feet and fell head first into masses of filled strawberry punnets meant for parents. When I stood up, I resembled a man who had been shot fifty times. My white school shirt, my trousers and my face were covered in blood-coloured strawberry juice and crushed berries. Luckily for me, the housemaster's wife was so upset by the ruined speech-day strawberries that she never got round to questioning why I had fallen into the punnets in the first place.

There were other times when I was not so lucky. In the first year of my 'A' levels, my penultimate year at Oakham, I was suspended, along with a number of other boys, for a week. A rather cocky third year walked up to the sixth-form area and started mouthing off to a group of us. We grabbed hold of him in what was supposed to be nothing more than a slightly boisterous but still jokey flexing of our sixth-form muscles. Then it all went wrong. One of the older boys appeared with a BB gun (an airsoft or pellet gun) and shot the third year in the knee. There could not have been anything more than some cork or a paper pellet in the gun because the third year laughed about it and walked away. He had been giving as good as he got. It was not uncommon at the school. I remember being repeatedly shot at by older boys with BB guns loaded with paint balls when I was in year three, both inside and outside the school buildings. It was all a bit of a wheeze back then, although, as a slightly more mature person these days, I appreciate the dangers of shooting BB balls at people.

Much later that night I was woken by my parents wondering why the housemaster had called home so late and why he wanted to see me first thing the next morning. It turned out that the year three boy had complained to his parents, quite rightly in hindsight, who, in turn, had notified the school. The one-to-one interrogation I was subjected to the following day was intimidating. In the end, three other boys and I were suspended. The boy who had fired the BB gun was expelled, as was the gun's owner, who had played no part in the incident and could count himself unlucky that someone else had thought fit to borrow the gun without his knowledge.

There was uproar at the school. It was felt by most of the other sixth-form boys, some teachers and the parents concerned that it was unfair to suspend what became the 'Oakham Four' because another boy had taken it upon himself to fetch and then use a BB gun. I was very embarrassed to be branded a bully by the school. Whatever faults I may have possessed, I didn't see being a bully as one of them, especially as I knew what it felt like to be bullied. I also grew increasingly angry at the injustice of it all. During the week out of school, the affected boys and their parents got together for a series of meetings. It was all rather exciting. The boys wrote a joint letter, aided by our parents, and Mum and Dad handed it in personally to my housemaster who, in turn, discussed the matter with the head. It did the trick. We were all reinstated, the charge of bullying was withdrawn and a notice sent around to that effect. I returned to Oakham feeling as if I had beaten the system.

As well as alcohol, I also dabbled in cigarettes and drugs, although both in a very minor capacity. I once used a bong (a kind of water-pipe, for those who don't know) to smoke some pot. I was 15 and with some schoolmates in a field outside the school premises one evening. The immediate after effects were these: one, I fell backwards into a thorn bush and lay there unable to move; two, I thought I was going to die; and three, I was in personal agony for ten minutes and vowed that I would never touch the stuff again.

One night, during my penultimate year at school, I was offered drugs by an older boy in a pub nearby. The tablets were in a small, see-through plastic bag and looked suspiciously like Es. Now, by then, I'd got drunk, been caught smoking, which led to me having to clear the school's pavements of chewing gum for two days, and smoked pot, but I drew the line at this. This was a different league all together and I wasn't interested. It proved to be one of my more sensible decisions. My friend, who was with me in the pub, accepted one of the tablets. A couple of days later I was dragged out of my classroom during a lesson – I still feel the increased heart beat from that moment – and found myself once more being interrogated by the housemaster on behalf of the head. The older boys had been caught dealing drugs. I was asked if I had been offered drugs and whether I had taken any, and whether my friend had. I admitted to being offered some but said no to the two other questions. The next day I was dragged in front of the housemaster again. This time he said they had overwhelming evidence that my friend had accepted some drugs. I felt under severe pressure. It was seriously scary stuff. In these circumstances, I confirmed this to be true. It turned into a major scandal for the school. Five boys were expelled from various years for drug-related issues, and even the national newspapers wrote about it. My friend, fortunately, received just a suspension. This made me feel a great deal happier about myself, although, to this day, I regret confirming the housemaster's evidence.

My two best friends were Jim Knowles and Simon Feek. Jim's now in the army and has seen action all over the world, from Northern Ireland to Bosnia, Iraq and Afghanistan. Feek was and is, it is fair to say, one of life's characters. I passed my driving test at my third attempt. The next day, Jim, Feek and I headed off to a nearby field, me driving the second-hand 1970s Volkswagen Beetle that my parents had bought for me, and Jim his motorbike. I loved my orange car, even if all my friends thought it was a heap of rubbish. It should have been a happy occasion. We had a beer, we played our music loud, and Jim let us ride his bike.

Then Feek asked if he could have a spin in my car. Jim, who unlike Feek was trustworthy, said he would sit alongside him to make sure nothing went wrong and it was difficult to see what could go wrong. Feek was going to drive my beloved Beetle up a straight 150 metre track, turn and come down again, while I continued to ride Jim's bike.

Moments later, an ashen-faced Feek appeared. 'Mate, I've had a night-mare,' was all he could say. He hopped on to the back of the bike and we sped off to where he had planted my car. Feek had hit a pothole, panicked and spun the car. My Beetle was now sticking out of a hedge with a wing hanging off. Somehow, using pieces of string, we managed to tie everything down and I drove the remains of my car home.

My parents were not Feek's greatest fans. They thought he led me astray. It was right at the end of my time at Oakham and I didn't see the point in dropping my best mate in it, so I told Mum and Dad that I'd crashed the car. They called me an idiot and insisted I paid them back the £800 worth of damages. It took me most of that summer, working as a waiter at Barnesdale Lodge on Rutland Water, to repay them.

Ten years later the truth emerged on my wedding day. Feek spoke about what had really happened that day during his best-man speech, and handed over an £800 cheque to my father. My parents were taken aback, both by the truth and by my loyalty to my friend. It was a special moment when a ten-year-long school secret was finally revealed.

There was still time for one more escapade, which Oakham may not be too happy about. On the final day of term – on the final day of my final year – I decided to steal the school flag, fluttering proudly beside the cricket pavilion while the first XI played the Old Boys. It was hardly a clandestine operation. It was speech day, for goodness sake, and half the school's parents and all the teachers were mill-ing around, but somehow nobody noticed a blond 18 year old pull down the red, black and red stripy school flag and sneak off with it. That was in 1996 and I still have the flag, back in my old room at my parents' house in Ketton. I suppose I should return it. They may have noticed at some point in the last fifteen years that their flag has gone missing!

My school days were over. That summer I received my 'A' level results. A 'B' in Design was fine, an 'E' in Geography not so impressive and a 'U' in Biology fairly disastrous. It takes a long time for a boy to become man enough to admit that he wishes he had listened to his parents when they advised him to work harder and to revise properly. I did neither because, in part, I knew I was good at sport and saw it as my future, but if I could live my life again, I would most definitely try much harder with my 'A' levels.

As it was, I did have somewhere to go after school. It may not have been Oxford or Cambridge University, but it was the Oxbridge of English rugby and it was called Welford Road.

2

TIGER CUB

The early years at Leicester

I first turned up at Oval Park, the Leicester Tigers training ground, at the ripe old age of 14, and thereafter I went whenever my school commitments allowed me, which, to begin with, wasn't too often. I was a nice public schoolboy mixing with primarily comprehensive boys from Coventry. One of them, Leon Lloyd, would become one of my best friends but back then he was keen to shove the pretty boy's face in the dirt. When I tried to tackle him in my first contact training game, I ended up on my backside. In the corner of the ground was a huge mountain of dirt and mud, which we were ordered to run up and down. It was a not-too-gentle eye-opener to me of the niceties of club rugby.

For two years, my parents, and usually my mum, would drive me for forty minutes from home to Oval Park and back again after school, and in the spring, when Oakham turned to hockey as their main sport, I would either play youth games for Leicester or watch the Tigers from the Welford Road stands, chanting 'Deano, Deano,' after the legendary figure that was and is Dean Richards.

Then, when I was 16, Brian Welford decided I should switch from centre to the back row. Brian was not only the junior rugby coach at Oakham but also the Midlands coach, who had a personal 'in' with the Tigers. Ian 'Dosser' Smith, the school's first-team coach and Tigers' head coach, was running his eye over me.

Dosser was another of those Leicester legends, a man who played 331 times as a flanker before Neil Back took over, and captained the

17

Tigers between 1983 and 1985. The stories about Dosser were many and often mythical, although the fact that he once played for the Tigers with two torn hamstrings appears to be true.

I was far from happy with the idea. I'd been a centre all my life and, at first, playing at number eight, I felt as if my game had suddenly been neutered. In a county trial match, however, I was switched to seven and this was my 'eureka' moment. Suddenly, the field opened up and I carved my way through it. I knew right then that I had found my position. Within weeks I was picked for the England Under-18 'A' team, despite being a year younger than most of the others. It wasn't the best experience. We played the New Zealand All Blacks somewhere up north, and as a sub I stayed rooted to the bench for the whole game. This was back in the days when subs were not used unless there was an injury. I roomed with Matt Salter, who would go on to captain Bristol, he barely said a word and felt as if I was in someone else's world.

That summer I toured Ireland with the Leicestershire County Under-18s, which was my first proper rugby tour. Graham Willars, who played for the Tigers an incredible 338 times over a twenty-eight-year span as a blindside, was the team manager. That was a huge deal. Everyone looked up to Graham at Leicester, and it was the mark of the man that when cancer took him from us at a young age, more than a thousand mourners attended his funeral. Strangely, the stand-out moment from that tour was not one of victory or defeat, but a ridiculous incident involving our captain, Richard Pope, who in his pumped-up way sprinted to the halfway line after we first emerged from the dressing room, stooped to pick up the ball, slipped and ended up head first in the mud.

That autumn was my last rugby term at school. Even back then, Dosser taught me something that has never left me, and goes a long way towards explaining the way I play rugby, and the catalogue of injuries I have suffered as a result. The message was this: you do whatever it takes to help your mates in a game, whether it's getting hold of the ball, or stopping others from doing so. If this means taking a good kicking, then so be it. The ball, not your body, is paramount. That simple but powerful message has never really left me.

He also gave me my first insight into captaining a rugby team. I was the Oakham School first XV and also Midlands captain at the time, and at our end-of-season dinner one of the younger lads in the side got totally smashed on alcohol. I had already delivered the captain's speech and now, on Dosser's instructions, had to look after the kid. Ironically, it would be the last time I would captain a side – apart from a couple of occasions as a stand-in at Leicester – until Martin Johnson asked me to lead England in March 2010.

Earlier, in the spring of 1995, I played for the England Under-18s in the Five Nations campaign alongside Andy Long, Pete Richards and Joe Ewens, although we were nothing to write home about, and failed to trouble the better nations. I was also playing for the Tigers colts side, coached by Pete Low and Roger Dakin, Leicester men through and through, who were very old school in their approach to the game.

At one game, away from home, we walked out of the changing room through a tunnel of reserves and the coaches, made purposefully narrow to pump us up. One of our props, Simon Black, was a dangerous character at the best of times. Everyone knew him as 'Barnesy' after Barnes Wallis's bouncing bomb. The coaches were shouting at us to fire us up and when Pete punched Barnesy as he walked past, Barnesy responded by landing such a fierce punch in return that our main coach was knocked flat on his back. It was an unnerving sight to see as you made your way out on to the field of battle.

As school ended, I contemplated joining the army but an event occurred during the summer to change my mind. The previous August, rugby had suddenly – too suddenly for many – turned professional and, out of seemingly nowhere, I had the chance to make a living out of a sport I loved. A guy called Pete Lloyd planted the idea in Dosser's head that I should be given a chance to join the Tigers' senior squad. Pete was just about the club's biggest fan. He was neither a player nor a coach, although he ended up being an unofficial scout, but he was a friend of all the players and had their ear. I was an 82kg (13 stone) streak of piss at the time but Dosser took the gamble and invited me to join the senior squad for the summer.

I remember absolutely bricking it on the first day I arrived at Oval Park as a senior squad member, driving the same orange Beetle with a grey wing that my mate Feek had mangled weeks before. For the previous four years I had always changed in the youths' dressing room but on this day I made my way to the first-team's area to be met by the incredulous faces of my hero, Dean Richards, and Dorian 'Nobby' West.

'The youth team's dressing room's down there, lad,' proclaimed Deano, waving his giant paw in the general direction of where he thought I should be.

'Er, actually Mr Smith has sent me here,' I replied, barely able to look at them. To Dean and Nobby it was Dosser, but to me, fresh out of Oakham, it was 'Mr Smith'.

We had to run three times round the whole Oval Park area, taking a break between laps. On the first two I caned everyone by a good 200 metres. During the third, which I again led by a good distance, I feared that the senior players would consider me to be a cocky twat, straight out of school, on my first training session, and absolutely burning all the well-known players. Richard Cockerill, the then England hooker, was closest to me and I took the ridiculous decision to let Cockers pass without making it obvious. I didn't want to be seen as an upstart. Now I look back and wonder, 'What the fuck was I thinking?' I should have shown the boys from day one that I was not the type who would ever give up. Despite all the success that would follow in later years, I look back on that incident and regret it intensely to this day.

In August, Leicester hosted a four-team pre-season tournament, with Boroughmuir, Agen and a Welsh side. It was at Welford Road, in front of a sell-out crowd, and I would be making my first-team debut in Leicester's first-ever game as a professional rugby club. In the team that day were Rory Underwood, John Wells, Graham Rowntree and many other legendary Tigers players. Dean was on the bench but he brought the forwards into a huddle when we met in the Mission for the Blind over the road from the stadium for a pre-match team talk.

'What's the back-row calls, Lewis?' he asked me.

Of course, I had no idea, which was a fairly inauspicious start to my first-team career. I'd been put on the spot and floundered, a trait that rears its head sometimes, even now.

We walked over the road and changed in the bar, which would soon be renamed 'Deano's Bar'. Dosser decided this would be a good moment to calm me down.

'As soon as you walk out of that door your heart will be beating out of your chest,' he said, pulling my face close to his. 'Fifteen thousand people will be screaming out there. All you need to know is that we are Leicester. We are Leicester. WE ARE LEICESTER.'

Far from calming me down, all this had the reverse effect. Then came his *pièce de résistance*.

'You need to remember three things,' he went on. 'One – tackle.'

I thought, 'Right, got that, what's two? Don't give penalties away? Stay low? Put your body on the line?'

'Two – tackle.'

Now I was really struggling to imagine what his third point would be.

'Three – tackle.'

Midway through the first half I received the ball from John Liley, looked up and saw that Rory and I were against only Iwan Tukalo. Now Tukalo was a 37 cap former Scottish international winger but Rory was waving his arms and shouting, 'Go, go,' so I went and managed to outsprint Tukalo to the line. In the second half I scored another try from a long way out. Leicester hammered Boroughmuir, we went on to win the tournament, and I felt on top of the world.

As we walked off the pitch, Rory came up to me and said, 'So, you're the one.'

It was immediately after this performance that I was offered my first professional contract with Leicester. Peter Wheeler, the former Tigers and England hooker who was, and still is, the club's chief executive, sent me the details. They would help me through a business-studies course at the De Montfort University in Leicester and I would receive £6,000 a year. I was to meet him to iron out the finer details.

My dad decided that this was the moment when his boy should become a man. He gave me a pep talk about how to negotiate with Wheeler, and added that I must not let him walk all over me. I was nervous but determined. I had twenty points to discuss with Wheeler, and I bloody well would not leave until I had my way.

Half an hour later I finished the meeting feeling that we'd had a good chat and that I'd contributed greatly to the discussions. Out of the twenty extra requirements I sought I managed to succeed with exactly none of them. It was one of Peter's many strengths that he could appear very nice while having it all his own way at the same time.

Dad wasn't too impressed with my efforts. We decided that he should be my agent for a while, although as his name is also Lewis Moody, he came up with the pseudonym Ken Basil – his father's two Christian names in reverse. It was genius, of course, until he turned up at the club representing me and everyone pointed out that he was, in fact, my father! In all the years he represented me, he never took a penny off his son nor the club. It was through him that I eventually discovered my own worth ethic.

It would be a while before I made my first start for Leicester in a Premiership match. I sat on the bench for the first five games of the season and never made it on to the field at all. At last my chance came, away to Orrell. It was September 1996 and for reasons that will become obvious Darren Garforth, the tighthead prop who would shortly win the first of 25 caps for England, comes to mind.

Garf was part of the famous 'ABC' club that formed the Leicester front row when the Tigers wore letters, not numbers, on their backs. Wig (Graham Rowntree) and Cockers (Richard Cockerill) wore A and B respectively.

I was still, to all intents and purposes, a schoolboy who had suddenly been transported into a man's world. I was also terrified as I found a spot in the away dressing room at Orrell and began to change, thinking about how I was going to tackle Orrell's Frano Botica, the New Zealand rugby league and union legend. What didn't help was the sight of Garf, completely naked, lying on a plinth, asking the physio to stretch his back by pushing his legs down on to his chest. From where I was sitting all I could see were two large bollocks flapping around. It was a hideous and strange introduction to pre-game shenanigans with the Tigers.

The thing you needed to know about Garf is that when the team were brought together in a huddle in the changing room just before running out on to the pitch, you avoided standing opposite him at all costs. Anything that stood on the floor in front of Garf or in the middle of the huddle – be it a ball, a kitbag or a bucket – would be kicked with all the might of an angry, dangerous scaffolder cum prop. Whoever stood opposite would invariably end up with a bucket smashing against their knackers. I recall standing there wondering whether it would be a good moment to laugh. 'Probably not,' I reasoned which, for once, was a good call.

The game was not going too well. During a break in play, the captain, Martin Johnson, pulled the forwards together. There had been too much turning over of the ball, and the man who would end the season captaining the British and Irish Lions to victory in South Africa had had enough. 'Ball control's imperative here,' he ordered.

A few minutes later I grabbed the ball in space, knowing that Johnno was right behind me. As I got half-tackled, I flipped the ball behind me with the back of my hand and watched it rebound off Johnno's forehead. For a fleeting moment I actually believed that the legend that was Johnno would be impressed by the flip of my hand. He wasn't. Instead, while play continued around us, he grabbed me by the collar of my jersey and bellowed, 'I fucking told you to keep hold of the fucking ball!'

We stopped at a pub on the way back on the team bus and drank a bucket load of cider. As an 18 year old I wasn't the best drinker and soon found myself making my way from the front of the bus, where the juniors always sat, to the toilet, where I managed to throw up in the sink. By the time Stuart Potter had made his way down from the back of the bus, the vehicle had lurched around so much that my vomit had covered pretty much all of the toilet. My head was in my arms, lying flat on a table, but from the corner of my eye I witnessed Potter, who was a legendary drinker, take one look at the obliterated toilet and launch a projectile vomit from outside the loo inwards. It was a memorable way to end an eventful day. At the age of 18 years and 74 days, I was the youngest player ever to feature for the first team. Ollie Smith would break my record a few years later, then Ben Youngs and George Ford, but the man whose record I took was a certain Martin Johnson!

That season, in total, I played no more than half a dozen times for the firsts, including the game against Harlequins when I tackled Will Carling. For much of the time I was either a sub or played for the seconds. But my first season at the Tigers was a massive eye-opener, especially when it came to the intensity of training. The Leicester training mantra was a simple one: 'Train as you intend to play.' This is why the Tigers training sessions became infamous throughout the game, mainly for the fights that occurred.

Barely a session took place without a flare-up, and it was rarely ever handbags. Ridiculously, it often happened during touch rugby rather than the contact training games we staged. Everyone would stop, stand around and watch until the fight came to its natural end.

The first big one I remember was between Nobby and Cockers, with neither hooker giving way. Nobby was still a traffic cop at the time and not one to take a backward step. Cockers was that combustible character who famously abused the New Zealand haka at Twickenham when playing for England. It was like a poor man's Ali v Frazier, with both refusing to give way.

Others were not quite so even. The two players you never wanted to get in a fight with were Fritz Van Heerden, the big Boer second-row forward, and farmer Julian White, the England prop whose hooks floored many over the years and earned him a number of red cards.

Neil Back managed to fight both of them, although twice he did well to finish second. The first time coincided with the birth of his first child, so Backy's sleep deprivation merely added to his prickly character. When someone knocked the ball out of his hand during a touch game, he lost his temper and shouted, 'Don't fucking do that again.' Fritz repeated the action in the next play and Backy went for him. In no time, Fritz held him in an unbreakable head lock and pummelled him until John Wells, who had just become coach, broke it up.

When Whitey gave him the same treatment a few weeks later, Neil was pulled away and led back to the changing room with one eye split open. He was furious. 'Why did you drag me off him?' he asked the coaches. 'I was about to have him.' That was Neil through and through. In his eyes, he was never beaten, he never admitted defeat and he never backed down.

At Leicester, you were never to show any weaknesses. Invariably, the fight winner would receive the plaudits and the loser would be ridiculed, but when it was all over, that was that. Grievances were never harboured.

Training always came first, fights or no fights, injuries or no injuries. Once Will Johnson, Martin's brother, broke his ankle during a training session. It was obviously painful and he lay on the turf writhing around. What was John Wells's reaction to this, as coach? He simply moved us on to the next pitch to continue training while Will waited to be collected by the ambulance.

Naturally, I became a figure of fun, not because I was involved in any fights, but because I was being me. In late autumn, I was driving my beloved Beetle along the dark, unlit country roads of Rutland when a large deer ran in front of me. I was alone, travelling at 60mph and had no chance to avoid it. The deer smacked against my bonnet, shot over the roof and landed behind me on the road. Incredibly, when I stopped to investigate, the deer jumped up from the road and ran off. My bonnet had been hammered into a V-shape, and on my way home it flapped open. After repairs, my orange Beetle sported not only a grey wing but a grey bonnet. Austin 'Ossie' Healey and Will 'Shaggy' Greenwood in particular took the piss out of me whenever I turned up at Oval Park with that car held together by rope.

Other times, it was me, and not wildlife, who would cause great merriment and mirth within the club. I had not quite learnt from my experiences at school and failed to realise that a rugby-club dressing room is the same environment as a school classroom, and if a weakness can be found, it is ruthlessly exploited. After many years of being the butt of people's jokes at Oakham, I was still saying stupid things that gave my new and mainly older teammates fuel.

Many stories have been told over the years, mostly untrue or only part-true, but I will admit to a few. One is to do with an outstanding gas bill, which I was supposed to pay at university. I'd never paid a bill in my life and when red bills marked 'outstanding' kept turning up at the house where I lived, I believed it was good news until we nearly lost our gas supply. My flatmate discovered the truth, explained to me what 'outstanding' meant in this context and then told a player. After that, of course, the story spread like wildfire.

On another occasion, a few of the guys were playing the board game Risk and the subject of Argentina came up. The 1996 European football championship had just taken place in England, and I commented on how well Argentina had done in that tournament. Geordan Murphy, the new Irish full-back at the club, pointed out that Argentina was not a European country, so could hardly have played in the European Championship. I stood my ground and insisted that they had, thinking of the Falklands. Of course, I was flogged for that, too.

The next year, I lived with fellow back-rower Paul Gustard, centre Jimmy Overend and my university friend, Ali Smith. My room was at the top of the house, which meant I had Velux windows in the roof. One day when it was raining and I had left for uni, my mum phoned to see if I had remembered to shut the windows. I was supposed to be living in a man's world by then. Again, when news got round about my mum checking my windows, I was slaughtered.

Another time, I was watching a 'Jerry Springer Show' about cross-dressers with the lads in the house when someone was introduced on stage as 'John AKA Jenny'.

'What kind of a middle name is AKA?' I wondered out loud. The guys explained that it was short for 'also known as', which was news to me. Naturally, word soon reached the players.

There were times during my first year at the Tigers when the mocking reminded me of my earlier years at Oakham. I thought

I had left all that behind me but, through my own stupidity, it had reared its head again. If I had been stupid in not engaging my brain in the first place, I made it worse by simply taking all the crap and looking unhappy in the process. In hindsight, I should have lamped someone early in my first year at Leicester. It would probably have gained me more respect. These are life's lessons and sometimes you need to find out the hard way.

Luckily, I had an escape outlet. University, or at least my student lifestyle, may have been at odds with trying to be a professional rugby player, but it was tremendous fun, nonetheless.

I moved into Number 1, Tudor Road, which was close to the Holiday Inn Hotel and not far from Welford Road. Suddenly, my life changed from one full of rules and regulations at home to one completely without rules – and I loved it. My three housemates were completely random people. There was Craig, the Trekkie, who had a model of the USS Starship Enterprise in his room, and was massively into sci-fi; Olly, a French doctor, who had come to Leicester to work and improve his English; and Andy, a 24 year old ex-naval officer, who decided he wanted to become a student. In hindsight, it's Olly I feel most sorry about. The rest of us would spend whole evenings teaching him words such as 'bollocks' and terms of endearment that, of course, were anything but. One night he came home, saw Andy and greeted him, 'Hi Andy, you fucking asshole.' For a short while, Olly genuinely believed that this was a normal greeting in England. The fact that it was said with a strong French accent only made it funnier. It was Olly's windows that would be tampered with if the rest of us were locked out, and he passed several draughty winter's nights for that reason. Despite this, all four disparate characters bonded well, although my best uni friend was Ali Smith, whom I met on the first day in a queue to sign for courses in business studies. He was, and is, one of life's comedy characters and a truly loyal friend.

At 16 he lost a leg after the quad bike he was riding crashed into a tree. His artificial leg caused him some awkward moments as a student, most notably on a night out when he disappeared for a piss while the rest of us queued outside a nightclub with some girls we were intent on pulling. He had bought what was basically a bin man's jacket for £110 because this was his way of impressing the opposite sex. What did not impress them was the state of Ali when he finally reappeared twenty minutes later, covered from head to toe in mud. He had leant against a post while he relieved himself, the post gave way and Ali fell down a manhole. He struggled to haul himself out of the hole but had to wait for the next person to come by to take a leak to help him. Not knowing whether to laugh or cry, we dusted him down and had a good time in the club, feeling we were well on the way to succeeding with our guests.

The moment we decided to impress the girls further by buying them kebabs it went hideously wrong. It was raining, so we deposited them in a telephone box while we went to buy the food. Ali was especially keen on one of the girls. Unfortunately, as he opened the telephone-box door, he tripped on the bottom rim and somehow managed to throw the kebab all over this poor girl's head. Her hair was covered in meat, lettuce and mayo. We didn't have any luck that night, or indeed most nights with the female of the species.

It was not an untypical incident in a year of sheer farce. One morning we woke in Ali's flat to discover that we had returned home the night before with a 15 foot high lamppost, various hubcaps and a metal street sign that had the name 'Beaver Street' on it. The lamppost was returned to its rightful place, but we kept the street sign – obviously.

That summer I was selected to go on tour with the England Under-21s to Australia, although I was just 19. As one of the youngest on a tour that also featured Paul Gustard and Phil Vickery, I was out of my comfort zone and offered little. I played in two friendlies, against Queensland and New South Wales, and came home little better for the experience. Clive Woodward was in charge of the squad, but as a forward on the periphery I had little to do with him, although I do recall one morning looking up from training with the forwards and seeing the backs at the other end of the pitch running about wearing brown paper bags over their heads. Woody had come up with the idea that the backs had to play with what they saw in front of them. That was the first time I witnessed Woody's left-field ideas in rugby, but it would not be the last.

On my return to Leicester I quit my business-studies course at De Montfort. I was doing neither my course nor my place at the Leicester Tigers justice. Something had to give and it was obvious which of the two it would be. I moved into a house with Ali, Nick Townsend and a red-haired northerner called John Tinsdale who was training to be a lawyer and worked hard. I attempted to study a single course in business at De Montfort but gave that up too when I realised I was doing no work.

My hedonistic lifestyle continued, however, and in Ali and sometimes John I found willing companions. We'd take the middle out of Ali's door handle and lock him in his own room, before rolling lit fireworks and bangers under his door. Highly dangerous? Yes. Highly stupid? Yes. But we were students, so that was all right, then! Another time, we tried to balance a huge bucket of water on John's door, it fell off and flooded the room. We also lodged his bed so tight against the door that it was impossible to enter his room. John was not amused and ordered us to sort it out, but after three hours of trying the only solution was for me to barge the door down. This was not quite what John had in mind. Today he is a lawyer. Thankfully, he was just a law student back then.

Despite all this, and the midweek drinking before training – we never touched alcohol on a Friday night before a Tigers game – my career began to flourish. What helped was that the victorious Lions squad, including quite a few Leicester players, returned from South

Africa after the season had started, which gave me and others the chance to shine for the first team.

The turning point came at Kingsholm, where Gloucester were meting out a hammering. Most of the Leicester Lions, making their first appearance of the season that afternoon, were sitting on the bench watching when Andy Goode scuffed his restart, I managed to catch the ball 20 yards on, and ran 30 odd yards unopposed to score under the posts. It was the first time I had ever really bothered to chase a restart but after that I was expected to repeat the feat on every occasion. Since that night, my restart chase has become recognised as one of my calling cards. The Lions came on, I stayed and managed to grab a second try as Leicester turned a large half-time deficit into an unlikely victory. Simon Evans, one of my roommates back at Oakham School, who was at the beginning of a career in journalism, was there reporting on the match for the local Gloucester newspaper.

Back in Leicester that night, the players re-assembled in The Soar Point, a favoured watering hole, and Will Greenwood and Austin Healey predicted that I would win more than 14 caps for England, and Geordan would do the same with Ireland. Nothing could have been further from our minds then, but in 2002, after I'd played for the fourteenth time for my country, under Woodward, I presented Will with my jersey as a reminder of what had been predicted back in 1997.

That autumn I started for the England Under-21s side against New Zealand in Newbury and then against South Africa at Twickenham. It was my first-ever appearance at headquarters and to cap it all we beat the Springboks, having also won against the All Blacks.

A young kid called Jonny Wilkinson featured in those games. It was the first time I had come across him. This time I was the senior player and this guy was the junior and, to prove my point, I thought I would run over him in training. It did not quite pan out as I thought. Jonny stopped me in my tracks and gave me a dead leg for my troubles. Even then he was a formidable tackler.

After the Twickenham game, celebrations went on long into the night and I, naturally, embraced the occasion. The drinks were flying, as indeed were the celebratory cigars. Just one player controlled himself, and that was Jonny. He drank only a little and, despite massive peer pressure from just about the whole squad, he steadfastly refused to puff on a cigar. That was an early insight into the focus he possessed, and I lacked. Within three months he was coming off the bench and making his debut for the senior England team in the 1998 Five Nations.

In contrast, I was called up for the England 'A' squad for the equivalent Five Nations. It should have been a major moment in my career, but turned out not to be. In Northampton, I was on the bench for the opener against Wales. During the previous week, Richard Hill, the England 'A' coach and former Bath and England scrum half, held one-to-one meetings with all the players. When it came to my turn, he looked me up and down and said, 'I don't know who you are, what you do, and why you're here. You'd better go and see Rob Smith.' Smith, the forwards coach, did know who I was, but I never stepped on to the field against Wales, and was then dropped for the rest of the tournament.

Back at Leicester, much was changing. Bob Dwyer, who had been in charge of the Australian team that beat England in the 1991 World Cup final at Twickenham, had been running the Tigers for about a year but was shown the door after senior player power won the day. To my mind, he helped usher Leicester into the professional era, as well as guided them to a losing Heineken Cup final against Brive in May of 1997. I got along pretty well with him, although he had massive fall-outs with Austin and always singled out Nobby's inability to find Fritz Van Heerden in lineout practice. 'Jeez, Nobby,' Bob would announce in his Aussie twang. 'I should have bought a shorter lock!'

Bob had no problem when it came to inciting the crowd, either. At Bristol, he once walked around the perimeter of the pitch shouting abuse at the home supporters. At Northampton, I was walking beside him when a local started to mouth off at him. Bob was holding a water bottle at the time and he calmly squirted water up and down the guy's head. The fan went mental but before he could physically get to Bob, stewards dragged him out of the ground.

Bob was not everyone's glass of amber nectar but I think only good things about him. He gave me the chance to play for the Tigers at 18 when there was no way the old guard would have countenanced such an idea, and he also gave me a mantra that has never left me: 'Lewis, always remember that good players have good games and bad games, but the best players have good games and great games.' I'm not saying he invented this, but it was the first time I'd heard it and it has stuck with me ever since.

When Bob was eased out of the club, Dean and John Wells took over as manager and coach and began a partnership that would become the most successful in English Premiership history. Joel Stransky, the man whose extra-time drop goal won the 1995 World Cup for South Africa against the All Blacks, was the club's stand off and became player/backs coach. The season ended without a trophy but with much to look forward to.

I'd become much more accepted as a first-team player, although I still flitted in and out between six, seven and the bench, depending on Backy, Paul Gustard and Will Johnson. But I was still living the life of a student.

One morning I was woken by a frantic Ali. 'Dean Richards has just called,' Ali said. 'He's been waiting twenty minutes for you to turn up to your end-of-season review. He doesn't sound very happy.'

I'd overslept after a night out on the tiles and completely forgotten about the appointment. My Beetle was still outside the first pub we'd visited, so I borrowed Ali's car, which, because he had only one leg, had the clutch and brake the other way round. I must have been forty-five minutes late by the time I finally arrived outside the room at Welford Road where the coaches had assembled. I knocked on the door and entered.

'Get out,' shouted Dean.

I obeyed his instructions, exited rapidly and waited until I was called back in again. I was not looking at my best, and the curry stain on my T-shirt hardly helped matters. Dean, Wellsy and particularly Joel started to lay in to me, calling me a disgrace. The Springbok eventually asked me to lift up my shirt so that they could inspect my schoolboy physique. There were three clear stud marks in a line across my torso. Wellsy nodded his head in approval.

'Fair play,' he announced. 'That's exactly why we like you.'

That summer I was selected for the senior England tour to Australia. Many of the better-known players were rested and we headed down under with a young and inexperienced group for what became known as the 'Tour from Hell'. Our party's time in Australia destroyed some international careers when they had barely started, and galvanised others, including Jonny Wilkinson's.

By the time I returned to the Tigers after an unforgettable time with England – unforgettable for all the wrong reasons – I knew once and for all that if I was serious about carving out a long and success-ful career as a professional rugby union player, I had to change my ways, and change them quickly.

3

THE STUDENT TEST PLAYER BUT A EUROPEAN CHAMPION

The 1998 tour of doom and winning the Heineken Cup

The news that I had been selected for England called for a double celebration. My flatmates, and especially my university buddy John Dinsdale, were delighted to discover a crate of Tetleys on the doorstep courtesy of England's sponsors at the time. John, almost single-handedly, managed to polish off the crate in no time. At home, my emotional parents cracked open a bottle of pink champagne, not a tipple I had consumed too often, and toasted my success. They were very excited and thought that all their journeys to training and matches in Bracknell, Oakham and Leicester had paid off. Their only son was about to play for his country and it was good to see how much it meant to them. The great shame was that I failed to live up to everyone's expectation.

Matt Poole, the Leicester lock who scrummed down alongside Martin Johnson in the Tigers second row, had a friendly word of advice for me.

'Mate, whatever you do, don't emulate me, go out on the piss and never win a cap,' he told me. Matt was highly thought of at Welford Road, possessing better attributes in some areas than even Johnno. It is one of rugby's mysteries that he never played at international level, but he clearly did not help himself. I heard his words, thanked him for his advice and proceeded to ignore it completely.

The squad assembled at the Petersham Hotel in Richmond before the long flight down under. A number of the biggest stars in English rugby were missing, including Johnno, Lawrence Dallaglio and, the day before departure, Neil Back, who withdrew. They were being rested after their huge exploits of the year before, playing for the British and Irish Lions. In hindsight, this was obviously a major blow, but as a naive student who happened to be an embryonic professional rugby player, I was just excited by the prospect of taking on the Wallabies, All Blacks and Springboks on my first senior tour. Besides, plenty of big-name players whom I had followed as a youngster were going on the tour, including Ben Clarke, Steve Ojomoh and Matt Dawson, the squad captain, as well as seasoned Tigers such as Graham Rowntree, Richard Cockerill and Austin Healey. In the squad, only Jonny Wilkinson was younger than I was, and with Richard Poole-Jones and Alex Sanderson named as the other opensides, I was confident I would enjoy a fruitful few weeks. I even managed to avoid abuse from forwards coach John Mitchell, who asked us all to strip off our shirts and bare our torsos for inspection. I was a skinny student sporting some puppy fat but when Duncan Bell, the prop, revealed himself, Mitchell turned on him instead. Two nights before we departed, Matt Dawson asked me to join him, Matt Perry and Ben Sturnham to judge a beauty contest in what was a qualifier for Miss England in Richmond. It was my first taste of minor celebrity – even if I was wearing chinos and large spectacles that made me look like a geek – and life was especially good. I had no inkling of just how hard the next few weeks would be.

A lot of the difficulty was down to the vast superiority of the opposition, but plenty of it was down to me, too, and it all started to go wrong on the very first night. The coaches were the same guys who steered England to World Cup glory in 2003, with the exception of

Mitchell. Andy Robinson had taken charge of the forwards by then. Clive Woodward was head coach, assisted by Phil Larder and Dave Alred. They were keen for us all to go out for a few beers on the first night as a bonding exercise. Pete Richards and I took them at their word, except for the 'few' part of the instruction.

It was all well meaning. In fact, Pete and I were the first back to the hotel but, after sitting by ourselves in the lobby for an hour, we grew concerned that we were not bonding enough and were in danger of starting off the tour badly. With all good intentions we ventured out again, and returned at six in the morning as drunk as you can be while still standing. We did not get into any trouble, and in my mind it became acceptable to behave like this on the tour. It set the tone.

On day two of my first-ever senior tour, with a Test match against Australia looming, I contracted a violent gastric bug that ruled out any chance of a debut cap. I was bedridden for the rest of the week, lost a load of weight and watched the debacle that befell England from my hotel room in Melbourne in growing disbelief. The 76–0 defeat is something that all of us in Australia, playing or not, will never forget. Jonny was devastated afterwards but found some strength from witnessing how high the bar was that he aspired to reach. My Leicester teammate, Stuart Potter, had a night to forget on his debut, although he was hardly alone. Potts was a magnificent player for the Tigers but it just didn't go his way on the night, and I felt for him. As I lay in bed, still not recovered from my illness, a thought suddenly dawned on me – 'Oh my God, what have we got ourselves into?' Up to that point I had known nothing but success in my rugby career, at school and at Leicester. This was new territory.

We moved on to New Zealand, and I continued to sample as many local beers as possible, along with my drinking buddies Messrs Richards, Bell and Potter. I failed to make the Test team, but played in two of the hardest midweek matches imaginable on any tour

– against the New Zealand Academy followed by the New Zealand Maoris – in front of my parents, who had flown out especially to watch their son. We got thumped in both. Playing the Maoris was an especially chastening experience for me. The final score was 62–14, I got flattened by Norm Berryman and, in my growing frustration, threw a punch. Afterwards, Roger Uttley, the former England forward, who was tour manager, had a word with me about the punch. 'I liked what you did out there,' he said. Roger was old school!

Looking back, it's easy to see why I was so frustrated. For a start, I had never – never – played in such a heavy defeat as 62–14 in my life – not at school, nor for my county, and definitely not for Leicester. I was embarrassed, especially when Berryman ran over me, and I was also angry that Pat Sanderson, in my eyes the third choice openside at the start of the tour, was playing in the England starting XV. Yet I had been, and continued to be, my own worst enemy. It was as if I was rugby's Jekyll and Hyde. Half the time I'd be as quiet as a mouse, sitting on the bus or in the dressing room. The England coaches were constantly trying to rid me of my shell. Put a few drinks down me, though, and I transformed into a larger than life character. I embraced the tour as if we were still in the amateur days, and I embraced the fact that, as an England player – even if this particular England were being demolished by every opponent – I suddenly found myself to be a bit of a catch for the local ladies.

This, obviously, was a completely new experience for me but one, as a single lad just out of his teens, I was glad to maximise. The fact that I had girls swarming over me in nightclubs meant that I spent many an hour in such establishments. Alcohol, naturally, was part of the package. How well did I fare? Let's put it this way. At the end of the tour, after we had been beaten by South Africa in a one-off Test, which I sat out, I was summoned to the front of the team bus and presented with a fluorescent yellow jersey by captain Dawson in front of the management team. This was the prize for the 'best shagger on tour'. I had to wear it over my number ones during the official, post-match function. At the time, I thought it was cool. Now I shudder at the episode, but not as much as at my antics following England's first Test defeat by New Zealand in Dunedin.

Once again, I watched another hammering unfold from the stands. This time England managed to score 22 points. Unfortunately, they also shipped 64! During the week I befriended some local students and went back to their houses a few times, or should I say student hovels. The inhabitants would lie on smelly sofas in sleeping bags, betting on horses, and when they emerged from their houses, smash cars into each other. I had been in the bar after the Test match for quite a while when some of the England players hobbled in. Can you just imagine what they thought when they saw the sight ahead of them? There was a stage in this bar and I was prancing around on it in the throes of performing the Full Monty in front of an audience baying for flesh. As each item was removed – my England tie, my England shirt and so on – I'd throw it into the crowd until I was left standing in just my boxers. Danny Grewcock, who has since become a close friend, was unlucky enough to witness this sorry sight, and he has told me many times what he thought: 'What the fuck does this joker think he's doing?' England had just been humiliated for the second successive Test match, and an hour or so afterwards, the battered and humbled players were subjected to the sight of one of their colleagues making a drunken idiot of himself. I was not alone in terms of being on the smash. At one stage, Clive Woodward started referring to Pete Richards as 'Besty' as in George Best, which was his homage to Pete's alcohol intake on that tour.

Thirteen years on I find it incredible that I should behave in such a manner and waste a golden opportunity to play for my country. At the time, I was living the dream. Now I realise I was a moron. Just thinking about it makes me cringe. I was an embarrassment to myself, to my family and to my country, even if I was not the only one. The reason why I got away with it, or thought I had, was because in what were very much the early years of professional rugby, tours such as this were still amateur in many ways. My body fat back then, for example, was 17 per cent. Now some of that was puppy fat, but a lot of it was down to the way I lived my life and to my amateur, student attitude. If an England player acted like that today, he would be sent home and labelled a disgrace by the press. For the past ten years, my body fat has been between 10 and 7 per cent, which is how it should be as a professional rugby player. Nothing, though, can remove the fact that I am disgusted with myself for acting in that way. If a new, young player behaved similarly with me as captain, I'd tell him outright to stop being a cock.

The fact is that, even though I thought I got away with it during the tour, I paid for my misdemeanours. They scarred me later. It took two and half long years before I got so much as a sniff of the senior England squad again, and that was only because many of the regulars were on tour to Australia with the 2001 British and Irish Lions. I have no complaints. I was lucky to play for England again after my performance in 1998 on the Tour from Hell.

The 'Boys on Tour' theme continued the week after we returned to England. Pete Richards and I went to Ibiza to do what young, single men do, although the holiday was marred somewhat by a moped crash on the second day. Although I was wearing a helmet, that was pretty much all I had on. When I slid headlong into a kerb, I was topless and wearing just beach shorts and flimsy flip-flops. I had a hole in my arm – my elbow shows the scar to this day – cuts and grazes all over my body, and most of my skin ripped off my right foot. We tried to grab a flight home but when this failed, decided to get smashed every night. And that is precisely what we did.

During a hedonistic night at the famed nightclub, Manumission, Pete and I decided to have our arms adorned with a henna tattoo. I was told that the snorting bull that could now be found on my bicep should be protected for the next forty minutes to avoid ruining the tattoo. After twenty minutes I grew impatient, went to the bar to buy some drinks and collided with someone. The end result? I would spend the rest of the week with an indelible, and huge, black smudge on my arm which looked distinctly uncool. Later that same night, having lost Pete, I flagged down a passing ambulance and paid the driver to take me back to my hotel. The only problem was that, in my inebriated state, I had no idea what the hotel's name was, or indeed where it was located. After half an hour of driving a rambling rugby player around the backstreets of Ibiza, the ambulance driver had had enough and threw me out – although he kept my pesetas. At one point, I vaguely recall attempting to pinch a scooter but failing to master the art of climbing aboard. I made it home, as you always do, at eight in the morning.

A few weeks later, I was back at Leicester for the important, pre-season run-up to the start of the 1998–99 season. On the first day of training, Dean Richards asked us to do what had become a tradition – run around Oval Park for a 3km fitness test. As always, I was stupidly honest and told Dean exactly what I had done to my foot, and how, as a consequence, I could not possibly produce such a run. Dean fixed one of his glares on me.

'That's not my problem, it's your problem.' he said. 'If you turn up to train, you train.'

That was that then. I produced one of my fastest times, despite the pain, partly to make a point to Dean, but mainly to get the run over with as soon as possible.

If this makes Dean appear to be a disciplinarian, he was, sometimes. On other occasions, he was as big a kid, if not bigger, than the rest of us. Take the rafting expedition in Annecy on pre-season tour. What happens when you get four rafts full of rugby players on some rapids in the South of France? Chaos! When Dean discovered that Nnamdi Ezulike could not swim, it was, of course, his goal to knock the winger out of the raft and into the water with his paddle. We tried to defend Nnamdi but Dean's determination won the day. As a screaming Nnamdi went overboard, he dragged Fritz Van Heerden with him and, in thrashing around in the water and clinging on to the big South African, almost drowned the lock forward. Nnamdi shouted for help, flayed his arms around and generally made a massive spectacle of himself while Dean sat in his raft and laughed. Soon we were all laughing when Nnamdi sunk to what he assumed would be a watery death only to discover that the water was four feet deep and he could stand up!

Another time on tour, the Tigers, including many household names and Test stars, acted like giggling kids in the classroom. We had a new conditioning coach whom we called Fifey, and one day he attempted to motivate us by recounting a story from the NFL in which two American Footballers were bench pressing in the gym, with one holding the bar and the other pushing it up and down. The player holding the bar had gone 'commando' that day and, midway through the reps, his cock fell out and landed on his partner's face. The point about the story was that the partner continued regardless, despite this unforeseen event. The moral from Fifey's story was that you must keep focused whatever hurdles stand in your way. Naturally, this was lost on all of us because we were in great pain trying to stifle our laughs and avoiding eye contact with each other.

The friendlies, if there are such things in France, were inconsequential, save for the clash with Bourgoin. I was on the bench with a slight niggle and watched in amazement as an initially small flare-up resulted in a thirty-man brawl, which became so physical that the game was abandoned with twenty minutes remaining. Dean was none too happy with his players for fighting, which struck me as ironic. If he'd been wearing the jersey that day, he would have been right in the thick of it.

Memories of that season are thin, despite the fact that I played in most of the games and it ended with a first Premiership title, which we achieved with a bit to spare. We sealed it at Newcastle with a hard-fought win. It was my first medal in senior rugby and a privilege to go on a lap of honour around the Kingston Park pitch alongside Johnno and the rest of the team, in front of, among others, my tearful parents.

A seasoned campaigner, Johnno was the epitome of Leicester Tigers. His articulacy has improved as he has aged and mellowed. Back then, he didn't say much. He simply led by example and I would have followed him to the earth's end on a rugby pitch. He had an aura about him. We felt it, playing alongside him, and opposing sides definitely felt it because Johnno was always fired up and always the first at the opposition. In training, it was the same. He was relentless, a rugby machine, and this became a key element of Leicester's success. Back, Rowntree, Garf, Cockers – they all possessed an impeccable work ethic. In their eyes, you could always train harder, and it created huge competition around the training ground and weights room. This became ingrained into the newbies at the club and, as they became seasoned campaigners, they, too, instilled this into the next generation. It was little wonder that the Tigers pack became the thrust of our play, although Paddy Howard would subsequently turn the backs line into one of the most potent in English rugby.

Paddy danced on the tables of a Newcastle nightclub on the night we won the Premiership in May 1999, wearing just his yellow Australian boxers. Shades of me in New Zealand the summer before? Not really. We hadn't just been thumped. We'd just won the league and it was a major cause for celebration.

After our next home fixture, we all took part in a three-legged pubcrawl of the bars around the ground. It was pot luck who your two partners would be but Craig Joiner, our Scottish international winger, had the gross misfortune of being sandwiched between

Dean and Peter Wheeler. Like Dean, Peter could knock back a few without blinking. There were twelve bars around the ground and the plan was to take a pint in each one. My abiding memory of Craig is seeing him throwing up outside Welford Road after being dragged, quite literally, around the bars by two large mutes who could have lapped the ground twice.

Two other events stand out for me in 1998–99, one ridiculous and the other life-changing. The ridiculous one concerns a Bee Gees concert at Wembley. Five Tigers – centre Jimmy Overend, flanker Paul Gustard, back-rower Oscar Wingham, lock Neil Fletcher and me – hired a car and driver to take us down to London. Nobody was a bigger fan of the Bee Gees than I was, unless you count Gussy and Jimmy O. In fact, Jimmy would often end the evening after a night out by changing into some shorts, putting on a cricket hat, pouring himself some port and singing and dancing along to his favourite Gibb brothers hits. We knew every word of every song. Until I was kicked in the throat during a game for the Tigers, I could even sing Bee Gees hits in the voice of Barry Gibb.

We were extremely excited on the drive down to Wembley, although goodness knows what other drivers thought when they saw five big lads in wigs, flares and dreadful seventies shirts. We'd managed to obtain front-row seats, albeit right at the side, and as we stood up, danced to the songs and handed a small bottle of vodka around to anyone who fancied a swig, we were oblivious of those sitting around us. Jimmy, in his excited fashion, tried to persuade the rest of the audience to dance. Four songs had been played, including my personal favourite, 'You Win Again', when the security men arrived. They had already asked us to calm down but this time they asked us outside for a quick word. In the process of removing us, Gussy accidentally caught one of the guards in the face with a flaying arm. It was unintentional but the guard went down in a heap, diving like Jurgen Klinsmann. The police arrived and stifled

Toddling around with a wrong-shaped ball.

Matthew Foster (*left*) is the boy who introduced me to the sport of rugby. Here we are at Bracknell mini rugby in May 1985.

The aspiring athlete – in track and field kit at Eagle House School with Dad. May 1987.

Making a break – in action for Bracknell minis Under-10s at the Newbury Festival.

Winners! Oakham Under-13s win the Leicester County Schools Cup and I get to hold the trophy (*kneeling, front right*).

Last day at school – Oakham leavers, May 1996.

If the cap fits – with Mum and Dad at Bridgewater RUFC, wearing my England Under-18s cap.

The love bug – my prized Beetle provoked much mirth at Leicester.

Tiger Cub – sporting my first Leicester kit.

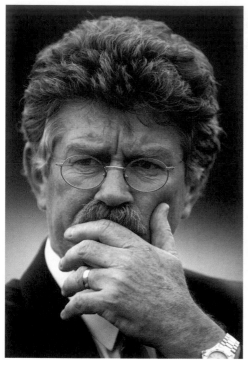

Bob Dwyer, the man who kick-started the Tigers revolution, in a rare quiet mood.

Coach Ian 'Dosser' Smith at Welford Road in September 1999.

My first start, versus Orrell, surrounded by Leicester stalwarts Dean Richards, Graham Rowntree and Richard Cockerill with hair!

Doing something right for a change on the Tour from Hell – in action against the New Zealand Academy in Invercargill. June 1998.

Try time! I manage to evade Dan Luger to score against Harlequins at the Stoop in February 1999.

Celebration time with two of my best buddies, Geordan Murphy (*left*) and Leon Lloyd (*right*), after winning the Premiership final by beating Bath at Twickenham in May 2001.

Man of the match Austin Healey in action against Stade Français as Leicester win their first Heineken Cup at the Parc des Princes. May 2001.

Doing the double! Leicester successfully defend their European title one year on and the champagne is flowing – (*left to right*) Geordan, Will Johnson, Glenn Gelderbloom, Perry Freshwater, Neil Back, Martin Johnson, me, Harry Ellis and Ollie Smith. May 2002.

Training time at Oval Park when it was always physical.

Deano! The legend that is Dean Richards in his role as Tigers head coach, in 2002.

Double attack, January 2003! My rival-cum-friend Josh Kronfeld and I are about to bring down Harlequins' Paul Burke, who later became the Tigers' kicking coach.

The unmistakable Clive Woodward watching England v Wales in the 2002 Six Nations at Twickenham. He later told me how impressed he'd been with my performance that day!

Breaking Wales's Iestyn Harris's tackle during my first Six Nations start at Twickenham.

Touchdown – but I know I am about to be crunched by two All Blacks. November 2002.

their laughs when they saw four rugby players (Fletch had cleverly disowned us by then) in platform heels. Nevertheless, it was deemed that we had been causing a nuisance and had to leave. And so, after just four songs, we headed back to Leicester, although Gussy and I lost Jimmy and Oscar when we split up to try to find our hire car driver, and ended up taking four hours, and various trains and taxis in fog, dressed like glam rockers, before we walked back into our flat. Jimmy, who had found the hire car driver but not us, had been back home for a couple of hours, and was throwing an impromptu party for a number of students. It was nearing its end by the time we finally arrived.

It was also in 1998 that I first met Annie Muggleton. I knew her friend Natasha quite well and met them both in the Students' Union at De Montfort University after they had been to Welford Road to watch a game. We went to a club called Mosquito Coast where Annie, having had one or two drinks, proceeded to jump on me on the dance floor. A week later we went to see *Halloween* at the cinema. Now I never liked horror movies, and still don't, so I guess that sitting through two hours of fear showed I wanted to be with Annie. Our first proper 'date' was on Bonfire Night. My plan was to take Annie to a fireworks display away from all the lads, who would think nothing of trying to sabotage my evening. Looking back now, I have no idea why I thought going to the Oadby Town FC display, which was directly across the small road from the entrance to the Tigers training ground, would guarantee no players seeing me. As soon as we walked in Will Johnson, Jamie Hamilton, Dave Lougheed and Craig Joiner all came over to say hello, barely disguising their smirks.

A week later I drove to Liverpool to meet my school chum Feek and fulfilled a lifelong ambition by going for a drink in the Cavern Club famous, of course, for discovering The Beatles. I downed a skinful that night and became involved in drinking games with a local, which turned into what I thought was just banter. When he asked me if I wanted a fight, I went outside with him, believing, in my now inebriated state, that it was playful. That changed the moment he landed a right hook full on my face. From out of nowhere five of his mates appeared and proceeded to kick the crap out of me. When I woke in the morning, I discovered, amid my black and blue face, that two teeth had been broken in half. I'd been with Annie for a fortnight but I was on the phone asking if she would still love me if I was ugly. Within another week or two I had taken her to meet my parents, which must have been disconcerting for Annie, but a relief for my mum and dad, who were wondering if I ever would have a proper girlfriend.

Miraculously, Annie and I became a settled couple and we have been together ever since. Annie, apart from becoming my wife and mother of my two children to date, also became the rock that I often needed to fall back on over the next decade of very high ups and very deep lows.

In 1999–2000, Leicester managed to defend their Premiership title. Again, I started for much of the season, even scoring the game-turning try at Bristol, where we secured the title, finishing off the move with a massive swallow dive that Chris Ashton, whose swallow dives for England caused such a fuss, would have admired. To win back-to-back titles in the face of some serious challengers in English rugby was a tremendous feat and, on the way back from Bristol, we stopped off in a pub in Gloucestershire to down a few drinks. There, in the corner, was Zara Phillips and her then boyfriend, jump jockey Richard Johnson, who were more than happy to join us in drinking games. That was the first time I met Zara, and I've got to know her better since she's been a regular visitor to the England team to be with her new husband, Mike Tindall. I liked her then, and I like her even more now.

During the summer, my nan on my dad's side passed away. Nan, who was a widow by then, had fallen down the stairs and she died in hospital two weeks later. Dad spent a lot of time with her in the hospital but on one occasion when he dashed home for a change of clothes, she slipped away. My cousin phoned me and I had the sorry task of breaking the news to Dad. Even now, many years later, I grow emotional just thinking about this moment. Dad was always fairly strait-laced and never fully revealed his emotions, and this was the first time I ever saw him cry. I'll never forget it. Later I broke down in tears with Annie as I told her about it, and when Dad asked me to be a pall-bearer with him at Nan's funeral, I was only too willing to help. Dad said something to me on the day of the funeral that has stuck with me ever since. 'Mum carried me into this world,' he said. 'I'm going to carry her out.'

The next season, 2000–01, was even better for Leicester, although not quite so good for me. Not only did we win a third, straight, extraordinary league title, but we became champions of Europe for the first time. The downside was that I suddenly found myself out of favour, spending more of the season than I would have liked sitting on the bench, or even playing for the second team. The management preferred to go with Backy, Martin Corry, Gussy, Adam Balding and Will Johnson, and explained to me that they were horses for courses selections. I still got a Premiership winner's medal, because I played more than ten times for the Tigers, but it was a frustrating time for me, which nearly resulted in my leaving the club.

In May, we faced Stade Français in the Heineken Cup final at a neutral venue. The neutral venue was the Parc des Princes in Paris, which is about half a mile from where Stade were based. Far from being a disadvantage, though, this seemed to work in our favour. We felt affronted by the unfairness of the venue site and used it as extra motivation, not that we needed any more motivating. This was a big, big day for the Leicester Tigers, especially Johnno and Wig and the others who had lost to Brive in the 1996 Heineken Cup final. As a club, we were desperate to put this right. We saw ourselves as the biggest club in England, yet while both Bath and Northampton had become European champions, we had failed to do so. This would be our day.

Even though I was on the bench, I felt so nervous on the day, because I knew how much this meant to my teammates and to the club. In the end, I played no part in the game, which proved to be an epic victory, but my memories are completely positive. To this day, the match is regarded as the best Heineken Cup final of them all.

On a blistering hot day, the team produced an outstanding collective performance to win the final 34–30, but three players stood out – Austin Healey, Leon Lloyd and Tim Stimpson. Man of the match Austin Healey produced a devastating run, which ended with Leon Lloyd scoring the winning try in the corner. Lloydy, in fact, scored two tries. This was the man who put me on my backside on my first day at Leicester as a colt and who became one of my best mates. When Tim 'Stimmo' Stimpson walked up to convert Leon's last-minute try, we led by two points. Stade had Diego Dominguez in their ranks, an Argentinian turned Italian kicking machine, who was striking every single kick home that day. If Stimmo had missed his conversion, there was every chance Dominguez could still snatch victory from the jaws of defeat. Instead, the Leicester full-back calmly threaded the ball through the middle of the posts, even though it was from the right-hand corner, and in the knowledge that so much was riding on the kick. As the final whistle blew, I sprinted on to the pitch and jumped on to Deano's back in celebration. This was our World Cup. The sense of euphoria was matched only by the sense of relief. Finally, we were European champions.

After beers in the changing room, we went to the post-final function in Paris, and then on a riverboat on the Seine. At the function, Austin handed the trophy to me in order to take a photo. As he did so, he attempted to kick me in the privates. My instinct was to protect my manhood, which meant using the Heineken Cup as a shield. The lid fell off and, as it landed, the little bobble on the top snapped off. I was mortified. I had managed to break the Heineken Cup an hour after Leicester had finally got its collective hand on it.

It nearly got worse. On the boat, the cup was filled with champagne and handed around the players. Ben Kay decided to take it outside for a photo. I joined him and watched as Ben attempted to put the cup down but instead dropped it over the side. Benny had the biggest panic attack you are ever likely to witness, followed by the biggest sense of relief when he peered over the edge of the boat and discovered, to his eternal gratitude, that the cup had miraculously hit a ledge and rolled back into the boat. By a huge dose of fortune the Heineken Cup was not lost to the murky, night-time waters of the River Seine.

The following day, back at Welford Road, the victorious squad embarked on an 'all-dayer' and it is just as well it was behind closed doors – well almost. You knew it was going to be carnage the moment Austin arrived fashionably late to make his grand entrance after winning the man of the match award the previous day. Seconds after his arrival, J.P. O'Reilly, our scrum half, threw a teaspoon at him from 20 feet away and struck him smack in the middle of the forehead. It was a 100 to 1 shot and well received by the gathering, save for Austin, of course, who retaliated by pulling the chair from under J.P., resulting in the number nine landing on his backside. It was going to be that kind of day. We had a jousting competition in the clubhouse with J.P., complete with a pan on his head, on my shoulders and Geordan, using a broomstick, on Cozza's (Martin Corry's) shoulders. A table was a shield. For some reason, I also decided to perform a naked sprint on the pitch, diving full length under one set of goalposts before turning around, racing up the pitch and diving under the opposite posts, too. Thank goodness there are no surviving photos from that day!

Throughout all this merriment, however, a dark cloud was hanging over my career. I had not been happy about being on the fringes of the starting XV, having previously been an ever-present. This was made worse by the news that Leicester had signed Josh Kronfeld, the All Black legend, and arguably the best number seven in the world, alongside Neil Back. I was struggling to make the XV with Backy around. Now there was Josh to contend with as well. The idea was that Josh would fill Neil's boots while Neil recovered from the 2001 Lions tour, but I could not see how I could force my way past both of them on Backy's return to the Leicester team. Even amid all the fun and games on the Seine riverboat I spoke to Dosser and several others about my predicament, and they all told me I had to do what I had to do, and if that meant leaving the Tigers, then so be it. I asked Dean if I could at least go out on loan to a southern hemisphere country to gain more experience, just as Johnno did in New Zealand when he played for King County, and Dean began talks with South African provinces. It was pretty much decided that the club would let me go for half of the next season.

What changed everything was my subsequent summer tour of America with the England squad in the Churchill Cup. Despite my patchy season, and mainly because of absent England players with the Lions in Australia, I was called up after a two and half year exile, and returned to England as man of the tour. It didn't do me any harm, either, that John Wells, in Andy Robinson's Lions absence, was the forwards coach. He returned to Welford Road to report to Dean.

Word had got around that I was on the verge of leaving Leicester. Within days, I had received big offers from Harlequins and especially Sale, whose Director of Rugby, Steve Diamond, told me during a telephone conversation to 'name my price'. I went to Dubai for a week's holiday with Annie and purposely switched my phone off. Seven days later I switched it back on again to discover tens of messages and missed calls from Dean. The bottom line was that I still wanted to play for Leicester, but the situation needed to improve. What had changed was my bargaining position, which was weak before I left for America but now, on the back of my performances for England and the offers from Sale and Quins, was strong.

Dad and I went to see Dean. The plan was that I would leave the meeting after just five minutes, and this is exactly what happened.

'I've had enough,' I told a somewhat surprised Dean. 'I want to play for Leicester so sort it out. A few weeks ago you weren't prepared to offer me anything but now I've had great offers from two leading clubs.'

My agent (i.e. my dad) then thrashed out a new deal. Dean explained that he saw Josh and I playing together, and when Neil returned, we would all alternate. I also received a much improved financial offer. As a result, I remained at Welford Road for the next nine years.

In the 2001–02 season, Leicester, incredibly, made it four successive Premiership titles on the bounce and, even better, successfully defended the Heineken Cup. The great battle between the Leicester opensides never fully materialised, because injuries to Josh hampered his ability to start every week in the first-choice XV. I began the season on a mission to oust the Kiwi. I wanted to hate the man, and in the first few gym sessions I attempted to match him. This was a futile gesture, bordering on insane, because Josh Kronfeld was one of the fittest and strongest rugby players I had ever come across. My efforts to equal his efforts, whether it was performing weighted chin-ups or bench presses, ended with me finishing a very poor second.

The irony was that we became very good mates. Josh had the kind of personality that made him difficult to dislike. What I found especially intriguing was how you could be as good a flanker as Josh, and yet be the complete antithesis of Backy as a person. The pair of them were polar opposites. Backy was 'rugby, rugby, rugby'. His intensity made him the player that he was. Josh was so laid back he was almost horizontal. He played piano and guitar, he was a surfer dude and very little changed his chilled-out demeanour. I realised I didn't need to be like Backy or Josh but should be myself, and that meant ending up probably someway in between the two of them. In terms of playing, Josh and I featured when Backy was away or rested, and when he was with us, Josh, more often than not, would be on the bench.

The league seemed harder to win that season. Paddy Howard had returned to Australia to play for the Brumbies and Rod Kafer had come in as a like for like replacement. A good number of Tigers were absent for large swathes of the regular season on England duty in the autumn internationals and the Six Nations. It said a great deal about Leicester's strength in depth, and mentality, that they could still win the Premiership title without, for major slabs of the season, Johnno, Backy, Wig, Benny Kay, Austin, Nobby and me. Some clubs undoubtedly suffered because their international stars were away, or, when back with their clubs, were still being stars. At Leicester, this was impossible. The club made you very aware that the only players who mattered were those who wore the jersey that week, and if someone was wearing yours in your international absence, you had to work hard to win it back, England or not. We were all very conscious of showing how important Leicester was to us when we returned from international duty, and again, Johnno, the England captain by then, epitomised this spirit. You might have thought that, in his position, he would take it easy on the Monday after a Test match, and five days before a club game, but Johnno would be first out of the blocks in training forty-eight hours after leading England.

There was nothing Johnno did that was anything less than committed, even the taking of the back seat on the Leicester bus. The rule was that the newer players would try to take a seat at the back, but this meant physically forcing the old guard – Johnno, Wig, Cockers, Nobby and Garf – out of theirs. Backy would sit just in front of the back row and act as what he referred to as 'the sniper', so this became quite a challenge, and almost always fruitless. I tried it on numerous occasions with the same results – clothes ripped, pants placed on my head, slapped, kicked and stamped on. Paddy Howard succeeded once in Northern Ireland on a pre-season tour when he slid under the seats unnoticed by the back row, who were otherwise engaged, beating up some newbie. Peter Short jumped on Dean's back once and ripped off one of Dean's ears, which had been surgically removed and sewn back on again only the week before. And Johnno managed to break a seat on the bus when wrestling with his brother, Will. Under the weight of those two the seat uttered an almighty crack and disintegrated!

Although winning the Premiership meant a great deal, my abiding memories from May 2002 are of winning the Heineken Cup for a second, successive time. *En route* we beat Llanelli in a quarter-final at Nottingham Forest's City ground. A last-minute penalty from Stimmo struck both the post and the bar before the ball plopped over. That was also the day when Harry Ellis announced his arrival on the big stage, gassing Stephen Jones for pace before scoring a solo try. This time, I was selected to start in the final, although I almost missed it after contracting a blood infection from a tiny scratch sustained at Gloucester the week before. It meant I did not train all week but the antibiotics did the trick and I ran out with my teammates at the Millennium Stadium to face Munster.

The day before the final I went on a walk around the Millennium Stadium pitch with some teammates in order to get a good feel of the place. A groundsman was painting the sponsors' logos on the pitch and was making a fine job of it. Unfortunately for him, we were throwing rugby balls at each other, American Football quarterback style. One of my efforts missed a player, but nailed a paint pot, splashing huge dollops of paint all over the carefully constructed logos. The groundsman responded by sinking to his knees in despair, holding his head in his hands. It was an accident but I've felt guilty about it ever since!

In a tight, tense encounter, Leicester won the final 15–9, thanks to Austin's individual try from stand off and Backy's own version of the 'Hand of God'. We were six points up and eight metres from our own line facing a scrum late in the game with a Munster put-in. Peter Stringer, their Irish international scrum half, was about to roll the ball into the scrum when Backy's hand shot out and knocked it out of Stringer's hand. The referee was unsighted at the other side of the scrum, so we got away with the infringement. The Munster players went absolutely nuts, and understandably so, and the media later likened it to Maradona's 'Hand of God' in the 1986 football World Cup. As hardened rugby players desperate to win, my Leicester teammates and I applauded Backy's ability to think and act under pressure. It was typical of him. Like any good openside he pushed the boundaries and, more often than not, got away with it. That said, I was happy for Munster when they finally got their hands on the Heineken Cup four years later.

Another 'all-dayer' followed, first back at Welford Road and then at the Walkabout pub, where our friendly landlord arranged a lock-in. Predictably, it was carnage. Josh spilled a tray of filled pint glasses, smashing them all on the floor. I woke up scrum half Jamie Hamilton, who was asleep on a sofa, with a blast from a fire extinguisher, resulting in a full-blown fire-extinguisher fight and a floor covered in foam. Then wing Steve Booth, forgetting about the broken glass, which was now hidden by the foam, decided to perform a sliding dive into the foam, and emerged lacerated from head to toe in cuts.

Those four, magnificent years at Leicester, years of outstanding success, would not be repeated again, at least not on a European level. My student mentality, except for the odd drinkathon to toast Tigers trophies, had long gone and I had transformed into a seasoned professional.

For the last two seasons of the previous century my entire focus had been Leicester, but in the first three seasons of the new century, England had come back into my life. After years of mediocrity something very special was brewing under Clive Woodward and Johnno, and a little belatedly, I would find myself playing a small part in it all.

4

THE CREATION OF CHAMPIONS

England, 2001–3

First came the disappointment. Clive Woodward, who was not part of the British and Irish Lions coaching set-up for the 2001 summer tour of Australia, chose what he deemed to be his strongest starting XV out of those English players surplus to Lions requirements for the fixture against the Barbarians at Twickenham. I was not involved. Gloucester's Andy Hazell played at seven that day, and I knew that I would be travelling on a full-cap tour to Canada and the United States as third or even fourth choice behind Hazell and possibly both Sanderson brothers, Pat and Alex. I made a mental note. The way I saw it, after my antics on the 1998 Tour from Hell, this could be my only opportunity to play for England again.

It wasn't so much that I'd played badly three years earlier. I was steady enough on the field, but off it I was way, way wide of the mark. I saw the Churchill Cup as my last-chance saloon, and vowed to be as professional as possible throughout the tour in every sense, including not touching a drop of alcohol until my work was done. How serious was I? Very. I'd get up at 6.30 each morning for a swim and a stretch before training. I'd turn down offers of a night out with the lads, preferring either to chill in my room or go to the cinema with quieter company. North America is normally a good tour to go on, for its rugby and its social life, but I was having none of it.

With Woodward in charge, and Leicester's John Wells the forwards coach, I was determined to make the most of my final chance.

I wasn't the complete angel, though. In Markham, near Toronto, before the first Test against Canada, I first learnt to abuse the RFU's credit card. Kyran Bracken was the tour captain and Clive gave him his card to spend on the boys on a team meal out. Since I wasn't drinking, I thought I should at least reward myself with something nice from the menu, and I persuaded Steve Thompson to join me in ordering some beluga caviar. Obviously, I'd never sampled this dish before in Leicester. It arrived, if you looked hard enough, in the top of what appeared to be an ashes urn. If we were disappointed in the size of the meal, we were even more let down by the taste. It was one of the most disgusting foods I'd ever eaten. Thommo agreed and we left nearly all of it. The price? £220.

The week proved to be an interesting one. Ellery Hanley, the former Wigan rugby league legend, was our defence coach in Phil Larder's Lions absence. He was always immaculate in appearance, and never seemed to get his training kit dirty. We were all in awe of him because of his fine record as a league player, but we weren't exactly clamouring to be his training ground guinea pig, at least not after what he did to winger Paul Sampson. When Ellery asked Sammo for his help in showing a certain way to tackle, assuring him and us that this was a simple, harmless training ground procedure, we all assumed he would go easy. Instead, he picked up Sammo, turned him upside down and proceeded to throw him head first into the ground. It was as good a spear tackle as you will ever see. Obviously, after seeing that, none of us wanted to be at the front of the queue and, if we were, we prepared ourselves as if we were about to face the Springbok pack. Ellery did say one thing to me, however, that has stuck. 'If you are wearing the shirt, then it's yours,' he said. 'Do everything in your power never to let it go.'

It turned out to be a good week for me. Although I'd failed to feature in the pre-tour Baa-Baas game, Clive and Wellsy selected me to make my first start for England in the first Test against Canada in Toronto. As a nice touch, Clive asked Wellsy, my Leicester coach, to present me with my shirt the night before the game. Steve Lander, the former referee whom Backy had, infamously, pushed to the ground during the 1995 losing cup final against Bath, was part of the management set-up, and he was hugely helpful in advising me concerning the breakdown area and how to avoid giving away penalties. Alex Sanderson, on the other hand, wasn't quite so helpful. As he was not involved in the Test match, he went out on the Friday night. The problem was he was sharing a room with me. I went to bed at 10.30 and was woken up at 2.00 by Alex, who was not only shouting, but also turned on all the lights and sat on the end of my bed looking for a good chat. It was a weird way to prepare for your England debut.

It was pretty weird the next day, too. Winning my first cap was very special, of course, but the scenario was not quite how I had dreamt it would be. I'd imagined I would run out in front of a massive crowd in one of the great rugby stadiums of the world. In reality, it was in front of 3,000 people either sitting in temporary stands or playing with their kids on grassy banks, while we got changed in a shed. The important point, however, was that we won 10–22 and I had a very steady game. Seven days later, this time in Vancouver, we won again, this time 20–59, and I had an even better game. The England back row that day consisted of Joe 'Worzel' Worsley, Steve White-Cooper and me. Steve's sister was going out with Gianluca Vialli. Although they were chalk and cheese, Steve and our uncompromising prop Julian White got along famously. Since then, Steve has become an affluent figure in the City while Julian is a farmer.

I had a lot of time for Whitey, and still do. He was at Bristol then but was about to join Leicester, and what a signing he turned out to

be. He may not have been your modern day, all-singing and dancing prop forward. Indeed, Whitey would run a mile just to avoid
handling the ball. But I'd have him in my team, any team, any day
of the week for his sheer ferocity and ability to pulverise the opposition pack. Without the ball, most of the rest of the team cannot
operate, and the reason why the backs received so much ball for
Leicester and England was because of Whitey and players of his ilk.

That said, I could never train too close to him because just watching him cracked me up every time. Whitey has a marvellous self-
deprecating sense of humour. He is aware of his strengths and of his
limitations, and often plays to the latter. In San Francisco, during the
build-up to our third and final Test, against the US Eagles, all Whitey
had to do was throw the ball up in the air, run and catch it. The problem was he'd launch the ball 20 or 25 feet up, then sprint furiously
after it before often collapsing to the ground without laying a finger
on the descending ball. This was the funny side of Whitey, but you
didn't want to cross him on a rugby pitch. Earlier that season Wig
had head-butted Whitey in a Leicester v Bristol game and Whitey
responded by launching a few right hooks. I defended my teammate
by punching Whitey and, for some reason, he was sent off and Adam
Balding received a yellow. Luckily, by the North American tour, all
that had been forgotten!

It was in California that I first went to the cinema on a Friday
night before an England match, something that has now become
a ritual before I play for my country. It takes your mind off the
next day's game for a few hours, and once I started I became
too superstitious to stop. I'd already been doing it for a while
at Leicester, in any case, with Geordan Murphy, Leon Lloyd and
Glenn Gelderbloom. In fact, we concocted a plan to re-enact a
scene from whatever film we'd watched the night before if any of
us scored a try on the Saturday afternoon. The first time we tried
it was after seeing 'Dude, Where's My Car?'. When Geordan scored,

we all produced the 'Z' symbol with our hands. Another time, after sitting through 'Crouching Tiger, Hidden Dragon', we rushed towards Geordan, when he scored, with our fists together and our heads bowed, and such was the force of our run that we accidentally head-butted him. After we'd watched 'Meet the Fockers' the plan was to copy Robert de Niro's 'I'm watching you' actions, when he used two fingers to point towards his own eyes. I scored at Gloucester the next day, but the problem was that it was a solo try. None of the guys were anywhere near me, so there was I, rather excitedly after scoring one of my best tries, repeatedly sticking two fingers into my own eyes while standing alone on the Gloucester try line. The others came to join in, eventually.

In San Francisco, Joe Worsley, Leon and Steve Thompson joined me for a trip to the cinema. We inadvertently chose one of the roughest areas of the city and when we emerged into the night air and stood waiting for our ordered taxi, we looked like lost tourists, complete with buckets of popcorn. From seemingly nowhere, a large car with blacked-out windows sped up and stopped in front of our feet. There it stayed, engines running, its occupants no doubt eyeing us up. After five minutes of this I became convinced I was going to die in a shower of bullets on the eve of what would have been my third Test match. I'll never know what the driver and friends had in mind because our cab arrived and four large but scared English rugby players quickly jumped in.

The match against the US Eagles went even better than the others had done. We won at a canter, 19–48, and completed an unbeaten tour, although the sense of occasion was somewhat dampened by the fact that we got changed in a municipal swimming pool and had to walk around the swimmers to get to the pitch. I scored a try, won the man of the match award and, later, the man of the series as well. Then, and only then, could I let my hair down and, it is fair to say, that is exactly what I did.

It began with the realisation that my suit trousers had slipped off the hanger and were lost. Pat Sanderson kindly leant me his brand new Abercrombie and Fitch jeans, bought that week in San Francisco. I spent much of the post-match function lurking in the shadows, because I was the only person not wearing a full suit. Then I was asked up on stage to accept my awards. It hardly looked good, being in jeans, but luckily, I was fortified by some vodka and Cokes I had been downing with Whitey. After a few more drinks at the function, the team ventured out into the night. Mark 'Ronnie' Regan was among us and, being the old school character that he is, insisted I drank from a whiskey bottle in his possession. I needed no second invitation and that was what finished me off. The first victim was Worzel. I saw him standing in a bar doorway, some 30 metres away, and decided to tackle him. Worzel had no idea what hit him. I'd sprinted the full 30 metres and hit him hard with a flying tackle that sent us both flying out of the door and into a car that, subsequently, sported a dent in its bonnet. Leon tried to help me as I sat on the pavement. Every time I fell to one side, Leon would catch me with his foot. Unfortunately for him, just as he called the others over to watch, I vomited on his shoes.

Pat Sanderson took me home in a cab and by the time I arrived at the team hotel I had temporarily lost the ability to walk. It was only 9pm and the team management were sitting in the foyer, waiting to go out for the night, but I had not touched a drop of alcohol in four weeks and needed Simon Kemp, the team doctor, to find a wheelchair to shepherd me from the taxi to my room. As the man of the series was wheeled past Woodward and company, he had some sick down his shirt. On reaching the lift, I fell head first into it, but somehow the doc managed to push me to my room. I was half asleep by now but awoke with a start to find a man – Simon, as I realised later – trying to take my trousers off as I lay on my bed. The England team doctor was then the recipient of a torrent of flaying fists, but he still sat with me for the next hour to ensure I survived. An unknowing Graham Rowntree, my roommate, returned in the middle of the night to discover a wheelchair in the room and me asleep in the recovery position.

Despite all this, I had at last made my mark, so to speak, with England. When Woodward assembled us all together again, the big boys from the Lions tour had returned and what lay in front of us was a one-off, postponed Six Nations clash against Ireland in Dublin. Their fixtures had been put back from the previous March due to an outbreak of foot and mouth disease. We came to Dublin having won our four previous games and so, for the third year running, were chasing a possible Grand Slam. In the previous two years, England had blown it against Wales and then Scotland. This time, Ireland had lost to Scotland the previous week but at least had blown off the cobwebs. The first-choice England side, in which I suddenly found myself a reserve, had not played for seven months.

Despite the presence of many Leicester colleagues, I was the most nervous I had ever felt as I prepared for the game and then sat on the bench, watching events unfold. England, with the 'Holy Trinity' back row of Hill, Back and Dallaglio, appeared to be on top at first and may well have won the game had Peter Stringer not pulled off a memorable tap tackle on Dan Luger. Instead, when I came on to the pitch with seven minutes remaining, we were losing. Phil Greening, the hooker, had tried a chip kick that went horribly wrong – and he never played for England again – and Keith Wood, his Irish counterpart, was having one of his sensational days. I still felt I could make a difference but, through nerves, my legs felt incredibly heavy. One possible chance came when Mike Catt made a half break. If I had been on his shoulder, I could have made a lot of metres, but my legs wouldn't allow it, and the game, and the Slam, was gone. Ireland won 20–14. It would be another two years before we could finish that particular job.

I did enough, though, to retain my place in the squad for the autumn internationals, starting just a few weeks later. Although I had no involvement in the 21–15 win over Australia, I started the second game, against Romania. I tend not to count this 134–0 romp as my first start at Twickenham for my country, although it was, because it barely constituted a contest. I scored two tries and Charlie Hodgson, playing at ten, scored 32 points, which remains a record for an Englishman in a Test match to this day. For the third Test, against South Africa, I was back on the bench but managed a few minutes at the end as England pulled off an impressive 29–9 win. Although I played for just a short period of time, it was, without doubt, the most physical rugby I had ever experienced – as if I was back at school playing against men. If you have never played against the Springboks before, you cannot fully describe what it is like to feel their full force. I had been warned, players had tried to explain to me, but until you experience the full force of the Springboks for yourself, all the talk counts for very little.

Although I was still an inexperienced England player, I now knew enough about what it felt like to wear the white of your country, and all the nerves that accompanied it. The morning of the match was, and is, always the worst. I must pack and unpack my bag a hundred times, checking and double checking that I have remembered to pack my gumshield and contact lenses, cycle shorts and pants. The hours feel like days and the minutes like hours. The bus journey from the team hotel, then as it is now, Pennyhill Park in Bagshot, takes half an hour, although it seems like half the day. It's not too bad to begin with. There is usually a bit of banter and someone – back then it was Mike Tindall, Dan Luger or Andy Gomarsall – will have prepared a compilation CD to play, but the nearer you get to the stadium, the more alone with your thoughts you become. You also grow appreciative of the tens of thousands of people who are coming to cheer you on that day. You see them in the pubs, pouring out on to the streets. You see them taking pictures and waving as the bus drives by. And you see them waiting in the west car park and by the west stand as you arrive. It serves as a massive boost to see so many backing you, but it also adds to your nervous, nauseous state.

For us, there was always one moment of light relief and it concerned Ronnie Regan. On the way to the stadium the bus always passed a fish and chip shop called 'Regan's'. Without fail, Ronnie would break the silence by stating, 'Regan's fish and chip shop, still doing good.' Another tradition of the journey was waving to the inhabitants of the house on the corner by the roundabout when we turned off the A316 and headed towards the west car park at Twickenham. The people who live there have changed, but they always make a point of waving to us as we drive past, and a few of us have always waved back.

In the 2002 Six Nations, a couple of minor injury niggles meant that I missed the Calcutta Cup win over Scotland, and the defeat in Paris, in which the French side, through Serge Betsen, did a job on Jonny Wilkinson. Against Ireland, England, emphatically, avenged their Dublin defeat of four months earlier, and I managed to feature as a sub, coming on to replace Richard Hill in the 67th minute. What I consider to be my first 'proper' start came against Wales, a 50–10 thrashing of the Principality. The Slam had gone and the Six Nations title, too, to the French, which is why Clive rested a few of the big-name players, including Johnno and Lawrence Dallaglio, for the last game in Rome. I started again, and played well enough for Clive to pay me a strange compliment when he said to Wig, 'There's something nutty about the way Lewis plays, but I like it.'

Clive liked it well enough, it seemed, to send me to Argentina as part of a team that was barely even our second XV. We were due to play a midweek game and then a one-off Test in Buenos Aires, and Clive rested his big guns again. The year before they had played in a gruelling Lions tour in Australia, and when we all returned it would be for the start of a very long season, culminating in the World Cup.

Nobody gave the remnants of this England team much, if any, chance, especially after our 'A' team were defeated midweek by their Argentinian counterparts. For the Test match, our line-up included Geoff Appleford, Michael Horak, Phil Christophers and Ben Johnston, all good players but not guys who would feature too much in Clive's grander plans. Against us was Argentina's first-choice team, including Agustin Pichot, Felipe Contepomi, the Lobbe brothers and Freddie Mendez, all bristling with passion.

Then there were the conditions. The stadium was a concrete bowl with barbed wire and a deep trench to stop the crowd from invading the pitch. This worked, although it didn't stop them throwing objects on to the pitch. We felt like modern-day gladiators as we entered the fray and the locals threw bottle tops and coins at us. Charlie Hodgson had to contend with all kinds of objects landing at his feet as he prepared to take his kicks, but he still managed a supreme display with the boot. Under the quiet but inspirational leadership of Phil Vickery, we all did.

Phil is a lovely guy off the pitch, and a bugger to play against on it. He was more of a doer than a shouter, but when he did speak, his softly spoken tone required complete attention. I experienced a great deal more of Phil's captaincy five years later during the 2007 World Cup, but back in 2002, under him, we pulled off a magnificent victory, 26–18. Later, Clive insisted that win laid the major foundation stones for the incredible eighteen months that followed. It did wonders for the confidence of England players who were seemingly on the fringe, such as Ben Kay and me. We returned from Buenos Aires believing we were good enough to take on and beat the best. Clive also saw how some of us could step up to the plate.

Phil Christophers succumbed to the traditions of a first-cap evening, which involves having a drink with every member of the squad. Just to help him along we slipped a Viagra into one of his drinks, although that didn't seem to have too much effect.

The alcohol did, though. Phil was so drunk he threw up at the dinner table during the official function, and then fell asleep in his dinner.

Before returning home, Worzel, Adam Balding and I flew to Las Vegas to enjoy three, reckless days in the Nevada sun and in the casinos. None of us had been there before and, naturally, we were three very excited little boys as we hit the Strip. On the first night, in between losing cash in the slot machines and at the blackjack tables – Balders blew all his tour money in two nights – we befriended an American fireman, who had worked during 9/11, and his friend, who was acting as his best man. The next day, in the white chapel, he was to be married. Collectively, we got horrendously drunk. In the early hours we were phoning the fireman's bride-to-be to tell her what a great guy her future husband was. By six we had discovered that Wes Brown, the Manchester United and England footballer, was in the vicinity and started buying him JD and Cokes. Wes took one look at the drinks and refused flatly to touch them, which meant I ended up downing them. In retaliation, I began to flick his bollocks with my hand every time he rose to his feet – an annoying habit rugby players tend to inflict on each other, called 'plum shots'. Eventually, he asked Balders to ask me to stop repeatedly attacking his privates.

The sun was rising by the time we got back to our room. A 60 year old cowboy, complete with 10 gallon hat and beard, helped Balders with me. A few hours later, the three of us rugby players made it to the wedding, where our newly married friend introduced us to all the families present. We didn't expect to be attending a stranger's wedding on our short sojourn in Vegas, but it was that kind of trip! Afterwards, we bumped into the cowboy again. I had no idea who he was. He asked us if he could stay in our room since he had no money and nowhere to stay. We told him we already had five in the room. He insisted he would be happy to sleep on the floor. In the end, we gave him $200 basically to go away. All in all, it was a strange thirty-six hours, and I spent most of the remaining day of our short break in bed.

That autumn I made a significant breakthrough. Up until the first game of the autumn international series, against the All Blacks at Twickenham, I had been on the periphery of the first-choice starting XV. I had played well when given my chance but was most definitely behind the Holy Trinity in the pecking order. Then, on the Monday night of the week leading up to the All Blacks match, Neil came up to me and offered his hand in congratulations.

'Well done,' he said. 'You're starting ahead of me.'

It was news to me, but very good news nonetheless. It was also very big of Backy to act in this manner. For a man with such pride and competitiveness, it must have been hard. This was the first time I had been selected for the strongest England team on merit. Funnily enough, I always felt that getting the nod over Backy would happen at England before it would at Leicester, such was the depth of feeling towards him up at Welford Road.

On the Friday night I was made to feel embarrassed in front of the whole team. Earlier in the week, Jerry Guscott had interviewed me for the TV and asked how the first-time New Zealand players would be feeling, running out at Twickenham. My reply was, as usual, uttered without any thought whatsoever. 'They'll feel like me, running about like a bunch of happy spastics.' The piece, understandably, wasn't used but a video tape reached the large hands of Ben Kay. Clive finished off his eve of game team talk and then added, 'There's one final thing to show you,' at which point on came my interview with Jerry. Of course, everyone found it hilarious that I had made an idiot of myself. I, on the other hand, was massively unhappy about it. I was the new boy trying to fit in and felt belittled in front of the whole squad just before the biggest game of my life.

I had words with Benny afterwards and, to be fair, he explained how he thought I'd take it well, and apologised.

The game was a classic in which I played my part. It began, as always, with the haka. I have never had any problem with that. In fact, I enjoy it. The way I deal with it is to focus on one player. When Richie McCaw is playing, it is always him. If not, whoever takes my fancy on the day. It becomes a staring match. If you are intimidated by it, you shouldn't really be out on the park in the first place.

Jonah Lomu was past his prime but he was still a nightmare to deal with. At one point, he bulldozed straight through Phil Vicks, which is practically impossible to do. I remember watching Vicks land on his backside and thinking, 'What chance do I have?' Moments before half-time it had been nip and tuck, with Lomu scoring the first of two tries and Doug Howlett out-sprinting us, but with Jonny slotting over penalties and drop goals. Then, in the fourth minute of injury time, I found myself with a clear run to the corner and the try line after good work from James Simpson-Daniel and Jonny. Although I was confident I would make it, I also knew that, a split second after diving over, I would be crunched by Chris Jack and Howlett. I had plans for a try celebration based on the film we saw the previous evening but instead lay there writhing on the turf winded. No matter, it meant we led 17–14 at half-time. This became 31–14 thanks to tries from Jonny and Benny Cohen and, although the All Blacks struck back to make it a nervous end, we came through 31–28.

Next up was Australia and I kept my place, although Backy, predictably, returned to the team, this time at the expense of Lawrence. Lol, by his high standards, had an average game against the All Blacks and Neil was stretching every sinew to get straight back into the team. He would play at seven and I would be at six. Clive's message was clear enough. Nobody, not even Backy or Lol, was indispensable.

During the week, Phil Larder's expertise in the drift defence was highlighted. I've often felt Phil never received the credit he deserved for his part in turning us into the best team in the world. He ensured that we had complete trust in each other as players. One morning he turned the video camera on to film us tackling each other. Johnno asked me to 'end him, jackass style' with as ferocious a tackle as I could muster in front of the camera. I launched myself at my club and national captain and we both ended up in a heap on the ground laughing. I'm not sure it did my shoulder any favours because, later that day in a training session, I mangled it. My first reaction was that I was out of the Wallaby match but forwards coach Andy Robinson told me to get on with it. On the day a handful of Ibuprofen did the trick. I always took them orally, although the painkillers reached the bloodstream quicker if you used a suppository. That was not for me, although Austin would have it no other way!

The game was another classic. The world champions led 31–19 at one point but 22 points from the boot of the incomparable Jonny and two rampaging runs from Benny Cohen saw us home at the death. We were building some momentum now with the World Cup just one year away.

Seven days later it was the turn of the Springboks to come to Twickenham for what turned out to be a travesty of a Test match. South Africa's premedited plan was to throw as many cheap shots as they could at us, and this is exactly what they did. We all knew that the next time the two teams met would be in the key group game the following October in Perth, which would probably decide who would enjoy the easier quarter-final draw. Their savagery backfired horribly on them. England thrashed South Africa 53–3, helped in part when Jannes Labuschagne was sent off for a late hit that poleaxed Jonny. It wasn't even the worst incident on the day. James Dalton, Robbie Fleck and especially their captain, Corné Krige, all landed cheap-shot punches and hits, and we were awarded a penalty try after a high tackle as well. It was a pretty desperate day for Test

MAD DOG - AN ENGLISHMAN

match rugby and not a great one for me, either. I left the fray after just 15 minutes, clutching my shoulder.

My mood was hardly improved by what went on later that night. I was planning on having a night out with Annie but she and her best friend Natasha (the future Mrs Danny Grewcock) had knocked back quite a few drinks by the time I ventured out into the Richmond night. I wandered up the road to find a taxi and when I returned I was met by the sight of Annie with both her arms wrapped around Prince Harry. I knew the Prince a little because he had popped into the England dressing room to say hello earlier in the autumn series, and later I introduced him to Annie in the bar at Twickenham.

'You've got to look after this one,' he said to me with a smile. 'She's a good girl, take care of her.'

Great. So I had knackered my shoulder and come off the field after just 15 minutes. I was stone cold sober while my girlfriend was blind drunk, and now I was receiving advice about my girl from Prince Harry! He was only being friendly, of course, but it didn't improve my mood. The night ended back in my hotel room. Annie was asleep, her brother Andy and two of his mates were teaching me how to break dance and we polished off six bottles of Freddie Mendez's own wine from his vineyard, bought during the previous summer's tour to Argentina.

I went to see Angus Wallace, the well-known Scottish physician about my shoulder. He cleaned it out during a minor operation and I underwent six weeks rehabilitation. It was the first operation I had ever undergone in my life, but it would not be my last. By the time I was selected in the starting XV against France in the opening Six Nations game of the 2003 tournament, I believed I was fit and injury free. I was wrong. Four minutes into the second half I attempted to charge down a kick and knew as soon as I landed on my shoulder that I was in trouble. We beat France 25–17 at Twickenham, but my tournament was over.

While England went on to win the Grand Slam, I was having two shoulder operations, but not before I sought out Johnno for his advice. He'd gone through the same injuries and told me to join the 'Zipper Club', which was his way of saying go for it, even though I'd end up with a scar that resembled a zip on my shoulder. The shoulder ligaments needed repairing and, in the process, all the muscle shrunk. The Holy Trinity were back in unison as the first-choice back row, while Cozza and Worzel were going well, too. Never mind the Six Nations, had my World Cup gone? Had all that hard work to get into the first-choice team come to nothing? That was the fear that would haunt me for many weeks to come. I went to Dublin to watch England smash Ireland 6–42 and went drinking with Geordan's family, but it was a bittersweet day for me. Of course I was happy to see the boys win the Slam. I even picked up a winner's medal. But no player ever enjoys other guys wearing his jersey while he looks on helpless.

It stayed this way over the early summer. I managed to squeeze in a training session with the Tigers, my first session after injury, and ended up with twelve stitches in my nose and eye after a flying boot from Perry Freshwater caught my head in a tackle. While I was working my socks off to regain fitness, England went down under and recorded two remarkable victories in Wellington and Melbourne. The 13–15 win in Wellington was England's second-ever victory over New Zealand away from home, highlighted by the pack's magnificent rearguard action when reduced to six men. The 14–25 win over the Wallabies a week later was England's first-ever in Australia, and a particularly impressive display. It was all looking very promising from an England World Cup perspective. The only question for me was would I be a part of it?

Two months later I received the news I was waiting for. Clive picked me to start against Wales in Cardiff in what was the first of three World Cup warm-up games for England. The team was mainly fringe players, captained by Jason Leonard against a strong Welsh side. Jason, of course, was and is a complete legend and a great ambassador for the game. I'll always remember him being one of the first of the senior members of the squad to welcome me when I became an England player. A genuinely nice bloke, he made me feel welcome from the start. He was also keen to remind the young players how important it is to give supporters some time, and he was and is absolutely right. Jason was a great example of how a rugby player should always respect anyone connected to the game, whether it is the RFU President or a small boy who had waited for an hour in the rain just to obtain your autograph. I still remember how I felt when Will Carling gave me his. Jason wasn't one to ram all his achievements down your throat, far from it. He was always willing to have a beer and a chat, and you have to respect the fact that, in a physically demanding position, such as prop, he should evolve with the game and play well over a hundred times for England. It was a mark of the man that when he retired from England, he retired from his club, Harlequins, too. He felt that if he did not possess the drive to play for his country any more, his club would no longer get the best out of him, either, even though Quins were more than happy to keep him on.

As for me, I cannot tell you how happy I was to be back in the fold, although I was by no means certain of making the World Cup flight down to Australia. It turned out to be a good day, though. We won 9–43, an unheard of score at the Millennium Stadium, and I scored the first try with a 24th minute effort after Simon Shaw caught the lineout ball and I was able to barge over, using Jason as a gridiron-style blocker. It was an incredibly emotional moment for me and I needed all my resolve to stop crying on the pitch.

A week later I was selected to start again, but this time in a much stiffer fixture, away to France in Marseille, where the French very rarely lost. They picked pretty much their best side. We were stronger than in Cardiff – probable first-teamers Josh Lewsey, Mike Tindall and Ben Cohen all started – but we were far from our number-one outfit. I was delighted for Nobby, my Tigers teammate Dorian West, who was asked to captain the side, but England's long, unbeaten streak of thirteen games came to an end. France won 17–16 to remind us that we still had much work to do. Clive was not best pleased with me, either. I had given away three penalties, two of which resulted in six points in what was a tight game. Two days later, back at the team hotel in Bagshot, he walked past me but stopped.

'Promise me you'll never give away so many penalties again,' he said.

The final warm-up game was the repeat fixture against France, this time at headquarters. The French selected a weaker but still strong side, while England, although not sporting our definitive XV, upped the tempo. It meant that I was on the bench, but I had my chance from the 57th minute when I replaced Cozza. England wrapped up their preparations for the World Cup in fine style, dismissing France 45–14 with Benny Cohen again scoring two tries.

I was thankful to have escaped injury after what had happened to Geordan Murphy earlier that day. My housemate was playing in Ireland's final warm-up game against Scotland when he suffered a double fracture of his leg. He had been on fire that season but as I watched the slo-mo of the incident on the TV, while waiting for the start of England's game, I knew his World Cup was over. I was devastated for him but also, in the back of my mind, remembered that whenever one of us got an injury, the other usually followed quickly afterwards. Today, as poor Geordie discovered, was not the day to contract an injury. After tackling Imanol Harinordoquy I thought, for a split second, that I had re-injured my shoulder. Luckily, it turned out to be an enormous stinger – when a nerve in your neck is momentarily trapped and pains shoot up and down your arm – and I was able to carry on.

It was a strange feeling afterwards. We had just thrashed fellow World Cup contenders but for many of us the overriding emotion was one of unease. The following day, Clive would be announcing the thirty-man squad and although Johnno, Jonny, Backy, Lol, Richard Hill, Matt Dawson and others could sleep soundly that Saturday night, for the rest of us it was like waiting for your 'A' level results. The thought of Clive's expected phone call was never far from my mind. Would he take five or six back-rowers? If it was six, would I be one of them? I was desperate to go and did not want to be told I was young and had more World Cups to play in. I wanted to play in this one.

I spent the following morning walking around Richmond with Annie. The phone rang a couple of times and my heart was in my mouth. Eventually, I received a text message. It simply listed thirty names. I scrolled down and came to 'Moody', and then I hugged Annie so hard I nearly squeezed the life out of her. I was going to the World Cup and my emotions right then were a mixture of relief and euphoria.

It would not be the same for two of my Leicester teammates and friends. Graham Rowntree had been omitted, ironically for Julian White. I was pleased for Whitey but disappointed for Wig. He had played throughout the Six Nations and been one of the 'Auckland Six' who withstood the All Blacks in Wellington that summer. Austin, too, failed to make it, despite managing to haul himself back to fitness after many months out.

Next stop for me would be Perth, though, and an opening group game against Georgia in the World Cup. It would, as every British sports fan knows, prove to be a memorable seven weeks.

5

THE BEST TEAM IN THE WORLD

The 2003 Rugby World Cup

By the time we arrived in Australia we had become the fittest England team imaginable. This was all down to the most intense training camp I or any of the other players had ever come across back at the Pennyhill Park team hotel in Bagshot. Mostly, the drills would be performed in teams. This meant we were always competing against each other. The sprints around the pitch, with little recovery time, would take a minute or so but by the end everyone was groaning with a horrific build-up of lactic acid in their legs. Jonny was the fittest, of course. In pretty much every exercise we were asked to perform he came out on top. Jonny just went for it, hell for leather. Even then, before we had arrived down under, he was incredibly motivated. He was, and has remained to this day, the ultimate professional who pushes himself to be the best he can be. It was constantly inspiring just watching him train.

Despite feeling utterly exhausted each night, there were plenty of light moments, too. I was continuing with my shoulder rehab, which meant spending plenty of time in the swimming pool, often with Barney Kenny, one of the England physios assigned mainly to me. One day I was in the pool, pushing hard against a rubber resistance band wrapped around my waist when it snapped. A split second later I heard a painful groan, looked back and saw Barney doubled up clutching his bollocks. Now no man respects Barney more than I do. He is utterly dedicated to his profession and to the England team, but I was still almost sick with laughing.

Phil Vickery used to have some fun at Barney's expense, and it was all because the England physio had an extraordinary amount of body hair. Every time Phil saw him he'd unleash the piercing howl of a werewolf. Barney used to pretend to ignore him by putting his head down and getting on with his work but Phil would howl and howl until Barney would eventually crack, look up and say, with a broad grin, 'Oh fuck off, Vicks.'

Austin Healey had done well to be on the training pitches at all. He had battled as hard as he could to regain fitness after a long-term injury, including spending many weeks in America with the well-known sports rehabilitation specialist, Bill Knowles. He knew it was touch and go whether he would make the World Cup plane, which is why he was eager to impress Clive at any given time. At the end of one training session, Clive wanted the forwards to carry out some receiving from kick-offs and needed someone to kick the balls. At first he asked Dave Alred, the kicking coach, but eager beaver Austin overheard and volunteered. 'No, no,' he shouted out. 'I'll do it.' By this time everyone was milling around and watching as Ossie prepared to launch the ball high towards the waiting England pack. Instead, he missed the ball, kicked the ground and rolled over on the pitch shouting out for the physio. Obviously, it wasn't that funny for Ossie, who twisted his ankle, but the disdain from Woody was priceless. 'Oh Christ,' he muttered, before looking over to Alred and shouting, 'Dave, Dave.'

Another hilarious sight was seeing the front-row boys trying to wear the brand new, state-of-the-art, skintight tops that Nike had produced for the England team to wear at the World Cup. There were a few teething problems with the jersey, what with it being easily ripped and, as was highlighted by the warm-up game in Marseille, making you unbearably hot. I know I hated wearing it at first, especially when it was going to be an all-in-one body suit. I was duly grateful that the International Rugby Board (IRB) decided we had to wear shorts in the tournament, but the skintight tops remained. Obviously, the back three boys loved them. Josh Lewsey probably went out at night wearing his. But the front-row boys, especially Whitey, were none too impressed. Let's just say it hardly flattered them. In some cases, just getting it on and off proved to be quite a palaver.

The final act before leaving for Australia was to break up my long-term relationship – with Geordan Murphy! I'd been with Annie a long time now and we wanted to move in together. I'd held off for a while because I loved living with Geordie. I wasn't the only one. Leon had also managed to steer clear of moving in with his long-term girlfriend, Lisa, but Annie and I had found a house and it was time to move on. I was nervous telling Geordan the news. It felt like I was ditching a girlfriend. I was equally nervous about telling Leon, because I thought that would force him to move in with Lisa, but it turned out that Leon was having the same thoughts himself. As soon as I moved in with Annie he moved in with Lisa, and now they are married with two children. Geordan took it well, too. By this time Annie had qualified as an interior designer, and she began to redesign the house while I went to Australia. The plan was that she would join up with me for the quarter-finals onwards, but first England needed to make it into the knockout stages, preferably by winning a group that consisted of Georgia, Uruguay, Samoa and, crucially, South Africa.

As I walked through the airport terminal at Heathrow to catch the Australia-bound plane – wearing flip-flops, of course – I felt a twinge in my foot, but dismissed it as nothing important. You often get twinges in your foot, after all. They are part and parcel of every-day life, but I felt it again as I warmed up for our first group game in Perth, against Georgia. I'd been selected on the bench. Hilly injured his hamstring 15 minutes into the second half and I came on to replace him. By then the adrenalin had kicked in, my painful foot was forgotten and I was pleased with my performance. As for the game, we won at a canter, 84–6, with 12 unanswered tries. Although the score suggests it was a routine thrashing, we all felt it the following morning. The Georgians, if nothing else, were huge, physical brutes.

I felt terribly for my friend Danny Grewcock. During the warm-up, Ben Cohen accidentally stood on Grewy's foot and broke a toe. This put him out for four weeks and when he returned against Uruguay, Grewy almost immediately broke his hand. This time there would be no reprieve for the big man. He was on his way home, having never really felt a part of the England World Cup success story, and Simon Shaw flew out to replace him. I understand why Grewy felt he played no part but he was wrong because he had been a constant throughout the team's rise to the top of the world.

I could, and even should, have joined Grewy on the way home but for a remarkable stroke of good fortune. After the Georgia game, I told Barney that my foot was still troubling me. He had a look but could not recreate the pain, and an X-ray showed nothing untoward, so we iced it and added it to the drills in the pool, which I continued to do even during the World Cup. I decided that it was all in my head and just trained and played through the pain. It was only after the tournament had finished, and I was back home in Leicester, that I had a CT scan and discovered that I had a fracture of the navicular. If this had been known during the World Cup, it is almost certain I would have returned to England. Luckily, it was not. The downside, however, was that, whereas instant discovery would have probably meant a three-month lay-off, not pinpointing the problem until seven games later resulted in a disastrous following season.

Richard Hill was just too good to be sent home, even though he had a hamstring problem that kept him out until the semi-final.

The man was just too immense. I really enjoyed watching him play his game. He was never flash and, in some ways, he never stood out, but he was the ultimate player's player. Whether it was with the work he did around the pitch, his support play, his cover tackling or his rucking, everyone knew just how good he was. His World Cup had just taken a huge hit but, Hilly being Hilly, he made sure his tournament was far from over.

Next up, at the same Subiaco Oval venue in Perth, were the Springboks, and this, with respect to the other three teams, was the game they and we had targeted for many months. Win this game and the likelihood was that we would win the group. Win the group and there was every chance we would face another group runner-up, Wales, in the quarter-final. Lose this game and second in the group would almost certainly result in a last-eight game against the All Blacks.

At first, nobody was sure that Hilly was out for this crunch fixture. I was under the impression that I would be on the bench until I received Clive's call on the Wednesday to tell me the news. I was with Grewy and Benny Cohen, Thommo and Worzel at the time, looking for a Starbucks and, instantly, my relaxed demeanour changed and I became a nervous wreck. This was the big one. This was the most important game in the World Cup, and the one game we had focused on since the moment we won the Grand Slam back in the previous April. Obviously, the knockout stages would prove to be of immense importance, but we had to get there first. Everything depended on the group game against South Africa. We decided to buy the Will Ferrell movie 'Old School' and watched it that night, which did wonders for my nervous state. By the end of the film I was back to normal thanks to 90 minutes of deep, belly laughs, courtesy of the ridiculous Mr Ferrell.

I was laughing again the next day, but this time at Danny Luger's expense. He, Benny Cohen and I had finished training with the rest of the England squad at a Perth school's gym and came across a pit full of kiddies' sponges, which, naturally, we could not ignore. Benny tended to be a slightly misunderstood individual, due in part to the fact that he suffered from some deafness in one ear. Some people thought he was aloof or arrogant when, in truth, he couldn't always hear what was being said to him. In the year before and during the World Cup, he had become unstoppable as a winger. He was very committed to his training, a dedicated individual who became a try-scoring machine. I'm not sure he ever quite received the plaudits he deserved but, as far as I'm concerned, he's one of the best wingers I've ever played with or against.

The point about the sponge pit is that, once you landed in the middle of the sponges, there was little purchase to haul yourself out of it again. Luges decided he wanted to jump into the pit and shouted, 'Lads, watch this.' Unhappily for him, Benny yanked his shorts down as he was airborne, resulting in a quite horrendous sight as he landed in the pit, where he stayed, furiously hauling up his shorts, while the locals who had come to observe the England boys training looked on in disbelief.

On a more serious note, we had the strange experience of having security guards assigned to our hotel floor for the last few days before the big game. This was because South African fans had begun to knock on our doors at all hours in the vain hope of disrupting our preparations. I felt sorry for the guards because all they did day and night was just sit in our corridor, but it did the trick. For the last two nights we all enjoyed our beauty sleep.

We beat the Springboks 25–6 but do not be fooled by the 19 point winning margin. It was a tough, close game, which was decided, as such games often are, by small margins. Jonny, as ever, kicked his goals while his South African counterpart, Louis Koen, missed with four penalties, although he did score from one that I had conceded after a high tackle. I was far from happy with my performance that night, but I did create the game's one try, scored, thank goodness, by Will Greenwood. Pre-match research had told us that Koen took his time with his clearances. Armed with this knowledge, I ran at the South African stand off and managed to charge down the ball. It could have flown anywhere. Luckily, it landed in Will's path, and after a kick forwards, he won the chase for the ball to score. That won the game for England and Lol was quick to congratulate me afterwards in his inimitable way. 'Awesome, mate,' he said, 'well done.'

I can't say Lol and I ever really saw eye to eye. That's the thing about sports squads. There were thirty of us in Australia and people may think that we were all best friends, but that was not the case. We were all professional and we all wanted to achieve the same goal, but we had our particular friendship groups.

As a player and a leader, Lol was awesome, but we had very different personalities, and with the whole Leicester v Wasps rivalry as well, it was difficult to be great mates. I think the two clubs saw themselves at polar opposites. We did things our way – not flashy, head down, getting on with the job; and they did it their way – in your face, all bravado, all very 'living the high life' in the big smoke. That's how I saw it at the time, anyway. I thought he and Wasps were arrogant, even though my mate Worzel played for them, but that was probably mainly due to hatred of a side who proved to be the only real thorn in our flesh over the years. That said, it was a fantastic asset to have Lol in the team, and he played a massive role in England winning the World Cup.

Even though my charge-down had proved to be so important to winning the game, I was down afterwards in the dressing room. I just didn't think I'd played that well. The Chief Executive of the Rugby Football Union, Francis Baron, compounded the issue. He used to pop in to the dressing room after games to shake hands and say well done or commiserate. This time was different. 'Not one of your best games, lad,' was all he could offer to me as I sat in my booth. I was 23 years old, we'd just beaten the Springboks to all but guarantee top spot in our group, I'd provided the game's turning point and he came out with that gem. I'd have taken it from Johnno or Clive, but not from a suit I barely knew, who had failed to play rugby to any reasonable level himself. It was just after the game and emotions were still high. If I hadn't been so weary, I may well have chinned him. When I told the players later what Baron had said, many replied that they were amazed how I'd managed to keep my own counsel. To a man, they said they would have decked him!

Later, Shaggy (as Will Greenwood was known) stopped me in the corridor in the bowels of the Subiaco Oval stadium.

'Mate,' he said, 'it means a lot to me that you gave me the chance to score tonight.'

Just over a year earlier, he and his wife, Caro, had lost their baby boy when he was born too prematurely. Now Caro, expecting again, was having complications and he was to rush back to England to be with her at what, especially in the light of their previous trauma, was an extremely worrying time. Both decided that he should play against South Africa first, however, and he was able to shut out his problems enough to score the winning try. At the time I didn't give what he said much thought. Now, as a father of two young sons, I understand more, and I feel privileged if I helped in any small way. It would end happily for Will and Caro, too, with the birth of their child.

Next up was Samoa in Melbourne, a game we always expected to win, but which turned out to be a great deal harder than anyone expected. Clive mixed and matched with his selection. I was back on the bench and Worzel came in to join Backy and Lol in the back row.

The game was always going to be physical because that's the way the Polynesians play – lovely people off the pitch, absolute monsters on it. Their captain, Sititi, stunned us by completing a wonderful try and, as the minutes ticked by and I sat on the bench full of nervous energy, the Samoans continued to lead. In fact, it was past the hour mark before we finally nudged ourselves ahead, and by then Vicks, Thommo and I had all entered the fray. The turning point was when Vicks bulldozed his way over to score. I was right beside him and half-expected the scoring pass but the Raging Bull does not score many tries and, from a short distance out from the try line, he was not going to be stopped.

From that rather late point onwards, we eased our way to a 35–22 victory but were far from happy with our performance. We were not happy about the incident at the end of the game, either, when Dave Reddin, our fitness man, sent on Danny Luger from the bench with Mike Tindall down injured, in the mistaken belief that Tins had left the field. For 35 seconds we had 16 men on the pitch, and as I came off, I witnessed the linesman, New Zealand's Steve Walsh, and Dave in such a heated exchange that it ended with Walsh lobbing water all over the England man. For a few days afterwards we were concerned about what the repercussions would be for innocently breaking the rules but it came to nothing, despite ridiculous calls from some members of the Australian media and former players to ban us.

There was one more game to go and, with respect to Uruguay, it was not a game we were ever likely to lose. The venue was the impressive Suncorp Stadium in Brisbane, and that meant a day or two of R&R on the Gold Coast. Clive told us to let our hair down. We were not suddenly on holiday but it had been a long, hard slog throughout the summer and the first three group games, so it was exactly the correct thing to do, but it did not go entirely to plan.

That night I threw a few vodka and limes down my throat along-side Grewy, Thommo and Whitey. Influenced by the alcohol, I gave Thommo a small tap in the nuts and he responded by cracking me on the jaw. It was all knockabout stuff, and as we both headed for the door, I gave Thommo a hefty nudge. At first I thought it was funny when his head cracked against the frame. My mirth changed to horror, however, when blood began to cascade from a head wound. I suggested we went to have the cut looked at, but Thommo refused, and I spent the rest of the night holding ice cubes to his head.

Despite this, Thommo saved my skin the next morning by waking me up five minutes before a team meeting. I was in a blind panic, and still fully clothed, but being late for one of Clive's meetings was tantamount to dropping yourself. I just made it and sat in front of Thommo, who loitered at the back of the room to hide his forehead. That morning in training he went down with a mysterious head wound. There must have been a clash of heads or something! It meant he could finally get some stitches. It wasn't the most convincing faked injury, but we managed to get away with it!

Josh Lewsey, Benny Kay, Worzel and I also spent a little time in the sea attempting to surf. None of us had ever tried it before except, of course, Josh! It was fairly comical stuff – none of us could stand up on a board, let alone surf. Josh ventured farther out in the vain hope of finding a wave in what was a flat sea. After a while, he was back, paddling furiously past where we stood waist high in the water. At that moment, I caught a glimpse of a large, grey fin shooting past my side. Later, our instructor, Munga, told us it was probably a dolphin. Probably! I'll never know, but if it had been a hungry shark, I would have stood no chance.

'Yeah, I saw it too,' Josh said as we hauled ourselves out of the water. 'That's why I suddenly came in.' He could have told us!

The game itself was a bit of a mismatch. England beat Uruguay 111–13, with Josh helping himself to five tries. Even I managed to get myself over the whitewash, my first and still my only World Cup try. The only memorable aspect of the game, save for Josh's personal tally, was when Worzel was sin-binned and, as he left the pitch to cheers from the English contingent, bowed his head repeatedly to them and applauded. Clive went berserk at the time, and maintained his anger the next morning when the squad assembled for the debrief. As Worzel and I entered the room, he whispered to me, 'Mate, I've got to apologise to everyone.'

'You're kidding!' I whispered back.

Joe was very nervous. It was a case of Clive striving for perfection in everything we did. You cannot really criticise him for that, can you, but I sometimes felt that Clive picked on Worzel a little. Joe didn't mean any harm in his actions. He was and is an awesome player. He just got his timing wrong.

Clive went through the game as he always did, highlighting the good and bad points, before reaching the climax of the meeting.

'I'd like to make it clear that there are some things that are unacceptable on a rugby pitch and I'd like Joe to now stand up and say something.'

I didn't know whether to laugh or cry. Obviously, in a room full of overgrown five year olds, there were funny elements to the whole fiasco. I kept my head down. So did most of the others. The last thing I needed was to catch someone else's eye and start to laugh. But I also felt dreadfully sorry for Worzel. Nobody in the team minded a jot, but it was all a little demeaning for him.

We stayed in Queensland for the quarter-final against Wales. They had finished second in their group behind New Zealand, but had given the All Blacks a run for their money in a highly entertaining, high-scoring encounter. We continued to train, if not right in the middle of the day, when it was still hot, and it began to take its toll on us. The quarter-final would make us realise we needed to slow down and pace ourselves better if we were going on to become world champions.

This was a very good Welsh team, including Stephen Jones, Shane Williams, Gareth Thomas and Colin Charvis, and they deserved their half-time lead, having scored a couple of very fine tries. I had started that day alongside Backy and Lol, and nothing seemed to be going quite right for us. Everybody felt knackered. You could see it on the pitch. We had smashed this Welsh team in the Six Nations and in the August warm-up game, but now we were making a good job of trying to exit the tournament. Poor old Luges was subbed at half-time, even though he was not injured, and that was the last we would see of him at the World Cup. It took a flash of brilliance from Jason Robinson to set up Shaggy for a second-half try in the corner, and with 23 points from Jonny's boot we squeezed home 28–17.

We were now just eighty minutes away from the World Cup final, but we were growing increasingly concerned about the way we had been performing. Samoa had not been too impressive, and neither had Wales. In the World Cup everything changes. Suddenly, teams go up a level or three and tend to beat teams who are supposedly better than they are. Look at New Zealand's record over the years. On most occasions, they had started the World Cup as favourites only to fall short. If we were to beat France in the semi, let alone go on to win the World Cup, something had to change.

The senior players called a meeting for the following morning, which the management attended. The main speakers were Jason Leonard, Lol and Johnno. Lol, as always, was very passionate. 'This is an eye-opener guys. We're not playing at our best.' Everyone agreed that we needed to cut down our work load and not assume we were the best. From this moment onwards, Johnno really came into his own. If we had a training session and he felt it was going well, he'd call a stop to it and that was that, without even checking with the management. You know a team's going well when the captain can take control of it like that. Johnno was a forthright figure, for sure, but he understood the players. The England team that won the 2003 World Cup was his team, no question, and I would have followed him to the end of the earth. He was, and in many ways remains, my captain.

With two games to go, Clive began to freak out. We were all nervous, of course, but we had a job to do and knew exactly how to do it. We moved down to Manly, a beautiful northern suburb of Sydney on the beach, in preparation for the semi-final at the Olympic Stadium. This was when Clive decided that we could no longer see our girlfriends and wives in the team hotel, the Royal Pacific. He wanted no distractions. In other words, he wanted no sex. Annie had been in Australia since the quarter-final and nearly all of the others had their partners down under, too. Our rooms were at the back of the hotel, which was handy because there was a back entrance through the car park. You can guess what went on. The management tended to sit in the main foyer of the hotel, so we avoided that area like the plague. Instead, we sneaked the girls up and down the back stairs to our rooms all week. The point was not to be disobedient. We needed to approach the semi like any other game. We knew it was massively important, of course, but this was not the time suddenly to change how we prepared for a Test match – in any way.

For the semi-final, Richard Hill returned to the starting XV and I dropped back to the bench. Coach Andy Robinson broke the news to me, emphasising that it was a very close call. I was disappointed but philosophical. Of course Hilly would play if fit. He was one of the best rugby players in the world at that time.

Again we fell behind to an opportunist converted try by Serge Betsen from our own lineout, and again we came back strongly. Jonny, who had been beating himself up about his self-perceived lack of form, scored all 24 points in the 24–7 win, consisting of five penalties and three drop goals in the driving rain. Jonny's perform-ance on the night was world-class but it had got to the stage where we expected nothing less from him. He was, and still is, that good. Every time he stepped up to take a kick we assumed we would score because it was a kick he had practised ten thousand times. It was clinical stuff by the team, and I was able to enjoy a 10 minute run around at the end, putting in a few tackles and making a couple of runs.

Afterwards, there was no elation, no euphoria at all. We had just won a World Cup semi-final and would be facing the Australians a week later in the same stadium, but it was as if we had done our job and got ourselves into the position we had aimed for, nothing more. I looked around the dressing room and saw only determined expressions on the England boys' faces. So far so good, but there was still one more game to play, and it happened to be the World Cup final.

Clive's head was almost exploding with the pressure now. This time he told us to stay out of the sun. We knew the pressure was on and were not planning to do anything stupid, but I still went out for my version of a surf at Manly, and visited my favourite milkshake parlour by the beach. It had to be business as usual. Life had to be as normal as it could be in the week of the World Cup final, which, considering I was 'papped' for the first time in my life by a photographer when walking with Annie, was not very normal.

The team remained the same for the final, except that Tins was back in for Mike Catt, who joined me on the bench. Catty had played a big part in our comeback against Wales in the quarter-final, and replaced Tins for the semi win over France, but Clive preferred the younger man for the final denouement, although Catty, typically, would still have his say at the end.

Friday night meant movie night. Most of the lads were intent on staying in. Backy even called a back-row forwards meeting, something he never usually did on the eve of a game. You can take it as either his thoroughness to ensure we got it right on the night, or his nervousness.

We were all nervous, which is why Thommo and I set off down the high road in Manly to the one, small, independent cinema to watch 'School of Rock'. Taking the ferry into Sydney was not an option, but when we got to the cinema, we were told that as nobody else had turned up, they were about to close. The projectionist was in the process of dismantling the screen and editing the reels. Thommo and I went into panic mode. They obviously didn't understand. We had a World Cup final the next night. We didn't want to watch a movie, we *had* to watch a movie; otherwise all our preparations for the big game would be in turmoil. This is the passionate speech we gave to the projectionist, who had plans that night involving friends and beer. He said it would take thirty minutes to put the film back together again. It didn't matter. We asked him what it would take to watch it. In the end, we handed over $300, bought a huge bucket of popcorn and extra large cups of Fanta and got to see our film. Thommo and I still talk about the most expensive trip to the cinema in history to this day. And although he does not know it, Jack Black played his part in our World Cup final.

I woke up in the morning sick with nerves. I tried everything I could to relax but failed miserably. I found myself just staring in the mirror, hearing a voice in my head saying, 'You're playing in the World Cup final tonight. You're playing in the fucking World Cup final.' I got up late, had breakfast, saw some of the guys, watched TV and went back to bed, but always there was a nagging worry in my head: 'Don't fuck it up.'

I can't recall a single word of Clive's team talk in the hotel before we clambered aboard the bus to take us on the forty-five-minute journey from Manly to the Olympic Stadium – official name, Telstra Stadium, now renamed Stadium Australia or ANZ Stadium – in Homebush Bay. I was totally numb. I can recall a rather surreal incident moments after we drove out of the hotel, however. There were hundreds of well-wishers outside as we walked to the bus. Jonny, as always, received the loudest screams on the night. Clive was the last on the bus, having made sure all his troops were aboard. As we drove along the seafront, everyone was in match mode, quiet, pensive and with headphones on, but a group of seven or eight Australians were waving furiously and trying to catch our attention. They certainly caught mine. As I made eye contact with a few of them, they suddenly turned and bared their backsides in a group moony. It was, I have to say, pure genius, and I commend them for doing that to the England bus *en route* to the final.

I sat on the bench alongside the other substitutes as the game began. Behind us sat the remaining squad members who were not part of the match-day 22. Ronnie Regan was regularly taking swigs from his Lucozade bottle. I found out later he had filled it with vodka and Coke. Lote Tuqiri scored early for the Wallabies but three penalties from Jonny and Jason Robinson's try in the corner handed England a big, potentially match-winning half-time lead.

Robbo's reaction when he dived over in the corner was remarkable, only because he was a man who kept his emotions in check. A quiet, born-again Christian who kept himself to himself, Robbo would have graced any team in the world that year. I didn't know him well but I respected him enormously. In fact, I'd sometimes ask him to run at me in training to sharpen up my defence. It was a thankless task in a one-to-one with the man, but luckily he was on our side, not anyone else's. It just showed how much it meant to him when he suddenly exploded with emotion, having scored the try in injury time, and it gave me a real boost to see it.

The lead might well have been more had Benny Kay not dropped the ball two metres out when all he needed to do was catch it and flop over. Had he scored that try it was pretty much game over. I felt bad for my Tigers teammate but, to his credit, he put his head down and just carried on performing like he always did. A lesser man would have been knocked for six by the realisation of what he had potentially done.

In the second half, the tide started to turn. Elton Flatley started to kick his penalties and our scrum was consistently penalised.

The South African referee, Andre Watson, had stated that he would 'put his house on never getting a scrumming decision wrong'. Our policy that day was not to have Johnno on his back, because it was felt that this might backfire, so it was Matt Dawson's job to be the cheeky chappie, a role that he revelled in. He and Kyran Bracken had an epic battle for the number-nine jersey in the tournament. In their different ways, both were world-class but Daws got the nod for the final and his job, as well as producing his usual sniping runs and being a total pain to the opposition, was to befriend Watson. Thommo, in what has become one of the classic World Cup quotes hardly helped, though. When the referee blew his whistle yet again to penalise us, Thommo had had enough. His head popped up from the dark areas of the front row, he looked across at the referee and said, 'Andre, you must have a shit house.'

For much of the game I was desperate to enter the fray. When you are on the bench, you feel all the adrenalin but have no outlet to vent it. Yet as the game progressed closer and closer to the final whistle, and as the Wallabies edged closer and closer to drawing level with England, I began to dread the thought of running on to the pitch and being the man who lost the World Cup. Flatley showed enormous bottle that night. Even though I was praying he would miss his penalties, I am glad he succeeded. I wanted us to win the World Cup, not Australia to lose it.

Three minutes into extra time I replaced Hilly. As I waited to join the game, Clive, his eyes almost popping out, had a final piece of advice. 'Keep a cool head and don't give away any penalties,' he shouted. It was pretty much the last thing I needed to hear right then. Clive had now gone way over the edge in terms of the pressure and the occasion. Everyone could see it in him. Luckily for me, a stray lineout ball fell straight into my arms and I was off and running. A few tackles and a couple of half-decent breaks removed any lingering nerves. Jonny kicked us ahead again, Elton returned the compliment and it all came down to the final minute.

We all know what happened next, although these things are never quite what they seem. I played a small part in the drama, for which I am forever grateful. It began when I half-tackled George Smith, the fine Wallaby back-rower. The ball went out to Matt Rogers in his own half and I was able to put enough pressure on him for the former rugby league star to slice his clearance. That meant we had a lineout inside the Wallaby half. Benny Kay called it and, one from the back, I was to receive. I'd like to think I may be remembered for a few aspects of my game, but being in the lineout is not necessarily one of them. On this night, though, in the most important lineout of my life, Thommo's throw found its way to his mate at the back. He'll be the first to admit it was not the perfect effort. It landed in my midriff, but the point about the next few seconds, which have now entered the rose-tinted land of sporting folklore, is that none of it was the polished move it was made out to be.

I flipped it to Daws and he made some valuable metres with one of his trademark breaks before being tackled. Backy, in the scrum-half position, attempted to pass to Jonny, who was in the slot and waiting for the opportunity to drop a goal. Instead, the ball hit Johnno, who was on a decoy run. Luckily, he managed to keep hold of the ball and, by taking it back in to the ruck, bought Jonny crucial time and shortened the distance to the posts. It was a classic case of there being no wrong decisions in the game, and everyone buying into what was taking place.

By now, I was on the other side of the pitch, virtually unmarked, waving frantically at Jonny. If he chipped the ball over towards me, I was convinced I would score. Happily, for the sake of English rugby, Jonny ignored me and, although he had missed with two previous drop-kick attempts, wobbled his third effort over with his right, and therefore wrong, foot.

Even then the game was not quite finished, and things didn't go to plan. Quite what an out-of-position Trevor Woodman was doing receiving Flatley's restart I'll never know but, thank goodness, he caught the ball before wisely shipping it out to Mike Catt. Catty had come on to replace Tins two minutes before the end of regular play, and it was left to him to punt the ball as hard and as high as he could out of the stadium to end the proceedings and confirm that we had become world champions.

Then, and only then, did the team erupt with emotion. The funny thing was, as happy as we all were, the overriding emotion was relief. Sheer relief. We were favourites to win the cup, after all. We came to Australia to do just that. We expected it. And now we had finally achieved it. Mum and Annie came down to the pitchside for hugs. Both were crying their eyes out. Dad was too, so much so that he refused to come down and be seen bawling his eyes out. A clearly irked John Howard, the Australian Prime Minister, virtually threw our World Cup winner's medals at us, and Johnno lifted the Webb Ellis Trophy. Mission accomplished.

Back in the dressing room it was time for celebration, but also reflection. I had photographs taken with Johnno, of course, and with two of my best muckers, Thommo and Worzel. Then the seven Leicester players in the squad decided to have a group photo. We were still covered in dirt, blood and tears, but these were the players who meant the most to you because you had played alongside them for so many years. Just as we posed for the photo, a woman's head poked its way into the huddle. I had no idea who she was and, caught up with the emotion of the moment, said, 'Excuse me, love, do you mind fucking off? I'm trying to have a photo with my mates.' She turned out to be Tessa Jowell, Culture Secretary in the British Government.

The night was not the huge piss-up you would expect. We saved that for later. This was a time to be with the ones you loved most in your life. It was almost as if I was disappointed the journey was over. I realised it was the getting there, not the being there, that mattered the most.

A few hours later, though, the mayhem began. It took us an hour to walk ten metres out of the hotel entrance, such was the demand for autographs and photos – a tiny taste of what was about to hit us on our return home.

6

TOUGH AT THE TOP, AND TOUGH ON THE BODY

Leicester, 2004–7

The long flight home was a time for reflection, a quiet time to savour with your teammates, and a time to sleep. For me, it was a gloriously chilled out journey home with the weight of the world lifted from all our shoulders. We posed for photos with fans on the plane, and signed autographs, while Clive and Backy took the World Cup down to the economy end of the plane to show the punters, which I thought was a nice touch. However, the relative serenity of the flight was shattered the moment we touched down at Heathrow. As the main door opened and we gazed out on to the airport tarmac, all we could see were hundreds of photographers snapping away at us. We assembled for the obligatory team photo on the steps to the plane and were then told to file into the terminal in twos and threes as there was a bit of a reception waiting for us. A bit? It is fair to say nobody expected the greeting we received from thousands of well-wishers, who had trekked out to Heathrow at the crack of dawn to cheer us home. Back in Australia, it had all gone quiet. The locals, having seen the Wallabies lose the World Cup final, got on with life. In England, the mayhem was just beginning. We appeared to have returned as household names, at least for a few weeks.

A new Renault was waiting for me at the Pennyhill Park Hotel as a welcome bonus for my exploits. Jason Leonard was given a car as well. We said our goodbyes in Bagshot and headed off on our separate ways, but not for long. When I arrived home – Annie had left Australia the day before me – I caught our new neighbours midway through decorating our house with 'Congratulations' and 'Welcome Home' signs. Considering we had only just moved in and barely knew them, it was a lovely thought. The goodwill continued. I was in a supermarket the next day when, suddenly, over the Tannoy a voice announced: 'Lewis Moody, World Cup winner, is in the store.' Out on the street a grown man ran up to me, hugged me and said, 'It was amazing. Thank you so much.' It was all rather bizarre, if cool. The sudden adulation was almost overpowering.

Then the opportunities started to flood in, as they do only after such sporting success. Thommo and I appeared on a TV show called 'Big Boys Toys' –a DIY programme in which we had to help build a rugby clubhouse – and I made my first appearance on the BBC's 'A Question of Sport'. Predictably, I made an idiot of myself when I needed my captain, Ally McCoist, to tell me that the answer to the question 'Who did Wales play recently in the World Cup quarter-final?' was, in fact, England!

One of the funnier events was when the whole squad became the subject of ITV's 'An Audience With … the England Rugby Squad', hosted by Chris Tarrant. I got to meet Kevin Whateley, who plays Lewis in the TV series of the same name and, before that, in 'Inspector Morse'. This was relevant because, for many years, I'd had Tigers teammates mimicking John Thaw's Morse character and shouting, 'Get me a beer, Lewis,' or, 'What about the girl, Lewis?'

The highlight of the evening focused on Worzel. The programme makers had asked around the families to see if any of the players had any other talents. Everyone said no except for Worzel's family, who told ITV that Joe was a pianist. This was true. In fact, whenever there was a piano in the team's hotel, sooner or later you would hear the tinkling of the keys and find Worzel playing his beloved Blues.

When we were sitting in the dressing room, waiting to make our stage entrance, a tiny bloke walked in, said well done to us all, shook a few hands and left again. It turned out to be singer, songwriter and pianist Jamie Cullum. Midway through the show, Jamie produced a superb, all-singing and dancing performance with the piano and a big band supporting him. Chris Tarrant then announced: 'And that's not all folks. We have another incredible pianist here with us today – Joe Worsley.'

Poor Worzel appeared on stage looking like a man facing a firing squad. He'd asked for a backing band, too, but was told just to play the piano. Even before Worzel began, I caught, out of the corner of my eye, Julian White's shoulders beginning to heave and the faint sound of a snigger. Silence descended, Joe took a deep breath and began. Now don't get me wrong. Worzel's a really good pianist, especially these days, but on this night, wracked with nerves, he had what can only be described as a complete mare. It was absolutely excruciating to watch, and to listen to. In his hour of need, he could have turned around and searched for support from his teammates and comrades. If he had, he would have witnessed Whitey slapping his knee and guffawing with laughter. The performance was so bad it was edited out of the recorded show.

We dominated the BBC's 'Sports Personality of the Year Show' that year. Jonny won the individual award, with Johnno second, and we won the team award. Johnno should probably have won the individual award, something that Jonny would happily accept. For all Jonny's wonderful exploits in Australia – including all the points in the semi-final and, of course, THAT drop goal in the final – the team that became world champions was very much Johnno's team moulded on him. Still, it was another memorable night for us all. My personal highlight was meeting George Best. I wanted to have a drink with him, of course, but when I bought one for him, his minders subtly removed it. George was on one of his detox sessions at the time. Pretty much the whole England squad attempted to have a drink with the great man. Every time the minders would say, 'Thanks, I'll be taking that then, George.' I'm glad I met him, though. And I was sad when he passed away.

I tried to persuade impressionist Alistair McGowan to produce an impersonation of Shrek especially for my Shrek-lookalike friend Thommo, and I also met my old Oakham School cricket coach, David Steele, the former England cricketer. David won the 1976 Sports Personality of the Year award after he took on the Australians in the Ashes, looking like someone's granddad! Jonny's dad, Phil, was especially pleased when I introduced him to the silver fox!

A week later, I was asked to switch on the Christmas lights, not only in Market Harborough, but also in Oadby. It was surreal as I wished the good folks of these fine Leicestershire towns Happy Christmas. Other treats included invitations to the premieres of 'Lord of the Rings' and 'Phantom of the Opera' in London; having a dormitory named after me at Oakham School; a civic reception in Leicester for the fans; being helicoptered to Twickenham straight after a Tigers game to parade the World Cup during the Baa-Baas versus South Africa match; and being named the Rutland Sports Personality of the Year. Yes, really!

The best, however, came last – our big day out in London. It began with the open-topped bus parade through the city centre streets. We all feared that no one would turn out. In the end, they reckoned half a million were out on the streets that day to celebrate with us. They were literally hanging off the lampposts in Trafalgar Square. The players took the bus while wives and partners stayed behind in the hotel to watch it all unfold on TV. As the trip was sponsored by Tetleys, Jason Leonard took it as a personal challenge to drink the bus dry of the stuff. When he discovered that there wasn't a toilet on the bus, he used the next best thing – an empty champagne bottle.

I know this for a fact because half of it splashed off the bottle and rebounded down my suit leg!

This wasn't exactly good news for me, especially as our next stop was Buckingham Palace to meet the Queen. Once there, we were briefed concerning etiquette. At first, we had to greet the Queen with 'Your Majesty' and then, after that, address her as 'Ma'am'. As we made our first greeting, we were supposed to bow as well. Nobby West, who prided himself on being a working-class former copper from South Leicestershire, stood there spluttering at these orders.

'I'm not bloody bowing to anyone,' he announced. 'And I'm not saying Ma'am or Your Majesty, either.'

We were standing in a horseshoe shape. The doors opened and in bounded half a dozen corgis. Every single one of them headed straight for me because of the former incident with Jason and the overflowing champagne bottle. I was still trying to shake them off my leg when a diminutive woman walked into the room. Johnno introduced the Queen to the players.

'This is Jonny Wilkinson, Ma'am, this is Lawrence Dallaglio, Ma'am, this is Mike Tindall, Ma'am . . .' The Queen would be getting to see a great deal more of Tins in future years – days earlier, he had first hooked up with her granddaughter, Zara. '. . . this is Jason Leonard, Ma'am. He's won more Test caps than anyone else in England. This is Dorian West, Ma'am.'

Nobby had got himself so worked up that he had no idea what to do next. In the end, in full view of everyone, he half bowed, half curt-seyed, and offered the limpest of hands as he said, 'Er, Your Majesty.' As you can imagine, Nobby was subjected to abuse for the rest of the day.

We all then sloped off to Number Ten Downing Street to meet the Prime Minister, Tony Blair. Annie, Luges and I were treated to a tour of the house by Cherie Blair, who proved to be exceptionally nice, and we all grouped around the PM for photos, like fans.

It was all tremendous fun, of course, and a series of once-in-a-life-time opportunities, but away from the new-found celebrity lifestyle, it was not going anywhere nearly as well. Four days after returning home from Australia, I was playing for the Tigers against Bath at Welford Road. My troublesome foot was proving to be extremely painful and Dean Richards suggested I came off at half-time. I asked if I could stay on just for the kick-off and then depart. As it turned out, I missed the ball but clattered straight into Mike Tindall, who was playing for Bath. As we both lay on the ground, Tins called me a dick and I told him how much it hurt.

The following week, I again couldn't last the distance, away at Stade Français. Then, in training, Will Johnson stood on the foot and that was it. A CT scan revealed that I had a minute fracture in my navicular but because this is the main loading bone in your foot, it meant that nothing could function. I was told I'd be wearing a boot for six weeks, and then I faced another eight weeks rehab. When the time had passed, however, and the foot felt exactly the same during my first training run back, I threw a massive wobbly. I'd just come back from winning the World Cup and all I wanted to do was play rugby at a time when I was enjoying my best form. Instead, I would miss the rest of the season, which included being absent from the return fixture against Stade Français. In Paris, I had conceded a penalty when I apparently brought down Diego Dominguez with a late hit. The truth is I never touched him but he went down as if shot by a sniper. It was so football-esque. I wanted to kill him in the return game but I was injured, and he then retired at the end of the season. It annoys me to this day that I was never able to get him back.

Times were tough at Leicester. A team so used to winning silverware was struggling, which was hardly surprising considering the toll the World Cup took on the team in terms of the best players being away and then so many of them injured afterwards. Not long into 2004 a cull took place, with various heads of department losing their jobs. I felt particularly sorry for John Duggan, a former player of great note and longevity, who had been a conditioning coach for a great deal of time. One day he came to work and received his marching orders. To make matters worse, his replacement, Darren Grewcock, was already in his office on the day he was dismissed. I felt that it could have been handled better, to say the least.

Up at the top, Dean Richards left the club as well. That defeat by Stade proved to be the final straw for the management board. They wanted to move Dean 'upstairs' but the big man was having none of it. I do not know exactly what happened, but Dean went from being Mr Leicester to someone who wanted no association with the club whatsoever. It was a great pity. All his memorabilia was taken down, 'Deano's Bar' was renamed, and the original Man of Leicester departed with barely a backward glance. To this day, no one's name has been chanted from the Welford Road stands quite like Deano's.

We went to Peebles in Scotland for our 2004–05 pre-season tour. In my first proper training session I felt the foot go again. I walked straight off the pitch. I'd been told it could be a career-threatening injury. Now I feared it was all over for me, and confided as much to Geordan. Like a good friend, Geordie rounded up Leon and Austin and they decided to take me out to the pub that night for what turned out to be an almighty bender. It was exactly what I needed. We stayed in the pub until two in the morning, then crept back into the hotel as drunks do – noisily. It didn't help that I was whipping Geordie with a car aerial and dragging Leon along on his knees. In the morning he discovered carpet burns! We continued the party in a room upstairs until an annoyed Whitey and Wig appeared and remonstrated with us.

In the morning, during the team meeting, John Wells, who had taken over from Dean, said, 'Please can those people who went on the piss last night make themselves known.' Rather sheepishly, the four of us raised our hands. Our punishment was to massage all the backroom staff. I felt it only right to tell Wellsy later that I had been very down and my teammates had rallied round me. Wellsy said it was a closed issue. He understood and appreciated me telling him this. We became known as the 'Peebles Four' as a result of this episode, a term we still use to this day. It may seem like a joke, but I prefer to see it as a reminder of a time when your mates stuck with you.

I missed the first five games of the new season. This was a dark, dark period for me. I recall sitting at home alone watching the Tigers win a big game with a last-gasp try from Danny Hipkiss. In typical fashion, Leicester had snatched victory from the jaws of defeat. Suddenly, all my emotions came to the fore. I started to cry, small tears at first, and then an uncontrollable sobbing. I was elated for my teammates, but gutted for myself. I wrote down my thoughts in a diary:

'Grow up. There are thousands of people worse off than you. But it shows just how much this game means to me, more than I could ever imagine. I realise that this is my forte, my gift. I knew hands down that on the pitch nobody would beat me. It is where I find my respect. When you are robbed of playing the game, you dream of scoring the winning try or making the game-winning tackle. When the old players tell you to make the most of it because you'll forever miss playing the game, you often wonder what they mean. I've been quite looking forward to life after rugby. But not now. Those guys would play again at the drop of a hat. Now I understand why.'

Five weeks later I was finally back training and so excited about being on the pitch again that I ended up having a fight with, of all people, Johnno, although perhaps the word 'fight' is stretching it a little. The session had not been going well. There were too many dropped passes, too many half-hearted tackles. Johnno called us all together and demanded that we started hitting the tackle bags hard.

Alesana 'Alex' Tuilagi started to hand off the bags, instead, and side step them before running down the pitch to score. I saw red. This wasn't what Johnno meant. All my pent-up frustration emerged as I sprinted after Alex and hit him with a diving tackle. From behind it may not have looked too good because all you could see was a swinging arm before the ball went flying. Suddenly, a large, dark shadow loomed. It was Johnno and he was not amused.

'What the fuck are you playing at?' he asked.

I swore back and within moments he had grabbed my shirt and, stupidly, I had grabbed his with my right, punching hand. Now there was no turning back. I couldn't be seen to back down and there was no way Johnno, our captain, was going to do that, either. While I contemplated hitting him, a large, right hook caught me flush on the jaw. I would have gone down, for sure, had Alex's brother, Henry, not raced up to break us apart. He caught me as I fell backwards, simultaneously throwing a left-hander that missed Johnno by a mile. So that was our fight. He punched me, I went down. Not exactly an epic! I continued training but was so dazed by Johnno's right-hander that I needed to lie down in the medical room. Afterwards, Johnno lumbered in to see if I was OK and to apologise. I didn't mind, far from it. I felt I was finally back and I was happy.

The rest of the season was largely uneventful at Leicester. I managed to get myself back into the England team, now under Andy Robinson, after Clive resigned in the summer. I also began to rediscover my form, highlighted by one of my best-ever performances in the Heineken Cup quarter-final, away at Leinster. We were not supposed to win, but everything fell into place at the RDS (Royal Dublin Society) Arena, and we came away with a famous victory, only to lose in the semi-final, to Toulouse. I remember sitting in the dressing room afterwards in Ireland, savouring the moment. I turned round to Johnno, in what was his last season.

'Mate, how do you replace a feeling like this?' I asked him. He looked at me for a long time.

'You can't,' he finally replied.

Worse still, we lost in the Premiership final to Wasps in what was Johnno's and Backy's last-ever games. This was not the way for two great careers to finish, but sport is no respecter of reputations. Afterwards, Wig stood up in the dressing room and told us to lift our heads.

'I want to thank two great friends of mine for the years we've had together playing the game,' he said. 'It's been a privilege.'

How we didn't all burst out crying on the spot I will never know. Maybe it was because at their last games at Welford Road the pair of them were presented with their replica pegs from the dressing room. After eighteen years' service, Johnno and Backy received a peg each. I thought it was hilarious, but that was the only thing that was remotely funny. With Backy and especially Johnno leaving, it truly was the end of an era. Add to this the recent retirements or transfers of Darren Garforth, Richard Cockerill, Paddy Howard, Dorian West and Will Johnson and it was easy to see that the guts were being ripped out of the team. It was a difficult time to be a Leicester Tiger.

Mind you, we nearly obtained Stephen Jones, the Welsh stand off. I say nearly because in the end he decided to leave Llanelli for Clermont Auvergne in the French Top 14, but not before he'd spent a couple of days with the Tigers. Peter Wheeler thought it would be a good idea if Geordan and I showed Stephen round. This was probably a mistake. After dinner with some of the other Tigers I suggested that Geordan, Stephen and I should find a pub nearby and we ended up knocking back sambucas at three in the morning. Five hours later I was in the gym when I saw Stephen walking around the club with Wheeler, and I found it very difficult not to laugh. Stephen looked like death and I wonder if Peter rued the decision to approach Geordan and me.

That summer I toured New Zealand with the British and Irish Lions. It did not go well collectively but I was happy with my individual input. On my return, Annie and I became engaged, although it didn't go quite how I had planned it. We had bought an apartment in Puerto Banus in southern Spain, and we headed off there for a break. I had arranged a romantic boat trip during which I would pop the question. The day before Annie had been reduced to tears when she asked me if we were ever going to get married. I told her I wanted to, but it wasn't in my psyche at the moment, just to throw her off the scent. The next morning the sea was too choppy and the trip was cancelled. Plan B was to take her out for a meal while a friend decorated the apartment. After a couple of hours, I feigned illness and when we returned, we discovered the place was decked out in flowers, petals and lit candles. There was even some champagne on ice waiting for us on the table on the balcony. Annie was so excited she started taking photos. At one point I got down on one knee to propose but she failed to see me and walked off, leaving me no other option but to get up again. Eventually, I asked her the big question. She laughed and replied, 'Are you serious?' It wasn't quite the reply I expected, but then she said yes and proceeded to phone all her friends.

Back in England, the ensuing season turned out to be an unmitigated disaster, at least from a Leicester point of view. A small shoulder injury meant that I missed the start of the season again. My first game was against the Leeds Tykes seconds, as they were then called. On the journey up, all the lads were talking about how arrogant the Leeds youngsters appeared to be, and especially someone called Jordan Crane. I listened to all this, and in my frustrated, angry way after missing yet more rugby, I took it all in. I started on the bench but came on and played well, scoring a try. Then Jordan and I both found ourselves running across the middle of the pitch after a line-out. When I saw it was him, I gave him a massive cheap shot, which landed on the bridge of his nose, to teach him a lesson. No one saw it, or so I thought. Jordan just felt his now bloodied nose, tore off his scrum cap and trudged to the sideline. It was a disappointing reaction. When Leicester's Richard Cockerill, by then a coach, and Simon Cohen watched this replayed on video, they could not believe his reaction to such unadulterated provocation.

'Well, he's not a Leicester player, is he?' said Cohen. 'He's not hard enough.' The following season Jordan moved from Leeds to Leicester.

Unfortunately for me, Ed Morrison, the referee, happened to be sitting in the Leeds stands that day, and he contacted the club to tell them to cite me. I phoned Jordan to apologise but it didn't prevent a six-week ban being meted out my way. There was little point in appealing. The video of the incident put me in a very bad light. I was disappointed in myself. I didn't normally deliver cheap shots but it was another example of how my frustrations over not playing rugby manifested in violence. As for Jordan, I now have a great deal of respect for him. He is a quality player.

I managed one game for the Tigers before the autumn internationals took me away on England duty. I should have returned for Leicester four weeks later but being sent off against Samoa after fighting with Alex Tuilagi – more of which later – resulted in a further nine-week ban. The club, rightly, fined us £3,000 each, which was donated to the Matt Hampson cause. Hambo, of course, is the former England Under-21 and Leicester prop who was paralysed during England training. The manner in which he has faced adversity and got on with life in an enthusiastic way is an inspiration to us all. Leicester were, understandably, unhappy with me. That was fifteen weeks of suspensions before I disappeared again with England for the Six Nations tournament.

By then, I had resorted to psychology to help deal with the anger that always seemed to boil over after periods out of the game. I had been reluctant to go down that route previously because I saw it, wrongly, as an admission of weakness, but life was becoming increasingly difficult for me as a rugby player and something needed to be done. Through my sponsors, Red Bull, I began to see Jamie Edwards for two-hour sessions at home, sitting in armchairs and using flip charts. The goal was to learn how to deal with seeing red, using distraction methods. The trick proved to be remarkably simple. Whenever I felt the first throes of a violent reaction, I was to look immediately at the referee. This not only distracted me from my intentions, but also reminded me that the ref would punish me severely, and it seemed to work. From the moment I returned to action, it was noticeable how many opposing players attempted to wind me up. I'm not saying that never happened before, but now I seemed to have acquired a reputation and plenty of people wanted to test it out, either by delivering some cheap shots – a slap across the face, a forearm in my neck or a stamp on my ankle – or in Europe, by gouging. Happily, I refused to react, and the longer I behaved myself, the less the cheap shots came. I ended up seeing Jamie for two and half years.

That summer, Annie and I were married in Bermuda, where a number of her relatives are from. Before then came the small matter of a three-day stag 'do' in Stockholm. Feek could not make it due to work commitments, Ali was branded 'worst man' because he was totally useless, and Geordan turned out to be a brilliant organiser, especially when it came to free drinks in Irish pubs. Each night I had to wear a ridiculous outfit, including a Fred Flintsone combo and, on the last night, a dress, which seemed to attract a good number of the Swedish gays who frequented a bar where we drank. The bar had a stage and a live band, who were persuaded by Geordan to let me sing Van Morrison's 'Brown Eyed Girl'. The first I knew about it was when I was introduced by the band to the crowd. I then proceeded to produce the worst rendition ever of Van the Man's classic, aided by Geordie shouting out the words from the corner of the stage, before diving off into the arms of the crowd.

The actual wedding was a small, intimate occasion on the beach. After a tropical storm in the morning, which threw my future wife into a tearful tizzy, we were blessed with glorious, afternoon sunshine. Feek, representing my school days, Ali for uni and Geordan for rugby, were my three best men and all delivered amusing speeches at the reception, although in Ali's case only because he heard Geordan's effort before the reception and stole all his gags. Geordie ripped up his now defunct speech and ad libbed for a brilliant fifteen minutes or so, while Feek owned up to my parents about crashing my Beetle.

Later, Annie's dad, Paul, and Geordan's then girlfriend, a good friend of Annie's, Lucie Silvas, performed the first song at the reception. Paul Muggleton used to be in a house band in New York and performed with the Rolling Stones and Jimi Hendrix. He was also a member of a band called the Savages who once reached number one in the Caribbean charts. He owns a guitar that Hendrix played. Paul is married to singer Judie Tzuke, best known for her massive 1980s hit 'Stay With Me Till Dawn', he and Annie's mum having separated long ago. Lucie, a very successful singer-songwriter, has known Annie since college days. She and Natasha, Danny Grewcock's future wife, were Annie's bridesmaids.

Still later that night, it was announced that occasionally I liked to perform Bee Gees songs. Naturally, I declined and, naturally, all the guests demanded I should go up on stage, so I did. I felt I was so good it could have been Barry Gibb singing, and the guests seemed to appreciate my efforts. When I came to watch the wedding video, I discovered how truly dreadful I had been, and how drunk everyone else seemed to be. As if any further evidence was required, Feek decided to take off his clothes and streak through the reception – aunties, uncles *et al* – before running into the sea!

Back in England, before the season began I travelled down to Berkshire to play cricket with my dad for his old team, Warfield. It was a bit of a reunion for him and his former teammates, and a joy

The start of a wretched six months. A shoulder injury forces me to leave the field at Twickenham, with physio Phil Pask in close attendance, during England's hammering of South Africa. November 2002.

I score against Wales in a World Cup warm-up Test in Cardiff, my first try since my shoulder operations, and suddenly the World Cup is back on track. August 2003.

Weight training at England's team base at the Pennyhill Park Hotel, Bagshot, August 2003.

Once a Tiger always a Tiger. The seven Leicester boys in the England squad celebrate in the Sydney dressing room after winning the World Cup – (*left to right*) me, Neil Back, Martin Corry, Dorian West, Ben Kay, Martin Johnson and Julian White.

The open-topped bus carrying the England team arrives in Trafalgar Square during the World Cup victory parade, December 2003. The crowds in London were amazing.

Receiving my MBE from the Queen at Buckingham Palace. Joe Worsley looks on. October 2004.

Mum, Dad and Annie came to Buckingham Palace to see me receive my MBE.

Leicester head coach John Wells, barking out orders during the Heineken Cup quarter-final win over Leinster at the old Lansdowne Road. April 2005.

Austin Healy and I grapple for the ball with Wasps' Mark van Gisbergen while Lawrence Dallaglio and Joe Worsley look on. Wasps were at Welford Road in December 2004 for a Heineken Cup tie.

Enjoying the moment with Geordan after the Tigers beat Leinster at Lansdowne Road in a Heineken Cup quarter-final. April 2005.

Johnno leads out the Tigers at Welford Road in April 2005. This was his last season.

Eight Tigers were named for the 2005 Lions tour to New Zealand – (*back row, left to right*) Ben Kay, me, Graham Rowntree, Martin Corry, Julian White; (*kneeling*) Ollie Smith, Neil Back and Geordan Murphy.

Lewis the losing Lion: 2nd Test v New Zealand, 2005.

New Zealand's Dan Carter destroys the British and Irish Lions in the second Test.

Don't effing panic! Gareth 'Alfie' Thomas scores for the British and Irish Lions in the second Test, which we lost, against New Zealand in Wellington, July 2005.

for me to play sport beside my father. During the game, I was bitten by an insect on my elbow and a couple of days later it had turned red. I have a history of infected bites, so I went to see the doctor. He, in his wisdom, thought I needed a drip in my arm, rather than antibiotics. Three days later, my arm was so swollen from shoulder to knuckle that I couldn't bend it. Full-blown cellulitis had set in and it was very obvious I needed to go straight to hospital. The hospital doctor took one look at it and arranged a bed for me immediately. I was placed on another drip, and also on a course of antibiotics, and stayed there for a week in great discomfort. It could have been worse. Much worse. The hospital doctor told me that if my arm had been left for another two days, there was every chance it would have been amputated. I'd missed the start of the previous two seasons through injury. This time I missed the first two games of the 2006–07 season due to sheer negligence. My initial doctor was struck off shortly afterwards, I later heard.

At Leicester, there had been more change at the top. Wellsy had left to take charge of the England Academy, which was his first step towards his future role as forwards coach with the England senior team. In his place, Paddy Howard returned from his pharmaceutical business down under to take the helm at Welford Road. Richard 'Cockers' Cockerill was his number two and my good friend Martin 'Cozza' Corry was team captain. Cockers was someone I never imagined would make a good coach, but I was wrong. He was astute at taking advice from senior players, such as Benny Kay, and soaked up every piece of information like a sponge. Paddy was a free spirit who encouraged everyone to have their say and bring in ideas, even if they were the wackiest moves or something taken from the school playing field. It seemed to work. After what had been, by Leicester's standards, a barren spell of four seasons without a trophy, we bounced back in 2006–07 to win the domestic double of Premiership title and Anglo-Welsh EDF Energy Cup.

This should have been a great excuse for massive celebrations, but every Tiger will still look back on that season with a tinge of disappointment because the elusive treble of Premiership, EDF Energy Cup and Heineken Cup was there for the taking. With the domestic titles secured, we kept our celebrations in check, because the biggest prize of all, to be crowned European champions again after a five-year absence, still had to be won, and we were just eighty minutes away from achieving this remarkable goal. We had to beat Wasps in the final, and we'd made 50 points against them in the league four weeks earlier. But sport doesn't always work as you might expect it to. Wasps did their homework on us, had a week off while we were playing, and stunned us with two blindside darts down the wing to score tries that won them the game and the Heineken Cup. Once again, we had lost a big final to our arch rivals. For us, in an incredibly long season, it proved to be one game too many.

Afterwards, I was very emotional, but not just because the Heineken Cup had slipped from our grasp again. My good friend Leon Lloyd was leaving the Tigers for Gloucester. He'd had some falling out with the coaches and was barely getting a look in any more with the first team, although for the final he was also carrying a small injury. The man who had played such a major role in us winning our first European title back in 2001 was sitting in the stands, and, being the proud man that he is, he was reluctant to come down to the pitch. But I waved him down because I believed he should savour his last few moments as a Tiger out on the grass with his teammates. I was desperate to win for him, and even contemplated giving him my medal. Later, at the official function, we both broke down in tears. Leon didn't even cry at his own wedding, so it showed how much this final day meant to him. I had one of my uncontrollable crying sessions and had to leave the room, followed out by Annie, who was concerned about me. I resembled the Robert de Niro character in 'Analyze This', the tears were that plentiful.

It had been an emotional day at the end of an emotional season. In fact, it had been an emotional time ever since the World Cup. Three and a half years earlier I was on top of the world, but then injuries, bad luck and a faltering club had invaded my world – and it had been no better at international level, with either England or the Lions.

7

THE WILDERNESS YEARS

England 2004–7 and the British
& Irish Lions 2005 tour

As everyone involved in the 2003 World Cup-winning England team will tell you, from the moment the final whistle sounded to confirm that we had become world champions, we dropped, collectively, on to our haunches. Everything had been geared to winning the World Cup. After that? Well, nobody had given it much thought. The retirements came, notably Johnno from international rugby, and so too did the injuries. Jonny suffered a horrendous series of career-threatening setbacks, and others, including me, were hit by long-term problems. I missed the whole of the 2004 Six Nations, and the summer tour to New Zealand and Australia, both of which went poorly, featuring England teams full of shattered players.

By the time I had recovered sufficiently to be selected for the England team for the 2004 autumn internationals, much had changed, starting at the top. Clive Woodward had walked out of his job during the summer. Most of us saw it coming. From the moment he began as England head coach, he had geared everything to winning the World Cup. It had taken over six years to achieve this and now, when he realised it would be back to square one, he felt he did not receive the support from the RFU that he required. His departure left a massive hole, which Andy Robinson, his dependable number two, was asked to fill.

Clive was not the best coach in the world, and he knew it. One of his qualities was to recognise his own strengths and weaknesses. He built up the best support team possible, while his attention to detail was extraordinary. Nothing was left wanting, but if you failed to buy into it, you weren't a part of it. The players soon cottoned on to this. It didn't matter if you did not believe in all of Clive's methods, only that you were seen to believe in them. For example, vision specialist Sherylle Calder was brought in to give the players eye exercises to do to improve their sight capability. Players were supposed to fill in the hours they had spent working on their vision skills on a board in the team room. Certain players did little or no eye exercises at all, wrote down the required amount of time on the board and received plaudits for doing so. Don't get me wrong. Clive was an incredible manager, the best in the world, but by the time we won the World Cup, the team, to some extent, coached itself. What Clive did was to ensure that we had everything in place to win.

Of course I owe Clive a great deal. It was him, after all, who believed in me when plenty of others may not have done. He had the balls to select me ahead of both Backy and Lol, which took some doing, and even after my ridiculous behaviour during the Tour of Hell he brought me back into the fold. He may not have been everyone's cup of tea but one aspect is beyond debate. Clive changed the psyche of English rugby at the highest level and turned us all into consummate professionals using any method he could at his disposal.

How do you follow that? As Robbo discovered, with enormous difficulty. As well as the retirements, the injuries and the post-World Cup hangover, every team in the world wanted to beat the world champions, especially as the champions happened to be England. I felt for Robbo. My respect for him was, and is, enormous. He and John Wells are the best forwards coaches I've ever played for, but now he was the boss and quite clearly unsure whether to be head coach or manager, or both. With the same coaching staff in place, Clive's shadow loomed all over the England squad.

It began reasonably well. I was delighted to be selected to start for

Robbo's first game in full charge, against Canada in the 2004 autumn Tests, especially as I had barely played any games for Leicester that season after my long-term injuries had kept me out of the game since December the previous year.

Jonny had been picked to captain England but withdrew with an injury. That was the start of his horrific catalogue of setbacks. Jason Robinson took the armband, becoming the first black man to captain England, the first former rugby league player to lead his country and the first full-back since the 1960s. Robbo was not a natural captain, and it was an interesting and novel experience for a forward like me to have a back in charge. As a player, he remained untouchable, the consummate professional, gifted with talents rarely witnessed in sport. In a 70–0 win over Canada he scored a hat-trick on his debut as captain and received a standing ovation from the Twickenham crowd when he left the field during the second half. I managed to get on the scoresheet, too, diving over from a maul to help England out of a slump of five defeats in their past six Test matches. It may have been as one-sided an international as you can get, but it still felt so good to be back playing in the white jersey after a year's absence, and to score at headquarters.

The following week it appeared as if all would be good in the new Andy Robinson era when we beat South Africa 32–16 to notch a sixth, successive win over the Springboks. Charlie Hodgson had not enjoyed too much luck over the years. For all his sublime skills, he was hit by either injury or the presence of Jonny, but with England's first-choice number ten out, and for some time, this proved to be Charlie's day. He scored a try, a drop goal, five penalties and two conversions in a 27 point haul. On this particular afternoon, Charlie looked like the best player in the world.

Seven days on, however, it was a different story. Although the 19–21 scoreline against Australia suggests a close-fought affair, there were too many errors and too many missed kicks. Henry Paul was replaced after just 25 minutes. I scored again, this time from a maul, but we just fell short.

Still, there was plenty of room for optimism as the 2005 Six Nations campaign began at the Millennium Stadium. I missed the game with a muscle strain, which was desperately frustrating for me, especially as I watched from the stands, helpless, as a huge Gavin Henson penalty won the night for Wales. I felt terribly sorry for Matthew Tait, who was making his debut and being taught a harsh lesson by Wales. Henson welcomed him to Test-match rugby with a huge dump tackle. Matthew was an immensely talented kid who had been built up by the media to be the next great hope, and was then knocked straight back down again after this defeat. Cardiff is, by anyone's standards, a difficult place to make a first Test start and he should have been given a second chance, but Robbo decided to drop him, just as he did Henry Paul. If he had his time again, I believe Robbo may have done things differently, but it was a tough learning curve for someone who, primarily, was an excellent coach rather than a manager.

I came back into the team for the next game, a dreadful home defeat by France, 17–18, after we led 17–3 at half-time. I played my part, giving away two penalties, which Dimitri Yachvilli converted, and somehow France, who played poorly throughout the game, beat us without ever going over our whitewash. These were games that England used to win by a point or a score. Now we were losing them by the same margin. Both Lol and Backy had retired from Test rugby – although Lol would make a return – so this was an awesome opportunity for Worzel, Cozza and me to form a new back-row trio as first-choice players. I'm not saying we failed to take it – Cozza, in particular, consistently played at a remarkably high level – but the run of poor results evidently failed to help our cause.

For me, another blood infection dominated the week of the Ireland game in Dublin. A small cut where the nail meets the flesh blew my finger up and, despite it being lanced and treated, the wound grew progressively worse to the point where I was admitted to hospital on the Wednesday night. I rejoined the boys in Ireland for the team's light run on the Friday morning, my only training of the week, and went on to produce a good performance in a game that we lost 19–13, sporting a huge bandage on my finger and dosed up on 48 hours' worth of IV drips. The result was disappointing. It was our third defeat on the bounce in the tournament, but at least I got to play against Geordan for the first time in a senior match. All week we had been exchanging banter and, even during what was a full-on, intense Test match, he'd be producing mock cheap shots, such as a pinch or a slap if we found ourselves at the bottom of a ruck. Towards the end of the game, he let a high ball bounce and I charged at him. Geordan could see this raving lunatic bearing down on him and hit the deck, which meant that he received a double knee drop in his back rather than a flying tackle. I think he was winded for the remainder of the game.

By now the criticism was flying at us, and especially at Charlie. He missed a tackle in Dublin, which cost us a try and, you could argue, the game, but in reality we all played our part in England's defeat. Charlie's misfortune was twofold – he was first-choice stand off in Jonny's absence at a time when the team were evidently going through a transitional period, and for all his qualities, his defence was not a patch on Jonny's. Jonny is one of the greatest number tens of all time, and he has set the benchmark in terms of defence.

The Six Nations had gone for England, and although we finished the tournament by beating Italy and then Scotland at home, it was a poor two months' work by us. Jason Robinson was injured for the Italy game, so Cozza took over the captaincy, and deservedly so. He would remain captain for the next eighteen months. You would think the Calcutta Cup at Twickenham on the final weekend of the Six Nations would be a major sporting occasion. It was not. All eyes were on Cardiff where Wales completed the Grand Slam over Ireland. It felt remarkably strange to be playing in an afterthought. Still, I will not forget the game, and for painful reasons. It is the only time in my career when I have been unable to carry on due to a kick in the bollocks. It was seconds before half-time and as I launched myself into the air, so too did Scotland's Jason White. Now Jason White is a big bloke with an awesome hit on him, and you definitely don't want his knees landing on any part of your body, especially your privates. It was like a blowtorch to my crotch. I lay on the hallowed turf in a foetal position as the half-time whistle blew and everyone else trooped off the pitch. Eventually, Phil Pask, the England physio, helped me to my feet and to the medical room where Simon Kemp, the long-suffering England doctor, had the dubious pleasure of rearranging my crown jewels. It was not my finest hour and you can bet it wasn't Kempy's either, especially when he had to ask, 'Er, would you mind moving that out of the way.' I have gone on to have two children so no lasting damage was inflicted, but I was in no state to carry on that day. Were my teammates bothered? Hardly. To them, after so many years of receiving plum shots, it was the greatest case of retribution.

I finished the season well for Leicester and this, coupled with a predominantly English management team, was enough to gain me selection for the 2005 British and Irish Lions summer tour to New Zealand. Clive had been appointed manager, and with him at the helm and Robbo and Phil Larder on board as well, the party that made the long flight south to the hardest venues of all had a very English look. Backy had been coaxed out of retirement, as had Lol, while Jason Robinson was retiring from rugby straight after the tour. Ian McGeechan and Gareth Jenkins would take charge of the midweek team – a questionable decision given Geech's impeccable past record as a Lions head coach – while Clive would be in charge of the Test team, aided by Robbo and Irish head coach Eddie O'Sullivan.

All my life, my dream had been to play for England. I grew up watching the English teams of the 1980s, rather than the Lions. I just didn't see becoming a Lion as the pinnacle. Part of it was because I was so desperate to beat the very guys who, in the Lions, were suddenly becoming my teammates. We are taught to hate each other when it comes to the Six Nations and World Cups, especially the Celtic nations. Mefin Davies, who joined Leicester, even went so far as to refuse the invitation to become a Lion that year partly on the grounds that he did not believe, as a Welsh-speaking Welshman, he could get on with the other nationalities on the tour. I think he knows that was a wrong call, but I can understand his reasons. By the end of the Lions tour, of course, I was totally smitten. Then I understood what it meant to be a Lion and I was keen to sample another, more successful, tour.

We gathered at Celtic Manor for a pre-tour international against Argentina to be played at the Millennium Stadium. By any team's standards, this was a big call, considering we had a week to prepare for a Test match using a group of players who had never set foot on the same field as members of the same team before. Two days before the game, we were working on our questionable lineouts, using a Scottish hooker and an Irish second-row partnership. The session was interrupted midway through because we had to attend a meeting with Alastair Campbell, Prime Minister Tony Blair's spin doctor, whom Clive had appointed as head of communications for the tour, to discuss how to deal with the media. So, forty-eight hours before taking on the Pumas, an unprepared team working desperately hard to perfect their setpiece are told to attend media studies instead.

I didn't have a problem with Campbell. We seemed to get on fine during the tour. Once, Alfie (aka Gareth Thomas) overheard him talking to the PM and demanded, in his purposefully comical way, to have a word with him. I was astonished to see Campbell handing over the phone and to hear Alfie bellowing down it, 'Now then, boyo, can I have a word about my taxes.' This is an example of how Clive thought it best to lead the tour. He treated it like a business, a well-oiled machine, where off-field concerns were as important, if not more important, than what happened on the field. Geech understood a Lions tour better. He knew that it depends on a group of guys getting to know each other and working together to put that bonding into practice in the games. Old school methods, at least to a degree, are essential on a Lions tour, more so than on any other type of tour. I don't think Clive ever grasped this.

The Argentina Test ended in a 15–15 draw, and that was only thanks to a last-minute equalising penalty from Jonny right from the corner. Argentina were a good side, but not as good as the team that finished third in the 2007 World Cup. As I trudged off the pitch, with three Tests looming against an All Blacks side that were on fire, I couldn't help but think, 'Fuck, this is going to be difficult.'

My view did not change once we landed in New Zealand. For a start, all the players were assigned individual rooms. England were used to this, but the other nations were not. Besides, on a tour where player bonding was imperative, it was the wrong call. It wasn't the only one, though. I found it bizarre seeing Geech in charge of just the midweek team. Not surprisingly, his team remained unbeaten throughout the tour. I played a few games under him and at the end of the tour, all those who had played for the midweek team received from Geech a T-shirt with the slogan 'Midweek Massive'. The Test team proved to be the opposite, and the jostling at the top hardly helped matters. Clive was in charge but it was fairly evident that Eddie O'Sullivan also wanted to be head honcho, hence the continual clashing of heads.

The Test team trained the day after a Test to help the midweek team prepare for their game, and the midweek team trained the day after their games to help prepare the Test team in a reciprocal arrangement, resulting in all the players feeling as if much of the tour was spent out on the training paddock. We had a few days off, of course, including one spent on a shoot that will always be remembered as the turkey massacre. While some of the boys played golf, I joined a dozen others, predominantly English, who chose the other option.

The day began as it would continue. The farmer who owned the land asked Josh to open a gate. Josh eyed the electric fencing suspiciously and asked if the power had been switched off. 'Yeah, sure,' replied the farmer. Josh took hold of the gate and proceeded to shake and rattle, his hands glued to the offending area, his eyes popping and his hair moving suspiciously upwards. Naturally, the rest of us found this hilarious. Josh did not quite share our delight.

We ventured into the area where the turkeys hung out and began to stalk them, not that it was exactly difficult. They all just stood around in large groups, eating. I started to feel a little uncomfortable about it.

'Should I send a warning shot in the air?' I asked the farmer.

'No, mate, just shoot.'

I fired a shot with my pump-action shotgun and three of them fell over. Then Wig scampered up a hill like Rambo before shooting another turkey. To my growing discomfort, this one was the mother of six chicks, following dutifully behind. Even though she had quite clearly been killed, we had to endure – as did she – thirty seconds of running around in her death throes. Backy shot her again from close range and then, to put her out of her misery, picked her up. The farmer had told us to pick up a turkey by its head to break its neck, but Backy forgot, picked her up by her legs and swung her around like a hammer thrower. It all felt so very wrong. Let me tell you how much of a challenge it was to shoot these birds. Grewy had a shot at one sitting on a branch. He missed the bird but snapped the branch clean off. The turkey remained sitting on it, even as it landed on the ground. The only positive from the whole day was that we returned to camp with twenty turkeys, albeit pellet-riddled, for the Lions chef to cook.

On another, happier, day, we were treated to a traditional Maori welcoming song and dance at the king and queen's holy sanctuary. Our response was to sing in unison the ridiculous 'Four Nations' song that Clive had commissioned for us for the tour. Matt Stevens led us in what was a truly woeful reply. It hardly helped that few of us knew all, or indeed any, of the words.

In New Zealand, I took the opportunity to ask Annie's stepdad if I could marry her. He and Annie's mum were living there, and he had helped bring her up from an early age. When I said I wanted to ask him something, his initial response was, 'What do you need, money?' He was delighted when he realised I wanted to marry his stepdaughter, but almost blew it later that night when an unsuspecting Annie, back home in Leicester, called me and then asked to speak to her stepdad.

'Congratulations,' he blurted down the phone, but as I waved frantically and shook my head in front of him, panic setting in, he added, 'Er, congratulations on moving into your new home.' Luckily, Annie, who had her stepsister, Larna, living with her while I was away on tour, did not suspect anything. I think she was too wrapped up at the time, setting up her interior design business, Anneidi, with her partner, Heidi.

Back in camp, we managed to upset the locals by sending just a handful of Lions to a meet-and-greet session, which gave the newspapers plenty of fuel to attack us with. As a result, we laid on an open training session. Everyone was invited, from media to punters. This was two weeks before the first Test and everyone was trying to catch the selectors' eyes, including me, but I managed to pull Simon Shaw on to my knee, which responded with a loud 'pop'. I spent the next two days with my foot up in the air, continually iced, but fell short by maybe a day from declaring myself fit for the first Test.

I was not the only casualty. Lol's tour was already over after he broke his ankle, although this did not stop him delivering a passionate speech to the troops before the first Test. Hilly was also injured, as was Simon Taylor and Malcolm O'Kelly. Matters were not helped by the paranoia that seemed to settle on the management's mindset. Some of it was justified. We knew from past experiences that New Zealand would go to any lengths to gain an advantage over their opponents. God knows how much money had been spent on the fencing we erected around the training pitch to keep out prying eyes, but on the eve of the first Test, a game that would go a long way towards deciding whether the tour would be a success or not, it was decided that all the lineout calls would be changed. This was because we believed our calls had been worked out during the previous defeat by the Maoris. The management were convinced the All Blacks had rumbled us.

Needless to say, our lineouts were disastrous the next day in Christchurch, but then again, so was just about every other aspect of the game, beginning with the loss of our captain, Brian O'Driscoll, in the first minute after he received a double-spear tackle from Keven Mealamu and Tana Umaga. Brian never actually captained me because we never played together on tour, but he was obviously hugely respected for the player and man that he is, and it was a wretched way for him to end his tour when it had barely begun. Somehow the All Blacks got away with what they did to Brian, which left a sour taste in all of our mouths. We looked totally out of sorts, it was raining hard and New Zealand's Dan Carter played like the best player in the world. A 21–3 scoreline almost flattered us and prompted Clive to make wholesale changes, which leaned on the 2003 England boys to do a job. It was two years on, though, and time had taken its toll. I felt that more of the Welsh and Irish boys deserved a chance, although at the same time, back to full fitness, I was delighted to be given a first Test start.

Despite the huge gulf between the two teams in the first Test, we believed we could still turn it around in the second, in Wellington. On the Friday morning team run, Alfie Thomas, our new captain in the injured O'Driscoll's absence, uttered his comical command that has become part of recent rugby folklore. Gathering the starting 22 around in a large huddle, he said, 'I've just got two words to say. Don't fucking panic.' It must have been bizarre for the rest of the Lions squad, watching from another part of the field. The pressure was on, the intensity huge – one day to go before a Test match we had to win against the best team in the world – and there we were doubled up in fits of laughter. All of us. Alfie had not it meant to be funny. Unwittingly, he had been hilarious. I had a lot of time for him, as a person and a player. He was tough, he was hard and he was physical, and he was just what we needed at such a difficult time.

In the game the next day, he skipped over to score a try inside the first two minutes, and Jonny converted, encouraging us to believe we could even win. Instead, New Zealand, and especially Carter, slaughtered us. The 48–18 score was the Lions' heaviest defeat in a Test match, and Carter's incredible haul of 33 points was an individual record. As the final whistle sounded, I was embarrassed, devastated and humiliated. By the time the third Test was over, a 38–19 defeat in Auckland, I was ready to kill someone. Anyone. It had been a better performance, and I'd managed to score a pushover try – the only Englishman to score a Test try on the tour – but the All Blacks still ran out comfortable winners to wrap up the series 3–0.

Nevertheless, I look back on those few weeks with some fondness. It was fun to tour on the same side as Geordan, for example, and through him I got to know a lot of the Irish boys. Through Stephen Jones, who was still talking to me despite his visit to Leicester, I also befriended a few of the Welsh boys. Martyn Williams, for example, was not only an exceptional flanker, but an exceptional person as well. Yet I also feel deeply frustrated about the experience, especially as I missed the 2009 Lions tour through injury and may never again play in the famous red jersey. The challenge was tough for a makeshift team facing the very best, even before we made it harder for ourselves. In the end, I felt as if we were a pub team getting hammered. That's not the way to feel as a Lion.

The year continued to lurch disastrously for me. After the Jordan Crane suspension and a very brief return for the Tigers, the autumn series began with a good win over Australia, highlighted by man-of-the-match Andrew Sheridan's dominance of the Wallaby front row. The following week we lost to New Zealand, 19–23, but took great heart from the fact that the All Blacks were hanging on by their fingertips in the closing minutes. The autumn series ended against a depleted Samoan side and, on the face of it, a 40–3 win suggests there really wasn't too much to write home about. But this was the game in which I became the first and to this day only Englishman to be sent off at Twickenham, and indeed only the fourth English player ever to receive a red card. For all my other feats in the game, that record will stick with me forever.

The game, as always against the Polynesians, had been physical, and on numerous occasions, tackles and hits had been questionable. Mark Cueto, in particular, had been subjected to some horrendous tackles, notably a high one with a straight arm from Tanner Vili late in the second half, which earned the stand off a yellow card. Moments later my Tigers teammate Alex Tuilagi tipped Cuets over in midair and the England winger landed on his head. Cuets rose to his feet and ran angrily towards Alex, which is when I stepped in, initially to be the peacemaker. I've watched the video a few times since and you can see that at first I'm reasonably calm as I stick an arm out between Cuets and Alex to break it up. Then Alex punched Cuets and I lost it. I just felt that Cuets had been on the receiving end of three disgraceful tackles in the game and now he'd been punched. I unleashed a flurry of punches on Alex and received some back from the Samoan captain, Semo Sititi, who had entered the fray.

Referee Mark Lawrence sent Alex off for the tackle, and I knew I would be following him. As I trudged off the pitch, Sititi accused me of throwing some cheap shots, which was a bit rich considering he'd just landed half a dozen punches on me and after all the dangerous tackles that had been flying around. Although both Alex and I deserved red cards, it is incredible how Sititi received nothing for punching me repeatedly. When I heard him mouthing off at me, I was within an inch of walking straight back on to the pitch and punching him. Thank God I did not. The resulting ban could have been forever.

In the tunnel, Alex and I apologised to each other and hugged, but I was still seething. Robbo came down to check on me, but I was surprised to see my dad arrive on the scene as well. He had never done that in all the years of watching me play rugby. On this occasion, he felt the need to support me. Robbo looked at me and shook his head.

'You know, I love you as a player,' he said, 'but sometimes I have no idea what's going on in your head.'

He wasn't the only one. Cozza checked up on me after the game while Cuets kept apologising for what he saw as his part in my downfall. I spoke to Alex's brother, Freddie, who had played with me at Leicester, and to Sititi, who introduced me to his family. I spoke also to my hero, the Samoan coach and former All Black flanker Michael Jones. I apologised to all and sundry but I was still fuelled with rage at what I saw as the injustice of it all.

The irony of it was that I may not even have been on the pitch at that time. Contact with Tom Voyce's knee had forced me off earlier in the second half for medical attention, and although I felt dazed and groggy, I'd insisted on returning to the game.

The immediate aftermath was not too pleasant. The media ripped into me, while some Tigers fans, no doubt aware that another lengthy ban would keep me out of the Leicester side, wrote on the club website that my contract should be ripped up. Dosser Smith provided one of the few rays of light when he left me a message to remind me that, although I was in a bad place, I could always call him, something he has repeated on many occasions since then. The fact that he still keeps tabs on 'his boys' is a very endearing feature of the man who has played such an influential role in my career.

Still, it was a very low point in my career, possibly the lowest, and I realised something had to be done. When I watched the video, uncomfortably sitting next to Annie at home, who kept asking me what on earth did I think I was doing, all I could see was a shouting, swearing, angry, hate-filled, bleeding mess. I was unrecognisable as the person I knew. I realised that I had let everyone down – my family, England, Leicester and myself. It was after this that I began the anger-management courses, which continued for the next two and a half years. Six years on I can look back on the incident with a degree of humour. It's just typical of me that, for all the trophies and caps won in the game, I will be forever in the record books as the first Englishman sent off at headquarters. I'm not proud of it.

The subsequent nine-week ban was served in time for the Six Nations and Robbo, despite my red mist, saw fit to play me from the start against Wales. After half an hour we opted for a lineout close to the Welsh line, rather than kick the points, and from the resulting ruck I burrowed over to score a try. We went on to smash Wales 47–13 and it was a much, much happier occasion at Twickenham for me. Eighteen months after quitting Test rugby, Lol returned to England action, emerging from the bench with fifteen minutes remaining to replace our captain, Cozza, and to score a try. This was the start of an increasingly uncomfortable period for Cozza.

Next up were Italy, who made us work hard in Rome for our 16–31 victory, but after two wins from two, there was already talk in the media of a potential Grand Slam. Scotland had other ideas. In the rain and the mud of Murrayfield, they beat us 18–12. Lol replaced Cozza once again, this time in the 64th minute. It's difficult to criticise Lol. All he wanted to do was play for England again. But to my mind it seemed a very strange thing to take off the captain in a game we were losing but could still win. It simply served to undermine our captain. When people look back over the past fifteen years of England captains, they will rightly look at Johnno, at Lol and at Vicks in particular. Ask the players involved in that post-2003 period, however, and they will, to a man, stress how Cozza carried the England team to a large extent through a difficult and transitional period. He was hugely respected, he led by example and, in so many ways, he was Johnno-esque in the way he carried himself. I can think of no higher praise than that.

After that Calcutta Cup defeat, however, it all went downhill for England and for Andy Robinson. In Paris, we were humiliated 31–6, and the following week we lost 24–28 at home to Ireland when Shane Horgan just managed to squeeze over in the corner in the sixth minute of injury time, despite my close attentions. I should have done better.

Changes were made to the management. Joe Lydon, Dave Alred and Phil Larder all left, although Robbo escaped the axe, and Brian Ashton, Mike Ford and John Wells filled the vacant places. In Australia that summer we continued to fall, losing 3–34 and 18–47 in our two Tests. I played in the first but pulled out of the second during the team run with a damaged hamstring. I was desperate to play for my country, but also embarrassed. Three years earlier we had won the World Cup in the same country. Now we were ranked sixth best in the world.

On my return home, in a media conference I was pressed on the subject of the axed coaches, and said, to my eternal regret, that some of them had not been up to the job. In truth, Joe Lydon, rugby league legend though he previously was, struggled in his England role with the backs, but the way it came across was that I was attacking all the axed coaches. I received a call from Larder.

'Lewis, I'm heartbroken that you would say something like that,' he said down the line.

I apologised to him, told him how much I respected him, and added that his defence skills transformed England into world champions. I apologised to Robbo and, when I saw Joe, to him as well. It doesn't alter the fact that I meant what I said about Joe, but it was completely wrong for me to belittle him like that in front of the media, especially as Joe had no comeback. I look back on that episode with unrelieved disappointment in myself.

Despite new coaches, the autumn remained grim. We tried to attack New Zealand, gave it a go and were beaten 20–41 at our own game by the best attacking team in the world. That was bearable for the Twickenham crowd. The following week, however, was not. We lost 18–25 to Argentina, the so-called whipping boys in the autumn Tests, the first time we had ever lost at home to the Pumas. That's when the jeers began to rain down from the stands. They started at half-time, continued late in the second half and then, as the final whistle blew, they reached a deafening crescendo as we sloped off the pitch. My feelings towards this were mixed. At first, I felt betrayed by our supporters. We had given our all. The jeers and the boos did not have a positive effect on me at all. In hindsight, though, we had played badly, again. The fans had paid good money and were subjected to watching a seventh successive defeat. It was disappointing that they should vent their feelings in such a way, but can I completely blame them? Probably not.

By now, Robbo was clinging on to his job. Next up were South Africa and it was decided that I should be dropped to the bench. I have no idea why I was singled out after the Argentina defeat, but Pat Sanderson replaced me until I came on for him in the 57th minute. Vicks barged over late in the game to complete an English comeback and a 23–21 win. There were smiles all around, especially on the faces of Robbo and Cozza, but all it served to do was delay the inevitable. The following week it was back to the drawing board. Somehow we turned a 14–3 lead into a 14–25 defeat against the Springboks in our second, successive Test against them. The boos returned, this time louder, and fans even left the stadium before the final whistle. It felt like a public execution.

It was a miserable time to be part of an England team. No one was playing well and we were losing game after game. I felt as though the press were picking a constantly changing team half the time, and you could see Robbo sinking deeper and deeper into the mire. I've always admired and respected him. I've already expressed my views about him as a forwards coach, and Robbo has always been completely honest with me, but we could all see how the pressure was getting to him. I had to take some of the blame. You can't simply put it all on the coach, but for it to go so horribly wrong meant changes were required, and that's precisely what happened. Robbo left his post shortly afterwards, to be replaced at the helm by Brian Ashton. It was just eight months before the 2007 World Cup, and we were supposed to be the defending champions!

Robbo took time out. He needed it. When he returned to coaching, his decision to join Edinburgh raised some eyebrows. I was absolutely delighted for him when he turned round Edinburgh's fortunes and then moved on to positions at the Scottish Rugby Football Union before finally becoming Scotland head coach. I think he has proved that his time in charge of England was a transitional period for him, and he has become one of the best coaches in world rugby.

His parting gift to me was to warn me about Brian. He told me that Brian didn't rate me and was not keen to pick me, and that he, Robbo, had been fighting my corner. He added that I'd have to play out of my skin to turn Brian around.

On the face of it, this may not appear to be the news you would want to hear but, strangely enough, it relaxed me. I just figured that it was down to me to play my best rugby. If this was good enough to get me selected to play for England, fine. If not, then at least I had tried everything. A couple of weeks later, I scored a hat-trick for the Tigers against Bourgoin in the Heineken Cup. Two weeks before the start of the Six Nations I played my part in Leicester's historic Heineken Cup win over Munster at Thomond Park, the first time the Irish province had ever lost there in Europe on what was their last appearance before the ground was redeveloped.

I was absolutely loving playing for a winning team again and my form, despite Brian's reservations, forced him to name me on the bench for the Calcutta Cup, which was the opening game of the 2007 Six Nations. I never made it to Twickenham, though. The injury to my left shoulder reared up again during the week and I was forced to withdraw. I had scored five tries in my previous six games and felt on fire. Now, after having my shoulder pinned again in hospital, I was to miss the whole of the Six Nations in this, a World Cup year. I was devastated once again. I could only watch in despair as Magnus Lund, Tom Rees, James Haskell, Nick Easter, Worzel and Cozza all packed down in the back row for what would be another mixed tournament. It began well enough with a convincing win over Scotland, dominated by the return of Jonny, spluttered a little after a laboured home win over Italy, then came crashing down when we were beaten out of sight at Croke Park by the Irish. A much better display saw off the French at Twickenham but the tournament ended with defeat in Wales and a final position of third in the table.

A weakened England got battered, twice, in South Africa during a short June tour. I was not involved in that but when the World Cup warm-up games began in August, I was on the bench as we demolished a decent Welsh team 62–5, highlighted by four tries from number eight Nick Easter. I managed a quick, 11 minute cameo, replacing Cozza. A week later, I was not named for the 15–21 home defeat by France, nor for the return fixture in Marseille, which the French won rather too easily, 22–9.

We would be travelling back to France for the World Cup pretty much in a shambles, and I had no idea whether I would be going at all. Four years earlier, I had been playing in the World Cup final and now my place in the team was hanging in the balance. However, after a few sleepless nights, the happy news came through that I had made it, Wellsy having probably chewed Brian's ear. There was no doubt, though, that I was some way down the pecking order.

There was still time for a rather unusual way to conclude final preparations. We thought we would be flying to Portugal for a week's training in the sun, even though the choice of Southampton airport as the departure point appeared peculiar. Instead, on arriving at the airport, we were told of a change of plan. We would be spending the week training with the marines in nearby Poole. Our kit was taken off us and we were given boots and fatigues. Our mobile phones were swiped, too, even poor Charlie Hodgson's, despite the fact that he had been married just the day before.

The week turned out to be a good, team-bonding exercise, or so we thought at the time. We had to meet all kinds of challenges, from working in the pitch dark having to find dummies and bags, to a high-wire course involving standing with three others at the top of a narrow telegraph pole. This was to build trust. The four of us had to link arms and lean out. Another test was to catch a trapeze bar and swing away, albeit tied to harnesses. I was especially pleased to come through these exercises because I have a latent fear of heights. On the Lions tour, I was close to being physically sick with fear at the top of the Auckland Tower.

Amid the challenging physical tests were, as always, moments of comedy. During a canoe race across Poole Harbour, when Jonny jumped into the sea to help drag us, his lifejacket blew up, leaving him floundering in the water. Benny Kay, James Haskell, Ronnie Regan and I had to run across the beach carrying the canoe over our heads. It was agony, the more so because Ronnie couldn't keep up with the rest of us. So he sabotaged the other teams by grabbing hold of their canoes. Not surprisingly, we won that particular challenge – an enjoyable end to the week.

After that, we spent the following few days in Portugal, where we had thought we would be all the time, and during this warm-weather camp I heard the happy news that Annie was pregnant with our first child. She had already undergone a pregnancy test before she called me, but then, once I had found a quiet corner, she proceeded to test herself again while I clung to the phone. 'Yep, I'm pregnant,' she announced down the line. My emotions were mixed. The news made me crave to be back at home with Annie but, at the same time, I was overjoyed and phoned Geordan first to share the news. My parents would have to wait until I returned from France, by which stage the first few weeks of pregnancy would have safely passed.

On a personal front I had just been given a major boost. On a professional front I was about to embark on my second World Cup. I should have been brimming with anticipation and excitement but I couldn't get rid of the nagging feeling that we would be travelling to the World Cup as unprepared as we had been prepared under Clive Woodward four years earlier. We would be starting the tournament with no form at all, no results and no settled team. None of us had any idea who the starting XV would be, let alone the 22. It really was no way to begin a defence of the World Cup.

In 2003 England went to Australia intent on becoming world champions. In 2007 we couldn't see any further than a quarter-final place, at best.

What happened next is something that, to this day, remains incredible to comprehend.

8

AGAINST ALL THE ODDS – ALMOST!

The 2007 Rugby World Cup

For the opening pool game against the US Eagles in Lens, I was named on the bench, and I had mixed feelings about it. A part of me realised that I had been lucky to make the squad at all, so little had I played for Brian Ashton's England, but another part of me was disappointed to be just a substitute – especially as this was a warm-up before we took on South Africa in a game that we suspected would decide who would win the pool and who would be runners-up.

We couldn't say this beforehand, of course, but we expected to hammer America. After all, that's pretty much what our second string XV had been doing year in, year out in the Churchill Cup. Instead, we stumbled our way to a 28–10 win, which was actually closer than the scoreline suggests. The US Eagles played their hearts out, even winning the final half-hour 7–0. We, in contrast, were truly abysmal. Jonny had a slight injury and didn't play, which meant Olly Barkley was at ten, and he scored 18 points. Vicks tripped up the American centre, Paul Emerick, earning a subsequent citing. I was granted the grand total of 11 minutes, replacing Worzel, and in that time the Eagles scored a converted try.

If we had any self-belief before that opening match – and we didn't possess much – it was shattered after a display so limp that we failed to grab a try bonus point. It was no way to prepare for South Africa six days later at the Stade de France in Paris, especially as Vicks received a two-game ban and then Olly Barkley pulled up in training with a damaged hip muscle, and Jonny was still out.

Just about the only plus in my eyes about the first game was the World Cup debut of scrum half Shaun Perry, with whom I got along well during the tournament. Pezza had not even been a full-time, professional rugby player four years previously when we won the Webb Ellis Cup, but a welder who played part-time rugby in the Midlands. He took his chance when an offer came from Bristol, impressed everybody in the game and forced his way into the England set-up in World Cup season. For him, it was an absolute dream to be playing in France at this time.

For the rest of us, it was fast turning into a nightmare. The situation was a repeat of our 2003 pool with what appeared to be the same fruits. Win this game, with all respect to Samoa and Tonga whom we still had to face, and the group was ours. Lose and we would finish second, which would mean a stiffer challenge in the quarter-final. During the week everything seemed calm. We did and said all the right things, and the irony of it was that I was quietly confident we could pull off a surprise against a South African outfit who were Tri-Nations champions and probably favourites to win the World Cup.

On a day off, we spent some time at the First World War battlefields under the guidance of Will Greenwood's former history teacher. I was deeply interested in seeing them, not just because of my fascination with history, but also because my namesake, Lewis Walton Moody, my great-grandfather, had fought there. What stood out for me was the portland stone memorial at the Somme. The Devonshire regiment held a trench, against all odds and despite suffering appalling losses, so that others could advance. A simple but powerful inscription on the memorial reads: 'The Devonshires held this trench, the Devonshires hold it still.' I get emotional even thinking about it. Later, we met a mayoress who was alive during the battle and who presented us with coins representing those traumatic times. It was a thought-provoking day, for sure, and one I will never forget. Whether it helped our preparations for the key pool game is a moot point.

I don't think anybody foresaw the crash that was about to hit us. On the face of it, we had a good team that fateful night. Robbo and Josh, Catty, Cozza, Benny Kay and Faz (Andy Farrell) all started – I was named on the bench – but the problem was that we had next to no structure to our game. Against the rampant Springboks, this was revealed in all its horror.

I came on in the 53rd minute to replace Tom Rees, who had scored a try against America. By then, the score was already 23–0 and, although I was determined to reduce the arrears, the game was quite clearly lost. I remember sitting on the bench, watching the debacle unfold, and thinking, 'This isn't right in a World Cup.' We had no building blocks in place to enable us to play the all-singing and dancing style of rugby Brian wanted us to play. In many ways, it still boiled down to small margins but, at this level, five or six small margins can result in a pasting. I'm not sure what was worse – conceding 36 points, or scoring none ourselves.

In the dressing room afterwards, the scene was one of utter desolation, and I wondered to myself how an England team at a World Cup, with players at the pinnacle of their careers, could finish so resoundingly second in a two-horse race. I'd played thirty-six minutes of rugby in two disappointing games so far, and immediately after the final whistle I could not see how it was possible for us even to escape our group. On the evidence of the first two pool encounters, we would not beat either Samoa or Tonga, especially as Robbo had left the field with a torn hamstring that put a question mark over his role in the rest of the tournament, and Jamie Noon's last-minute injury meant his World Cup was already over. Everyone thought Robbo would be gone as well. I don't think a single person among the team or management, save for Robbo himself, believed he would be back. At that precise moment, I felt as low as I'd ever felt as a professional rugby player, and that includes being sent off eighteen months previously against our next opponents.

Yet, even in a moment of utter darkness, there was farce. The dressing-room door opened when Brian was speaking to the team, and a French medical officer wheeled in Noony, who was now confined to a wheelchair, pushing him first into the centre of the room, and then towards a corner, where he left our man facing the wall. The timing was impeccable. The orderly turned round and marched out as Brian was still trying to speak, but by then he had lost us, or at least me. All I could do was stare at Noony, facing a wall from a couple of inches away, with his back to the rest of us. I didn't laugh. The occasion, after all, was sombre. But I did find it hilarious, and a little surreal.

There wasn't too much hilarity, though. The World Cup, after two games, could not have gone much worse and, to cap it all, Mike Ford, our defence coach, had suggested to the media that selecting Faz had not worked. The next day, Mike stood up and apologised to the team, having already sought out Faz, and this meeting turned out to be the one that changed everything.

We knew to a man that on our performances to date, Samoa, and possibly even Tonga, could and possibly would beat us. Some of us were mindful of 2003, when the Samoans were ahead for over an hour in our pool game. We had no direction, we had poor results and we had an ever-changing side. It was clear that the management were butting heads. Wellsy, as a traditional practitioner, was finding it difficult to integrate his ethos into Brian's expansive philosophy. None of it was working.

So the players demanded a meeting on the Saturday. Mike uttered his apology, Brian said a couple of things, and then the floor was left open for the players. This is what took place, to great effect, after we scraped home against Wales in the quarter-final four years previously, but this time it was more full on, and a little nearer the knuckle.

A lot of the players had their say, including Jonny, Faz and me, but the three main speakers turned out to be Lol, Catty and Olly. We focused on our lack of structure. Every so often, I'd look across at Brian, standing in the corner with his head bowed, and felt for him. He had the vision, but we needed the structure to be able to realise it, and although the essence of what everyone said was supposed to be constructive, it still appeared to be an attack on Brian and his methods. His power eroded away during that meeting. The reality was that from that point onwards, he had lost the players.

At the end of the meeting, Wellsy and Wig told the players to go and have a good night out. They would arrange a bar for us, and after a long and not especially fruitful slog up to this point in the tournament, we deserved a break and some bonding time. Wig had only just been appointed England scrummaging coach but, seemingly in no time, he had become an integral part of the coaching set-up. It was a little strange for me at first, because just the season before we had been Leicester teammates, but having recently stopped playing proved to be one of Wig's strengths. He kept himself remarkably fit and he knew exactly what it was like to be a player in a fast-evolving game. His empathy with us was vital.

As we trooped out of the meeting and began contemplating a night of merriment, Wellsy pulled me aside.

'Go out and be as idiotic as you want,' he said. 'Enjoy it. We need to create something here with this team.'

My coach had just provided me with a passport to mayhem and I instantly relaxed. Up to this point, I had been stressed out to my eyeballs. The World Cup had not been going to plan, either collectively or personally, Annie was heavily pregnant, I felt unwell and I had no cause for optimism concerning the next few weeks. The night ahead, however, following on from the players' meeting, changed the environment just when it was imperative to do so. So what happened? With Wellsy's endorsement ringing in my ears, I drank myself to oblivion.

We had two bars sectioned off just for the England squad and this meant drinking games, attempting to eat a pint of peanuts in one minute (I failed), drinking straight out of jugs of vodka and Red Bull, and then springing off tables, Spider-Man style, landing on a seated Mark Cueto. Some French gendarmes were permanently attached to us, and the All Blacks also had their band of guards, because the English and New Zealand teams were deemed to be most at risk from terrorist attacks. At the end of the evening, two of the gendarmes dragged me back to my hotel, and when I say dragged I mean dragged. Annie had arrived the day before and was leaving early the next morning. I slumped on to the bed at six in the morning but soon felt it necessary to visit the bathroom. My wife, to her eternal credit, cleared up before departing for Leicester. She realised that it had been going terribly wrong for us and understood the need for a night such as this. Still, if ever anyone deserves to be made a modern-day saint, it is Annie.

A couple of days after the World Cup tournament had finished, a photo from our night out appeared in one of the British tabloids, of me jumping off tables. I shudder to think what the public reaction might have been if it had come out at the time. England had just been humiliated by South Africa, and we were out getting drunk! Few people would have understood why we needed to do this. As it was, the next day we all turned up to training, feeling a little worse for wear, but as if we had found a new direction. For the first time, I felt we were united.

The World Cup had now turned into a knockout tournament for us. Lose and we were out. The pressure was on and there's no doubt we were feeling it. I was yet again named on the bench and, this time, managed just ten minutes of the game in place of Worzel. My individual frustration grew even more, especially as I knew that the Samoans, including players such as Lemi and Mapusua, Sititi and the two Tuilagi brothers, were not going to lie down and roll over. That was how it turned out. As I trooped on to the field in Nantes, we led by just four points, but a couple of late tries from Cozza and Paul Sackey, and some points from Wilko's boot, made the 44–22 scoreline more favourable than it should have been. We were still in the World Cup and we had performed better, but we were hardly world-beaters.

Next up were Tonga, just six days later, in the same Parc des Princes stadium where Leicester won their first Heineken Cup back in 2001. To my joy, I was selected to start. No explanation was given and I did not really care. All that mattered was that at last I could be where it mattered most of all. I'd kept my frustrations to myself, save for a quiet word with Wellsy, who was adept at allowing a player to vent his feelings. He did not make any promises to me, but I still felt better for doing so.

As I sat in the dressing room, I felt incredibly nervous. We had to win this game and, for me, it was my first real opportunity. It didn't matter that I had won a World Cup, Heineken Cups, English leagues. The nerves still rot away in your stomach. As I sat there, Wig ambled up and sat down beside me.

'How much do you rate Andy Farrell?' he asked me.

I told him hugely. And I did. I watched Faz when he played for the all-conquering Wigan and Great Britain rugby league sides, in awe of the guy. He really was the Martin Johnson of rugby league. Some people gave him a hard time when he switched over to union. His problem was twofold. Firstly, he missed the whole of his first year through injury, and secondly, when he did finally regain fitness, he was played at six before being moved out into the midfield.

The England team in France loved Faz because he was a fantastic team man whose ethos in everything he did was exemplary. I can't say I knew him particularly well. We didn't hang together or even have too many conversations, but my respect for him was total. Wig digested what I said.

'Well,' he said, 'Faz has just told me that he'd have you down as first on his team sheet every single week.'

That's all Wig said. He rose to his feet and walked off. I felt like a million dollars. It was such a special moment for me, and it has lived with me ever since. I never mentioned it to Faz. I didn't have to. But my nerves disappeared, and as I ran out on to the Paris pitch, I knew I could do something for my country.

This story also reveals a great deal about Wig. I didn't really give it much thought at the time, but now, looking back, I can see it was a moment of genius from my former Tigers teammate.

However, it was nearly over for me inside the first five minutes. In attempting to charge down a clearance by Vungakoto Lilo, I received an accidental knee to my head and was knocked clean out. I was unconscious for nearly five minutes. All I can remember is the distant sound of Matthew Tait saying, 'Moodos, Moodos'. Simon Kemp, the team doc, suggested I should come off. I told Kempy where to go. I'd waited this long to get my chance in the World Cup, and there was no way I was walking off after five minutes. A lineout followed and I had no idea what was going on. Cozza went through the move beforehand and, a minute or so later, I had come round properly. Ironically, I was knocked out for a second time in the second half, although not for as long. This time my head was jerked back by the force of an arm smashed into my face by Nili Latu, the Tongan captain. I think he was attempting to kill me!

Once again, just like against Samoa, it took time to kill off the Tongans' challenge. After 55 minutes we led by just six points. A Tait try eased us away but the killer score came from Faz, who touched down for his only try in his union Test career. If you saw how the rest of the team reacted to the try, you will understand that it was not just because we knew the game was now won, but also because it was Faz who had scored the crucial try, and no player was more popular than he was within our ranks. A late converted try for Tonga made the eventual 36–22 scoreline a little closer than it needed to be, but it made no difference to us. We had made it through the pool and into the quarter-final where Australia, the strong favourites, would be waiting for us in Marseille.

A trip to Euro Disney followed the next day. This was optional but, of course, I went and Annie came along, too. The problem was my head was spinning from the double blow I'd received the night before. Midway through my first ride – Aerosmith's Rock 'n' Roller Coaster – I felt so sick that I thought my head was about to explode. Annie had been under orders from the medics to check up on me every hour during the night until she gave up on me at five in the morning. Now, in my wisdom, I was lurching around a fast, indoor roller coaster with flashing lights and heavy rock music blasting. Every loop the loop was torture. Every jerk of my car was like having a needle shoved through my head. That was it. There would be no more rides for me. Instead, I became that person who sits holding all the bags outside the entrance of a ride. It wasn't just Annie's bag, either. It ended up being the bags of half the England players' wives and partners!

To the outside world, we stood next to no chance of beating the Wallabies, based on what had been seen so far in the tournament. As the week developed, though, our confidence grew. The coaches, and especially Wellsy and Wig, had discovered some weaknesses, which we were intent on exploiting. The Australians had not really been put to the test in a comfortable passage through the pool games. They would win the breakdown with one or two players. Mike Ford also did his homework on the Wallaby backs and decided that we should attack Berrick Barnes at every opportunity. What helped boost our confidence even further was the miraculous return of

Jason Robinson, who, if you recall, had damaged his hamstring so badly during the South African debacle that there seemed no possibility of him playing again in the tournament. Instead, just three weeks later, he was back. Enormous credit must go to the physios here. Phil Pask and Barney Kenney worked tirelessly, from seven in the morning until ten at night, ensuring that we were in as good a nick as possible for the next game. How they managed to return Robbo to the starting XV was a minor miracle. Credit, too, to Robbo, whose mental conviction that he would be back played a major role in his recovery.

Until someone pointed it out to me, I was unaware that the quarter-final, for which I would again start, would mark my 50th cap. Reaching 50 is removing the monkey from your back. It's a relief to get it out of the way, to be frank. When I was told I should lead the team out on to the pitch, the traditional way to honour your half century, I refused point blank. This day, of all days, was not about me, an individual. It was completely about the team. The only thing that mattered was winning, but Vicks, safely back in the team and captain again after his ban, insisted as we stood up in the dressing room and made our way out. I didn't want to cause a scene, so I made my usual entrance, which means sprinting out at 100 miles an hour. Normally, I am some way back as England emerge from the tunnel, so when I sprint I end up close to the front. This time I found myself alone in the middle of the pitch for seemingly ages as the rest trudged purposefully out. The next morning, I was criticised in one of the newspapers for trying to steal the show!

For all our trials and tribulations, we had been tested by South Africa, Samoa and Tonga. Australia had breezed through into the knockout stages. In the first few minutes, we won four turnovers because we piled four or five players into the breakdown. Then, whenever their stand off, Barnes, received the ball, both Andy Gomarsall, our scrum half, and I flew into him. Even at 10–6 down at half-time, after a Lote Tuqiri try had given them an edge, we were confident we would win. Two penalties from Wilko nudged us ahead, and that's the way it stayed, although we had a late scare when Worzel, who came on for me in the 66th minute, conceded a penalty with two minutes remaining. Stirling Mortlock, the Australian captain, pushed the ball just wide from a difficult position, and, somehow, we had won.

As pleased as I was for England, I was more pleased for Worzel. It would have been horrific if his mistake had cost us our place in the World Cup. We deserved to win the quarter-final. It had been a tough, forward-dominated, defensive display from us, perhaps not aesthetically pleasing, but we had grafted our way into the semis. It was difficult to believe that we were now just eighty minutes away from another World Cup final, and that Robbo was a game away from winning his 50th cap, too. We reminded him of it amid the dressing-room merriment that followed.

A passing Wallaby may also have heard the bizarre sound of Kenny Rogers' song 'The Gambler' blaring out of our dressing room, and the equally strange noise made by thirty England rugby players singing along to an American country and western star. This had become our team song after Matt Stevens, our singing prop, who never needed any invitation to play his guitar on the team coach and sing, had played this particular hit so often that we all started to sing along to it. Immediately after beating Australia, we played the original version on our iPod. 'You gotta know when to hold 'em, know when to fold 'em,' was soon ringing around the room. Everyone from Wilko to Robbo, Vicks and me was in full voice, and we accompanied ourselves with a great deal of foot stamping.

Later, a few of us made our way down to the harbour area of Marseille. The atmosphere was terrific on that warm, balmy evening, mainly because the French had beaten New Zealand in a quarter-final in Cardiff, and were now due to face us in Paris the following Saturday night. For one night only, there was shared Anglo-French joy at our surprise victories over the might of the southern hemisphere.

During the week of the semi-final, our new biggest fan, Kenny Rogers, sent us a video message. 'Hey you guys,' said a white-haired, white-bearded 70 year old, wearing a tight-fitting England rugby jersey. He went on to wish us luck against France and promised that if we went on to win the World Cup, he would fly over and perform privately, just for the England team. I'm not sure Kenny had ever seen a game of rugby, let alone England play. I found the whole business hilarious, as we all did, but it played its part in uniting us even more.

As bad as we had been during the World Cup so far, I never had any doubts that we would beat France. In hindsight, it is obvious that their World Cup final was beating the All Blacks in the quarter-final. They could not pick themselves up again to take us on, even though it was played out in front of an 80,000 capacity crowd at the Stade de France. Once again, we had done our homework and identified that their stand off, Lionel Beauxis, liked to attempt drop goals from almost any angle. Gomars and I made it our mission to stop him.

The start could not have gone any better. Josh took advantage of a bobbling kick down the left touchline, grabbing the ball out of Damien Traille's hands before knocking over the big French full-back and scoring. The clock read two minutes. At half-time, three Beauxis penalties meant that France held a 9–5 lead. Wilko reduced the arrears to a point two minutes into the second half. We left it late, although clearly in the ascendancy. A 75th minute Wilko penalty nudged us into the lead, and a drop goal from the man the rest of world rugby still stood in abject fear of, finished off France.

We had won 14–9 and, against all the odds, had made it into the World Cup final. I had left the field in the 54th minute with an injured shoulder. I was already having cortisone injections in it after sustaining an injury in the previous game against Australia. Even as the final whistle blew and we celebrated, my overriding reaction was, 'Fuck me, do we really deserve to be in the World Cup final?' In 2003, we got everything right. In 2007, we had ripped up the blue-print. We had made it to the final having drained the last glass in the last-chance saloon. I felt almost as if we had done the 2003 boys a disservice by getting to within one game of matching their feats. Robbo would now be winning his fiftieth cap and we would have the chance to turn around the 36–0 hammering meted out to us by the Springboks. South Africa would be favourites, of course, but we knew we stood a good chance of completing one of the most unlikely comeback stories in sport.

In the small hours after the French win, I decided to wander down into the team room in the hotel. I struggle to sleep after most games, let alone World Cup semi-finals, and after hours spent toss-ing and turning in bed, I thought a bit of TV and food might help to counter my insomnia. I expected to be alone but when I walked into the room, Wilko was there, experiencing exactly the same problem. I'm sure many of the other players also struggled to sleep that night, but only Wilko and I ended up chatting into the small hours in the team room. It is not just the adrenalin that keeps you awake. A rugby forward's skin is so battered that your ears can stick to the pillows, while my painful shoulder and knee meant that I could never get comfortable.

I blame the fact that England ultimately lost the World Cup final on Danny Hipkiss. That's because we tried and failed to go to a cinema on the Friday night in Paris. My old cinema muckers, Steve Thompson and Ben Cohen, were not involved, so I had coaxed my Tigers teammate Dan to be my new movie partner. The problem was that the Parisian taxi drivers had decided to go on strike, so the roads were jammed solid with cars, making a journey from our hotel to the cinema virtually impossible. We tried using a driver but just sat in traffic. I was seriously contemplating finding a bicycle, which would have meant a ten-kilometre round trip. Dan put his foot down at this suggestion.

'You do know we have a World Cup final tomorrow and you want us to ride a bike for ten k?' he said. Dan had a point.

I was devastated. Why was it always so hard to catch a film the night before a World Cup final? Defeated, we returned to the hotel, where I borrowed Wellsy's DVD copy of '300', which I watched in my room. This is why we failed to defend our world title the next day.

The same night, Vicks called a team meeting. It was completely different from any 'eve of final' meeting I had attended before. Usually, the coaches take you through the moves and deliver final instructions, aided by the captain. This time, the coaches left and Vicks perched on the edge of a table in front of us all. In a very quiet voice he spoke of the journey we had all taken to get to this point. He reminded us of the dark days we had endured and how we had turned it all around. He implored us to give it our best shot. At times, Vicks was close to tears. It was that emotional, particularly for him. Vicks had been forced to miss two games after being cited, and had sat helpless as we were crushed by the Springboks in the pool game. He had been close to being the captain of the worst side ever attempting to defend a world title in the history of the tournament. Now we were eighty minutes away from achieving a miracle.

The problem was we had exceeded all our expectations, and South Africa, the pre-tournament favourites, and now the red-hot favourites to win the final, had not. We had been saying all week that it could be one of the greatest turnarounds in the history of sport, but subconsciously it was hard to escape the feeling that we had already achieved so much more than we'd thought possible. You could sense the feeling of relief with the players and coaches. To a man, we felt we didn't really deserve to be in the final. Still, that's where we were, and in a two-horse race you always have a chance.

We were minus Josh Lewsey. Poor Josh was injured during the semi-final win over France in which he scored that crucial, early try. During the final, after a 9pm kick-off on the Saturday night, we started losing more and more key players. At half-time, the score was 9–3 to South Africa, our points coming from a Wilko penalty. I had conceded the first points of the night when I tripped Butch James after he had chipped the ball. It cost us three points but, bearing in mind what had happened to Vicks earlier in the tournament, I was lucky not to have received a yellow card. Still, this would not be a repeat of the thrashing meted out to us five weeks earlier. It could have been much better, too, straight after the break. First, Taity went to within metres of scoring one of the most spectacular tries you'll ever see in a World Cup final, only for Victor Matfield to tackle him after a long, jinking run. Then, from the resulting phase, Cuets appeared to go over in the corner but was judged, after an agonisingly long wait, to have just placed a foot in touch by the TMO (television match official, or video referee). To this day, Cuets will tell you he scored. My gut reaction, as it happened, was that his foot was out. We will never know, but a converted try would have edged us into a lead, and then it would have been South Africa glancing up at the scoreboard.

Wilko managed to reduce the arrears to three points, but by then we were beginning to lose key men. First to leave the fray was our captain, Vicks, replaced by Matt Stevens. Robbo followed clutching his shoulder in the 47th minute, to be replaced by Danny Hipkiss, then Catty four minutes later. Ronnie Regan's final ended in the 63rd minute, and mine two minutes later. Suddenly, an awful lot of experience had left the pitch, and when Worzel, on for me, was removed from the action having torn both groins with nine minutes to go, the last man standing was scrum half Pete Richards, my old partner in crime from the 1998 Tour from Hell, who found himself playing as a flanker in a World Cup final.

It was just too much to expect a final miracle. My shoulder was in pieces, and as I sat watching the final denouement from the side-lines, my mood was philosophical and reflective rather than sad. South Africa won 15–6 and, despite Cuets's effort, few could argue they didn't deserve to win.

Had we become world champions in 2007, they would have made a film about the feat. The script would have seemed so far-fetched, nobody would have believed it. But it nearly happened, and many of us gained as much from our experience in 2007 as we did in 2003. We were knocked clean down during the group stages, having endured a year of wretched results in the run-up to the tournament. A true test of character in sport, and, I guess, in life, is if and how you get back to your feet. We managed to create an incredible journey that so very nearly reached an incredible ending. I think that is why the post-final dressing room was quiet, but not devastated.

On the team bus, as we left the stadium, this turned into unexpected merriment thanks to Rob Andrew's impromptu and unintentionally funny speech. Rob thought it might be a good time to soften the blow just meted out to us by South Africa, but his attempts to console resulted in some of the players failing to stifle their laughter. The gist of his speech went like this. 'Lads, well done. It's a great achievement to reach the final. Losing the World Cup final, though, will stay with you forever. It will probably haunt you for the rest of your lives.' Rob had been part of the England team who had lost the 1991 World Cup final to Australia, and it was as if he was attempting to exorcise his own demons and sixteen years of pain. Even though we had indeed lost a World Cup final, there was a vast difference between the England side of 1991, who may well have become world champions had they not changed their game plan for the final, and the England team of 2007, who had somehow lurched their way to the final. To be told that we will be 'haunted' by the loss for the rest of our lives was probably not the best way to console us. Rob's intentions were, of course, to help. His speech was heartfelt and all the boys had great respect for a man with a Test record such as Rob's. Maybe it was the right speech but at the wrong time. In the end, it was pure comedy.

The next morning we arrived back in England and posed for photographs on the steps of the plane again, where Olly Barkley de-bagged Matt Stevens. We said hello to airport staff and then wandered through the terminal. Four years earlier you couldn't move for well-wishers and supporters. This time we made our way out of the terminal almost unnoticed. The contrast was not lost on anyone.

9

A DEMEANING ILLNESS

It started just before Christmas 2004. I went to the toilet and discovered the water had turned pink. I thought it was a little weird but dismissed any real concerns. As the New Year came and went, however, I experienced more and more discomfort in my stomach, and I started having bowel movements four, five, sometimes ten times a day. Still I left it. I assumed whatever it was would pass. Then, during Easter time 2005, I noticed thick red blood in the water in the toilet. Now although I found this a difficult subject to talk about, I knew I could not just leave it any longer. Even someone as stubborn as I am understood this was potentially serious. I had a word with the club doctor at the Tigers and he recommended Dr Barry Rathbone at the BUPA Hospital in Leicester. It was during my subsequent visit to Dr Rathbone that some of my worst fears were realised – an anal examination for one thing. The doctor slipped a glove on to a finger, then some lubricant before inserting it into and up my anus. He followed this up with a tube that blew air into my stomach. This was very embarrassing and extremely uncomfortable. It also made me want to loosen my bowels instantly.

The doctor told me that I had colitis but I needed a proper examination in an operating theatre to discover how extensive the problem was. Colitis can affect the bottom half of your colon or, indeed, the entire colon. In worst cases, this means removing your colon and having to use a colostomy bag for the rest of your life. If this had been the case, my career would have finished immediately.

I researched into why, and how, I had suddenly contracted colitis. It soon became clear that this was the price to pay for all the operations and medical treatment meted out to me over the years. Overexposure to anti-inflammatories, antibiotics and pain-killers plays a part in bringing it on, which is pretty much what I had been living on for the past few years. Colitis can also be exacerbated by stress, which is something I was under, consciously or subconsciously, most of the time, either playing rugby or trying to gain selection. The stomach problems I had in my first year at Oakham were brought on, so the medical verdict said, by stress. Maybe this was the way my body showed itself to be under strain.

I reported back to the Leicester team doc but asked him not to tell anyone else, and this included the coaches. I didn't want them to see my condition as a point of weakness, or to give them a reason not to pick me for the team. The doc was compromised but agreed. I didn't particularly see it as a weakness, but I was convinced others would at the time. The coaches told me once how a board member at Tigers had accused me of not caring for the club because I was absent so often through injury and suspensions. I asked them which board member it was because I was going to find him and sort it out. Wisely, the coaches refused to tell me. I always gave 100 per cent to the Leicester Tigers. Unfortunately, and this was one of the moments, I was often emerging from long-term injuries.

Knockout drops were applied to the area during the biopsy. These partially paralysed me so I was able to watch an uncomfortable procedure played out on a TV screen. A huge tube journeyed up my backside, wriggling around on the TV screen, and a pincer on the end of the tube tore out a snip of the infected area. The biopsy confirmed that I had ulcerative colitis, which means ulcers on my colon, and I was given steroids and an enema. I was to use an enema every day, I was told, for the rest of my life. The whole thing was some kind of a cruel joke, and now I was being asked to shove something up my arse every single day. I took a stockpile of steroid cylinders with me on the Lions tour and the problem was controlled during my time in New Zealand, without anyone needing to know. Yet on my return, and for the next three years, colitis began to dominate my life.

There were times when I was virtually housebound, times when I couldn't leave the toilet. At its worst, I'd be going twenty-five times in a day. Occasionally, I failed even to make it to the toilet, even though I was in my own home. When we lived in Kirby Muxloe, I had a fear of taking car journeys in case I got caught short. The journey to the Tigers training ground was a relatively short one but I still needed to identify four or five places *en route* where I could go to the toilet. It was the same when we moved to the village of Arnesby. There was a pub, for example, where I stopped on many occasions in order to use the loo. As this was before opening time, the cleaners would often forget I was there, lock up and leave me trapped inside the pub with training still to make. I'd have to call up to the people who lived in the pub to let me out. They knew who I was. It was a Tigers pub, after all, but they never asked me why I kept needing to use their toilet at eight o'clock in the morning. On the way from Kirby I'd use a rent-a-car place. They began to ask me why I should just walk in, use their toilet and go again, but I was so desperate not to have an accident I'd just insist, walk by and no doubt appear rude.

There are very few more demeaning and belittling experiences for any man, let alone a Leicester and England rugby player, than when he shits himself. This, I am afraid, has happened on many occasions, too. The worst experience was on Christmas Eve in 2007. I was in Leicester city centre late in the afternoon, picking up a few final presents. This was before the birth of my children so it was just Annie and me, although my parents would be visiting, and I was reasonably well dressed. I was in the car park when I felt the first dreadful rumblings in my stomach that spelled trouble. I went into slight panic mode and sought out the nearby Phoenix Arts Centre to use their toilets. The door was locked. I then found a public convenience but that door was locked, too. The only other place I could think of was a nearby restaurant, but it, too, was closed. This was, after all, Christmas Eve. Now I was really starting to panic as the pain grew progressively worse, and as I walked back towards my car, I lost complete control of my bowels. I basically shat myself in the middle of the street. I waddled back to the back of the restaurant to find some bins, took my clothes off, emptied out my trousers, disposed of my boxers, cleaned up my trousers as best I could, put them back on and returned to my car to drive home. It was pretty rank. It was also an all-time low. A World Cup winner had just shat himself in the centre of Leicester, was forced to clean himself up as well as he could do, and then drive home on Christmas Eve, wondering just what had happened to him and his life.

Of course, I did not have cancer, or motor-neurone disease, or anything else which can kill or destroy you. But, at its worst, colitis stripped me of any self-esteem, and of any quality of life. You no longer feel like a human being. You are miserable because of the combination of the constant pain in your bowels and the humiliation of it all, and when you are confined to your bed, rushing backwards and forwards to the toilet and sometimes making a mess, that's as low as you can get. When colitis takes a real hold, your life is pegged back to bed, toilet, shitting yourself and making a foul mess everywhere. I use to wonder how old people can sometimes make a mess by having no control of their bowels. Now I understand. I just wish I hadn't need to find out in my twenties.

The Christmas Eve experience was by no means my only one. Getting to work every day proved to be a nightmare. I'd get up an hour and a half earlier than I needed to because I knew I'd be sitting on the toilet on numerous occasions before even leaving for Oval Park. It was stress that brought it on and the irony was I grew stressed by the thought of the short journey to training. The very first time I shat myself outdoors – it was happening all the time at home – was in early 2006, moments before arriving at Oval Park. I'd already been a few times at my now established toilet stops, but even in the three minutes between McDonald's in South Wigston and the training ground, I could not hold on. I was clenching my buttocks and grimacing in pain as my panic rose in the knowledge that I was in very grave danger of having a horrendously embarrassing accident yards from my unknowing Tigers teammates. A minute from turning into the car park my bowels emptied as I sat in the car. Luckily, I was wearing trousers and not my training kit, and I was the first to arrive. This became a purposeful tactic in order to avoid any teammates if the worst happened. I rushed into the first toilets – the women's – and spent twenty minutes cleaning up. It was obviously disgusting. I felt like a small child, or an incontinent 90 year old. Then I showered before training, which must have appeared odd to my fellow players as they arrived, although nobody wondered enough to ask.

From that day onwards I have always taken spare items of clothing with me in case of an accident. Once you get into training you focus on the job in hand. I was definitely man down that day but only really got to dwell on how my life had spiralled downwards when I returned home and sat talking to Annie about it. At this point Annie, my parents, the club doctor and Dr Barry Rathbone were the only people who knew about my condition. There was no way I was going to let my secret out to a bunch of rugby players who would then mock me mercilessly for shitting myself in public places. I ended up hiding it from them all for three years, not wanting their mockery or sympathy.

Looking back, I can see that I slumped into a state of depression. My condition prevented me from doing simple things, such as driving the forty-five-minute journey to see my parents, or taking trips to London for functions. Also, I could not possibly room share when the Tigers stayed away in readiness for an away fixture. For a long time, I'd make up a string of excuses for having a single room, telling Jo Hollis, the Leicester Tigers manager who organised accommodation, that I had a touch of flu, or a heavy head cold or something. Eventually, my condition started to become too obvious.

Just after my first son, Dylan, was born in 2008, I had operations on my Achilles, my hip and for the removal of four wisdom teeth. It was three weeks before I was due to play again and I felt in wonderful nick, close to full recovery. One day, after training, a few of us went back to Louis Deacon's house for some food and to chill. Often my colitis would rear up badly after surgery, maybe as a result of taking the subsequent drugs. At Louis's, I suddenly turned as white as a sheet and fell asleep on his couch, even though other players were making a noise around me. In the course of that week, I dropped a massive 10kg (22lb) in weight, an amount that had taken me months to put back on in the gym after surgery. That, in itself, was devastating. All that hard work had been for nothing.

Around that time, I had to blow Austin Healey out after I was invited down to London to appear at his testimonial dinner. I absolutely hate agreeing to something and then later pulling out, especially when the excuse given is 'stomach troubles'. I don't think Austin was hugely amused or impressed, although I'm sure he would understand now. Another time, I was incredibly close to crapping myself on stage in Lincoln at a Leon Lloyd testimonial dinner. At one point, I was asked a question and I was silent for a seemingly eternal ten seconds before answering. I came across as being pensive and giving the question the consideration it deserved. The truth was that I was using all my powers to prevent a major accident, up on stage, in front of an audience. Reading this, you may find such a thought to be hilarious, but place yourselves in my shoes!

One day I decided to tell my best friend at Leicester, Geordan. He had guessed something was up in any case, so when I spelled it out to him in the car, his reaction was not one of great surprise. Actually, his response, or at least my own reaction to it, surprised me. He was sympathetic, of course, but he didn't overdo it, and he also gently took the piss, which was ideal. I guess there is always a fine line when it comes to mickey-taking, especially concerning a subject as delicate as this. My fear was that everyone would get stuck in to me, but Geordan's light dealing with it made me begin to realise that perhaps it had not been the best course to keep everything to myself.

Later, I told the Deacon brothers, Louis and Brett, and Leon. Slowly, events made it inevitable that others would know. At the end of a three-day England camp in Loughborough, I was laid so low with it that I had to withdraw. I couldn't lift myself out of bed. The England management were more than understanding, as was the Tigers coaching team when I finally mustered up the courage to tell them. I told them that, although I tried not to be late for training, and never intended to leave early, from time to time my condition would force me to do both. More and more players at Leicester got to hear about it. I never stood up and made a public announcement, of course, but word got around, and when I had to dash off the training field, it soon became known as the 'Emergency Crap'.

Ironically, I became less stressed about my condition when people knew about it, which is what I had initially feared the most. Being stubborn about it and keeping it a secret had simply made life harder for myself. This also helped to explain my single-room obsession. I'm sure some of the lads thought I was simply being Mr Big Time. On one occasion, during pre-season, I had to share a room with Geoff Parling, the lock who joined us from Newcastle. The next day he asked me why I'd been up and down all night like a yo-yo. Once I explained to him, he accepted it without batting an eyelid.

During all this time, I became a nutritional expert. It turned out that it was not only stress, nor the drugs I'd been taking over the years, that caused my colitis to flare up. The other problematical area was my diet. The list of foods I needed to avoid was extensive. It included all spicy foods – so that meant no more curries – red meat, especially lamb, brown bread, surprisingly, caffeine and the protein shakes with creatine that I used religiously at Leicester to help bulk up. Even alcohol had to be taken in moderation. The reason why I crapped myself after the bender the England boys enjoyed during the 2007 World Cup in Paris was not the copious amounts of alcohol I'd consumed that night but my colitis. I began to experiment by omitting certain foods from my diet for a week or two, then returning to them to see which ones gave a reaction, and which did not. I pored over books and the internet to discover the best diet to follow when suffering from a severe bowel condition. My diet became an obsession. I also thought about contacting Sir Steve Redgrave, a fellow sufferer, who famously won gold at the Barcelona Olympics – one of five gold medals in five Games – while dealing with the dreadful effects of colitis. In the end, I didn't try to get in touch with him, but there were times when I was desperate for advice from people from whom I could take heart.

As we entered 2009, however, I felt I was getting on top of my colitis, although I was once caught short during a 5K run, hopped over a fence into a farmer's field and had only dock leaves to clear up the subsequent mess. Colitis accidents had been less serious, and indeed less in general, but I continued to be hit by serious injuries, which meant more surgery, more time out, more stress and more medication. Just before the infamous Heineken Cup semi-final win over Cardiff, of which more in the next chapter, I experienced a major trauma.

It began with what felt like a sore voice box. The more I shouted, which is what happens on a daily basis in training or during a match, the more painful it became. It grew so bad that I went to see an ear, nose and throat specialist at the same BUPA hospital where my colitis was first diagnosed. This resulted in a pipe with a tiny camera on it being pushed up my nose to check out the problem area. As uncomfortable as this was, at least it was a different orifice! The doctor came back to me to report that he wanted to carry out a biopsy because he had discovered a red area in my throat, which concerned him. He wanted 'to be safe'. When I pressed him more on this, he admitted that it could turn out to be nothing or, worst case scenario, cancer. He certainly wasn't prepared to rule out anything. Great!

I had ten days to mull over what he had said, the time it took to have the biopsy and then hear the results, and this was in the immediate run up to the Heineken Cup semi-final. The longer it went on, the more I feared the worst. Annie felt the same. In fact, if anything, she was more stressed than I was. In the back of her mind she contemplated becoming a young widow and single mother. Dylan was a year old by then and I had not yet turned 30 years of age. We braced ourselves for some terrible news. The result stunned me. I was perfectly OK save for a throat infection, but it was the reasons for the infection that hit me hard. It emerged that the steroids I'd been taking to counter the colitis had resulted in the infection. My condition had directly resulted in my wife and I having to endure some of the scariest few days of our lives.

This was bullshit. I was furious and depressed in equal measures. Life had been a litany of injuries, infections, operations, colitis and now a cancer scare. I'd just about had enough. That's when I decided to knock everything on the head. No more steroids, no more anti-inflammatories or antibiotics, and no more supplements unless it was completely necessary. From that day on, I turned my back on all of it, so that I'd never again react to so much being thrown into my body. Since then, save for the odd, lesser flare-up, my colitis has plateaued.

The condition will never go away completely. I am resigned to taking a minimum of four tablets a day every day for the rest of my life. On bad days – and they still occur, although not as bad as they have been – it is eight tablets. These have been passed by the rugby authorities because I have a Special Exemption clause – a TUE – which allows me to take them during my career under the laws of the game. Everything I do needs to take into account my colitis. A few years ago I used to grow terribly nervous before making a speech or being interviewed in front of an audience. Experience and age enable me to handle it much better these days but I still need to go to the toilet on numerous occasions beforehand. I must continue to watch my diet and monitor myself, especially when, as often still happens, blood appears in the pan.

Some people may find it uncomfortable that I have been so open about such a personal issue, but having felt so low because of the condition, so dehumanised and so humiliated, I wanted to share my feelings, especially on behalf of the tens of thousands of other people in the UK alone who also suffer from some form of colitis. I have grown far more comfortable talking about it now and if this chapter helps anybody affected by the illness, in any small way, I will be happy.

It is ironic that, a few years ago, in my younger, more immature state of mind, I might have found such a condition in a teammate amusing, and been one of the first to exploit it. Now I realise just how much colitis can affect you and how hard you have to struggle to prevent it from taking over your whole life. It will never go away. In that respect, it is a life sentence. Yet today, I feel as if I am definitely winning the battle.

10

BACK ON THE CONVEYOR BELT

The twilight years at Leicester, 2007–10

O nce again, it was straight back to business after the World Cup, and that meant turning out for the Tigers the following week. Richard Cockerill had been in charge at Leicester during the World Cup, but now a new man took the helm. He was Marcelo Loffreda, the coach who had guided Argentina so impressively to a third-place finish in the tournament, stunning the French in Paris in the third/fourth place play-off. Leicester, however, would be a very different proposition altogether.

On New Year's Eve, I treated Dad to a 65th birthday weekend at the plush Stapleford Park near Melton Mowbray. Annie and I made out we would not be joining him, Mum and their two best friends, Jan and Ray, but we surprised him by turning up during their pre-dinner drinks. The weekend, and seeing in the New Year in such nice surroundings, was my way of saying thank you to him for all his support over the years. On the dance floor, and over quite a few more drinks, we agreed it had been a mutually enjoyable few years.

Later that night I lay in bed and thought, for just about the first time in depth, about my father's pride in what I had achieved as a sportsman, and realised it was not simply the pride of a father, but the feeling of immense satisfaction and justification for the massive role that he had taken in the moulding of my life, and my career.

Kind almost to a fault, the decision my parents took to stick with just one child so that they could afford to give me the opportunities in life they could not have given two children was, in hindsight, breathtakingly unselfish. Dad worked as hard as he possibly could to provide me with the best education and chances, which led, of course, to my development on the rugby field. He worked his way up from being a 16-year-old apprentice to becoming a director of cement factories all over Indonesia. When I was still at school, I'd barely see him. He'd be up at five and off to work well before I rose from my teenage slumbers. He'd return at 7.30 or 8pm and often fall asleep in his chair. At times, I'd think he wasn't around that much, but that's because his incredible work ethic meant he was normally first in, and last out.

We didn't need to say too much to each other that night as we raised a glass. He knew his hard work had paid off, professionally and in terms of putting food on the table, but also because his efforts had provided me with the perfect platform to succeed in my chosen field. As I rolled over to sleep, my happiness was not merely the result of my own success, but of knowing that I had, after all, done my father proud, and there was nobody more deserving of this than he was.

Although I featured in a number of games for the Tigers, I was struggling with both my shoulder, damaged during the World Cup, and my Achilles tendon. My Achilles, in particular, grew worse and worse as the weeks went by. I started England's Six Nations campaign that February against Wales but after 15 minutes hobbled off, knowing that my Achilles was in trouble. The club gave me six weeks off to recuperate after a scan suggested I had tendonitis, but when those six weeks had passed, I could still barely jog. That's when it was decided I should visit one of the most pre-eminent Achilles specialists in the world, Haaken Alfredsson, who practised in Stockholm. Geordan, who also suffered from a niggle, England physio Barney

Kenny and Scott 'Topper' Tindall, the Leicester physio, travelled with me to Sweden to see Haaken.

Geordan was quickly diagnosed and took the return flight the following morning, bringing with him the happy news that he would be out of action for two weeks at the most. Typically, for me it was more dramatic. After another scan, Haaken told me that a build-up of fluid around the tendon was causing the problem and that, in a worse case scenario, I'd be out for eight weeks. First, though, I was to be operated on that same day, under a local anaesthetic, to release the fluid and relieve the pressure on the tendon. It was extremely strange to be face down and hear Haaken say, 'OK, so I'm now cutting into the problem area,' followed by a long pause and then, 'Oh!' That was enough to tell me that my bad news had just got worse. My Achilles had been sheared lengthwise, which is less common than widthwise, and I was being told it would take three to four months of rehab before I'd be fit again. I had flown out to Stockholm believing I had a four-week injury at worst. Now I was stuck in the Swedish capital with Topper for four days and three nights, because of the wound, and facing a four-month layoff, which, of course, ruled me out of the rest of the Six Nations and, indeed, the rest of the season with Leicester, too. I would never play for Brian Ashton's England again. Brian was axed after the Six Nations and, eventually, Johnno took over.

Topper called Cockers to tell him there had been a change in the diagnosis and the eight weeks had now become four months. We then made the most of our time in Stockholm, me on crutches with spikes in the end to deal with the carpet of late winter snow. The first night was a low-key affair since it had been quite a day. Geordan, Topper and I just had dinner and a few drinks. On the second night, minus Geordan, we had a few more, but the third night turned out to be embarrassing. We decided to go to the cinema but the only film on was '27 Dresses'. Unfortunately, we misunderstood the translation of the seating plan. We thought we had purchased a pair of extra-wide, 'superior' seats, but when we were shown to our place, it turned out to be a shared, two-seater 'love' sofa. So there we were, two Englishmen snuggled up together at the back of the cinema watching '27 Dresses'.

On my return to England, I went to see a London specialist to get my hip checked. What with my shoulder and Achilles, I had barely thought about the problem with my hip. The specialist told me that I had a major bone defect and cartilage damage, and said that, since I was out with a long-term injury in any case, I may as well have surgery on the hip sooner rather than later. A bone spur was grinding my cartilage away and this needed to be halted in its tracks. So I went under the knife again, this time to treat a micro-fracture of the hip joint. All these operations resulted in me requiring six months rest and rehab.

The timing, from a personal point of view, could have been better. Annie had just given birth to Dylan, our first child. Even before the operations, I was wearing a plastic boot and needed to avoid as much weight-bearing as possible. The subsequent hip operation meant I had to lie or sit as much as possible. We could have done with a straightforward labour and birth, especially Annie, of course, but this failed to materialise. Instead, Annie was subjected to a thirty-six-hour labour and a caesarean section when she was desperate to have as natural a birth as possible. For nearly all of this time, we were hospital-bound through fear of losing our bed and being told that if we left it would be taken. At one point, Annie ordered me to get some sleep so, after 30 hours of being up, I grabbed half an hour.

When the doctors realised that Dylan was facing in the wrong direction, any hope of a natural birth went out of the window. I was ordered out of the theatre for a while and spent my time pacing up and down the corridor until, after what felt like a lifetime, I was called back in to witness Dylan being lifted out of Annie. It was a pretty traumatic experience for both of us but as I watched Dylan arrive into the world, two thoughts raced through my mind. Firstly, Dylan looked more like a green alien than anything resembling a human baby; and secondly, my admiration for all women who give birth, and especially Annie, just shot through the roof. Quite clearly, it is the hardest job in the world.

Ordinarily, the thought of the mother-in-law staying with us at home for six whole weeks would not be massively positive, but Annie's mum, Nicky, arrived from New Zealand and baled us out completely. I was in my surgical boot and resting my hip, and Annie required rest for the first six weeks of Dylan's life. She wasn't able to do much at all, although she did win the argument over naming our son. The moment I saw her look when I suggested calling him Lewis, I knew I was never going to win. Thus Dylan Lewis Moody arrived into the world.

Meanwhile, back at the Tigers life had gone pear-shaped. I had managed to play a few games under the former Puma coach, including his first in charge when he let the existing management handle the selection and the style while he took time to gather his thoughts. We lost to Leinster in the Heineken Cup at the RDS in Dublin and played poorly. This was all Marcelo needed to see. He proceeded to take a catastrophic line in coaching and style.

This is what I wrote in my diary during that season. 'Marcelo's not the man for Leicester. He and his methods have taken us back ten years.' It was true. He decided to go right back to basics with our style, which was odd considering how expansive and free-flowing we had been under Paddy Howard the season before. He had the backs practising high balls and rucks for most of the time. We felt we were a top team full of fluidity, and then suddenly we were being taken back to the dark ages.

It was not all his fault, however. Indeed, I liked his love and passion for the game. There was no doubt he was a true rugby man but it didn't help that he arrived at Leicester almost midway through the season. Cockers had brought more players into the team because of so many World Cup absences, and when the guys returned, the squad ballooned up to fifty players. Then the guys who played in France but found themselves ousted from the first team started bitching and bickering, which only added to Marcelo's issues. His English was so broken that, behind his back, the players called him 'Borat', which hardly enhanced his standing with the squad. Marcelo arrived with a great reputation, his heart was in rugby and he knew what he wanted, but he just wasn't right for Leicester.

The coaches didn't make it any easier for him, either. They could not work out what he was trying to do and at no point did he gain their confidence. By the end of a trophy-less season, Marcelo was packing his bags and heading back home. We lost both the Premiership and EDF Cup finals and, blasphemous as it may appear to be, I believe it was a good thing that we lost them both. Winning silverware would only have papered over the cracks. It was a terrible time to be involved with the Tigers. Leicester was, and is, a club I care passionately about, and I felt a huge responsibility to help put things right, but there was little I could do, being out injured for so long.

During that summer I visited the Kibera slum in Nairobi in my role as an ambassador for the Hope HIV charity. I'd wanted to see for myself how the charity was working to good effect in such areas for some time, but the demands of rugby meant I could never venture too far for too long. Carrying a long-term injury, however, presented an opportunity, and I'm very glad I took it up. Based in England, Hope HIV supports mainly AIDS victims in sub-Saharan Africa. The month I arrived in Kenya there had been massive riots, and as I walked through the most appalling slums, a tall, blond and very pale Englishman, it's fair to say I stood out. Around three million people lived in one square mile. One man I met had been a glue sniffer. Now he lived here under a bridge with a sewer running past, and this was seen as a step up in life. It really was the biggest shithole in the world and, of course, it's moments like these when you appreciate just how much you have got.

In the middle of all this poverty, illness and filth was a tranquil haven, an area run by the Salvation Army and supported by Hope HIV, with trees, children playing and teachers teaching. One teacher, Beatrice, had been there for twenty-three years, and it was through respect for her that the local gang members, many of whom had been taught by her, left the haven alone during the riots.

It was a thought-provoking visit, and it prompted a big hug for Dylan on my return to Leicester, and a major donation from the proceeds of my testimonial year, which I was sharing with Geordan. It also got me to analyse my life, and what I was doing with it. In a diary entry, I talk about wanting to do more than just fulfil a job. I wanted to make a difference. Was I doing enough with my life? Was I doing enough for others? Was I ever going to be as good a rugby player again? This questioning reflected a heightened level of self-crisis, borne out of a combination of issues – my injuries, the birth of Dylan and the huge responsibility I felt for my family, and my emotional reaction to visiting Kenya. These were mentally tough times. At the start of the 2008–09 season I was still recuperating, of course, from my hip and Achilles operations. I finally ran out on to a rugby field in the colours of the Tigers in November, during the autumn internationals. I attended every pre-season meeting I could, however, including the referee's lecture at a Military School in Leicester. The first picture that came up in his slide show turned out to be his missus in a semi-naked pose, much to the delight of the whole Tigers squad of players and managers and to this guy's acute embarrassment. I've never seen a man move quicker to remove a shot from a slide show than he did.

By then, a new head coach had taken over the reins at Leicester. South African Heyneke Meyer arrived in the East Midlands with a big reputation, too, after steering the Bulls to victory in the Super 14 final. I thought he was going to be brilliant for us, I really did. He knew what he wanted, he had a structure, he was passionate and he was a great believer in making us a tight-knit unit. He'd even go so far as to instruct us to stay together as Tigers when we played for England, something the England management would not appreciate. He had a South African coaching ethos, wanting his big, ball-playing guys to carry the ball, and he did his best to gain an understanding of the club by talking to the senior players as often as he could about all things Leicester. His results were up and down, but any new coach is going to need a good six months minimum to get his feet under the table. Heyneke just about made it to six months.

In January 2009, a very good friend of mine and of many other Tigers died. Her name was Vina Patel and she acted as solicitor, advisor, accountant, counsellor and general friend to me, Leon Lloyd and a few of our colleagues. We'd often go to lunch and just talk about any concerns we had about anything in life. At first, the story was that she had fallen down the stairs in her offices in Leicester. Leon phoned me to report the news and we were both shaken by poor Vina's untimely passing. We both attended the funeral, as did her grieving husband and her partner at her office. Later the truth emerged. Her partner, John Cort, had paid a hitman to murder her and make it look like an accident so that he could get his grubby hands on the insurance payout. He was sent away for 28 years, and the hitman for 27 years. Whenever I think about Vina, I feel sadness for a lost friend and also shock that she was murdered.

I managed to play eight games under Heyneke once I had returned from rehab, and I hit the ground running. So much so, I was called up to the England squad for the 2009 Six Nations tournament. My excellent form surprised me. I was voted man of the match in just my third game back, and with two weeks before the start of the Six Nations, I felt as if I was in a good place.

Then another injury struck, and this one nearly proved to be an injury too far for me. It was an accident at the Leicester training ground. Alex Tuilagi chipped the ball over my head, I dived on it and Alex fell, landing on my ankle. I knew immediately that something was not right, although that gut feeling turned out to be wildly optimistic. I hobbled off and sat on the side, with ice packed around the damaged area. At the end of training, I sat in the physio's room, waiting to be taken off to hospital to be X-rayed. Cozza asked if I'd be fit for the game on Saturday. I told him I expected to be. It was probably just a strain. When the X-ray results came through, Topper and Haj Singh, the Leicester doctor, were with me. You could see in Haj's eyes that he did not quite know what to say to me. In the end, all he could muster was, 'Sorry mate.' I just lay back on the bed, placed my cap over my eyes and disappeared into my own world of pain.

In reality, by my standards, this was not one of my bigger injuries. A fractured ankle would mean eight to ten weeks on the sidelines. I'd had a lot worse, but it was the timing that broke me. I was more devastated by this piece of news than by any other concerning injuries and setbacks in my whole career.

After I had recovered from my Achilles and hip operations but before I injured my ankle, I had written the following in my diary: 'I'm not sure I can cope with another injury. You always doubt yourself afterwards. Can you be as good again, can you tackle, will it all just fall back into place? You always fear that the next time the answers will be no.'

There really wasn't anything anyone could say to me, although Alex made a point of seeing me to say, 'Sorry, Chief.' It wasn't his fault at all. It was just one of those things, a freak training-ground accident.

For the next half an hour I couldn't even ease myself off that bed. I was too upset to contemplate what to do next. I called my mum in an emotional state and told her the news. 'You're kidding,' she replied. I added that I felt as if I'd had enough of rugby. She told me I'd be OK in a few days and not to make any hasty decisions. I called Annie. She came straight to the training ground to collect me and, together with Geordan and his then partner Lucie Silvas, we went off to lunch. I sat there in the restaurant, contemplating the looming prospect of my eleventh operation, this one to put a couple of screws in the damaged ankle. I looked across at my crutches, now familiar appendages, and decided that I'd had a good career but enough was enough.

I conveyed this to Annie as soon as we got home. It wasn't because I'd stopped loving rugby, far from it, but I just couldn't face any more pain, any more operations, and any more rehab. If I was hoping for a sympathetic shoulder from Annie, I didn't get it. She told me to stop being so stupid. She added that rugby players had short enough careers without retiring early, and that it was a straightforward fracture that would heal soon, leaving me with many years ahead of me to play the game.

It was all I needed to hear. I genuinely believed that this was the final straw and that I would be announcing my retirement but, in reality, what I needed was a slap around the face. Annie delivered it and thus saved my career. The next day I reported to Oval Park.

'Right then,' I said to Topper. 'What do we need to do to get me back as quickly as possible?' And so the process of rehab started all over again.

One of my biggest gripes was not simply the personal trauma I experienced whenever faced with an injury, but the constant feeling that I had not played enough times for Leicester. In my 14 year career at Welford Road, I played 222 times in total, which included 170 starts. That may seem like a decent figure, but if I had been fit and available for every game, this would have been well over 400 appearances, just like some of the old-school Leicester players who still dotted around the club. I always found this difficult to deal with, especially when players younger than I am had played more times for the Tigers.

This was also my testimonial year. It was an honour to be granted a testimonial by the Leicester fans, and when the club suggested sharing it with Geordan, I was delighted and believed that the English and Irish interest would help make it a bumper year. Unfortunately, the recession struck almost immediately and money was hard to come by. Some was going to our chosen charities, and the rest coming to us. There were times, frankly, when I felt as though I was selling my soul, signing this and that, and turning up everywhere for autographs and photos. Some people may wonder why highly paid rugby professionals should pocket any testimonial money at all, but the majority of players do not make it to Test level and are therefore not highly paid. And all rugby players, even those who do get to play international rugby, reach the end of their careers by their mid-thirties at the latest, if they are lucky.

The timing of the testimonial may not have been perfect, but it was great to be sharing it with Geordan. From the moment he was the lone person in the de Montfort University bar to catch me as I dived off a stage in 1997, I knew that we would be there for each other. This was despite the fact that he didn't want to come out for a drink in the first place, and later that night, as he sat happily talking to a group of people, I picked him up and dumped him down on the table, scattering everything and everybody in the process. I consider him to be one of my very closest friends, the kind of person for whom you would drop whatever you were doing at whatever time he came calling.

We've both had testing times in our careers, and we've been able to lean on each other. The man has 70-odd caps for Ireland, so he's not exactly been a failure at Test level, but everyone at Leicester, and nearly everyone in Ireland as far as I know, believes he should have 100 caps. For some reason, the long-time Irish coach, Eddie O'Sullivan, preferred Girvan Dempsey at full-back over Geordan because he felt Girvan was a safer option. Now, I've got nothing against Girvan but he's no Geordan Murphy. Ironically, there's no one safer under the high ball than Geordy in my opinion. It's an example of how much coaches can affect your career.

On a personal level, Geordan is, and has always been, my 'go to' man. He has, for example, on many occasions been there for Annie and the kids in my absence, and as godfather to Dylan he has become, to all intents and purposes, an uncle. He would be round at our house all the time to see Dylan, pampering him with toys and calling him nicknames. First there was Elvis, because he was quite possibly conceived in Las Vegas, and then Sputnik, because it took ages for Dylan to grow any hair. Geordy was, and is, besotted with Dylan and happily babysits for us at the drop of a hat. There is not a nicer person in rugby and you would find very few players, no matter their club, who would disagree with that statement.

Still, despite my obvious anguish, injury and illness, there were good times too during the testimonial, notably the ladies night, when our academy boys had to serve five hundred screaming women as waiters, while ten of the Tigers enacted 'Lay All Your Love On Me', a dance on the beach from the film 'Mamma Mia', choreographed by Annie, who has a degree in contemporary dance, and her friend Keely. Five of us were dressed as men, and five as women – I chose the latter on the basis that I rarely needed any excuse to dress up as a female.

For this entertainment, I persuaded Tom Varndell, Marco Wentzel and Derrick Hougaard to perform a semi-strip down to their boxers, holding flippers, but as they made their stage entrance, one of the Leicester boys pulled Derrick's flipper away from him, which meant the South African, a staunch Christian, had to cover his privates with his hands while he danced. It was one of the funniest sights I've ever seen.

In my injured absence, Heyneke's short spell at Leicester came to an end. Family issues meant that he had little option but to return to South Africa. I had a lot of time for him and felt he was getting somewhere with his methods, but the fates conspired against him. During a team bonding session involving the management, the coaches decided to stage a 100 metre race, but two strides into it Heyneke tore his Achilles right down to the bone. It meant he could not be on the pitch all the time during training, but instead had to stand at the side, leaning on his crutches, a feeling I knew all about. Cockers therefore took charge of much of the training, and although Heyneke brought South African defence coach John McFarland into the camp, he served only to ruffle feathers with the rest of the coaching staff. To Heyneke's credit, once he knew he would be on his way back to South Africa, he stepped aside early and allowed Cockers to take full charge of the team. John McFarland phoned in to the club the day after Heyneke's departure to say that something had come up and he was unable to come to work that day. Cockers replied that if he failed to show, he would not be welcome any more. That was the last time anyone ever saw or heard from him.

It was during the latter stages of my rehab that my colitis flared up again, followed by my cancer scare. The Achilles, the hip, the removal of my wisdom teeth, the broken ankle, the stresses at home, all resulted in a setback with my illness, just as I was about to play again for the Tigers.

I made it back for the epic Heineken Cup semi-final at the Millennium Stadium against Cardiff. We should have won in proper time, but we let a large lead slip to end up drawing 26–26. I had a shocker of a game, no doubt the result of my terrible state of health and concern over the potential threat of cancer. In particular, I missed a tackle – especially galling since I pride myself in that area – and Jamie Roberts needed no second invitation to rampage half the length of the pitch to score a try. It resulted, famously, in a drop-goal shoot-out. I made sure I was way, way down the list of takers. In fact, only the props, Martin Castrogiovanni and Julian White, plus the reserves, were behind me in the queue, and I comforted myself that there was no way it would come to any of us needing to pop the ball between the posts. As it turned out, it got uncomfortably close. Our French scrum half Julien Dupuy had earlier been substituted, and when we turned to him to return to the field seconds before the end of extra time in order to take a drop goal after the final whistle, he could not at first be found. Julien had sneaked out of the stadium for a cheeky fag!

After five drop goals each, the score stood at 4–4, but after Martyn Williams missed his effort – a cruel twist for such a fine servant for the Cardiff Blues – Jordan Crane hit the target and we had made it through to another Heineken Cup final. My relief was complete. I had played badly, missed a crucial tackle, and was contemplating stepping on to the pitch to drop a goal in a sudden death situation in front of 70,000 fans. Thank goodness it never came to that. The following week, those who had not taken a drop goal in Cardiff all had a go in a mock drop-goal shoot-out. None of us got even close to scoring. Whitey's effort actually went out in touch!

Before the European final we had the small matter of the Premiership final, where we faced London Irish. I was once again on the bench despite scoring a late try to beat Bath in the semi-final play-off. We managed to scrape home 10–9 in the final to reclaim the domestic league title. It was hardly a classic, although I was pleased that, when I finally had my chance, I managed a cheeky off-load to Craig Newby whose pass gave Crane the chance to score what proved to be the winning try.

We needed to play better if we were to beat Leinster in the Heineken Cup final at Murrayfield, and we did, but it was not enough to see off a Brian O'Driscoll and Rocky Elsom-inspired Leinster, who won 19–16. Ben Woods again started at openside and scored Leicester's try, relegating me to the bench, and although I entered the fray on the hour, the momentum had swung the Irish province's way.

I wasn't happy, to say the least, about my continual selection on the bench, and I wasn't happy, either, about the way Cozza, one of the true greats of the Leicester Tigers, was treated. He had been injured and out of the side, but had been back and available for the last four games of the season, which included a semi-final play-off, a Premiership final and a Heineken Cup final. This would be his last season. Cozza would be retiring from all forms of rugby after the Heineken Cup final. He was club captain and fit, but he had to sit out these important games, watching from the stands. I'm not one for sentimentality just for the sake of it. Leicester are a hard-nosed club that makes hard-nosed decisions and I have no major beef with that. But in games such as major finals against stern opposition, you need your leaders out there on the pitch with you, lending attitude and experience. It wasn't just me. Everyone felt aggrieved for Cozza. To my mind, it was a complete injustice, and it gave me an insight into how the club was changing.

Any outside chance I had of being a late selection for the 2009 British and Irish Lions tour to South Africa had also gone after a handful of cameo performances from the Leicester bench. I have no idea if starts would have made any difference or not, but after the 3–0 thrashing by New Zealand in 2005 and the belated understanding of what it meant to be a Lion, I was desperate to have another crack at it, and devastated to miss out on what would prove to be an epic series.

On the back of all this, I did the unthinkable. I instructed my agent, Mark Spoors from Big Red Management, to start putting feelers out to the French Top 14. I was beginning to feel stale, and all my mates I'd grown up with at Leicester, bar Geordie, had left or were leaving. I told my dad how I felt and he agreed wholeheartedly. Annie was behind the idea as well, excited by the prospect of living in the south of France, learning a new language and living in a new culture.

Despite my growing reservations about the club, I enjoyed a successful pre-season and was fully fit, but nonetheless I was still picked on the bench for the first game of the 2009–10 season. I had kept my own counsel up to this point but felt an explanation was required from Cockers. He told me that the number-seven jersey belonged to Woods and it was up to me to prise it off him. I felt he was wrong, of course, and when I had my chance to replace Woods in the 50th minute I played well enough to start the next fixture. That's how it remained for the rest of the season.

With my colitis now under some control, and having had a full summer to remove any lingering niggles, I ended up having one of my best seasons for club and country, playing under Geordie, who was appointed as the new club captain.

I had mixed feelings about this if I am being honest. I was, of course, delighted for my best friend in rugby, and vowed to support him on and off the field as much as possible, but it was a role I'd quite fancied for myself, having been such a long-term servant of the club. I had been given the captain's armband for three games and managed to win them all, but Cockers felt Geordan was the better man for the job and he has gone on to lead from the front as Leicester continued to enjoy great success. In hindsight, it was, of course, the right decision. Geordan has been awesome with the captain's armband and his form and commitment can never be questioned.

The longer the season went on, and the longer I played well and featured regularly in the Tigers starting XV, so the doubts grew about whether I really wanted to leave Welford Road. I scored a try in a win over Leeds, then a brace against Newcastle. It was going well, from a personal viewpoint, in the England jersey, too. Yet before the end of the season, I had agreed to leave Leicester and signed for Bath for reasons I will go into later. It was not, as I will explain, quite how I wanted it all to end, but if I was going to leave the East Midlands after fourteen years at the greatest club in English rugby, I was determined to go out with a bang.

Ironically, we played Bath twice between me signing for them and the end of the season, once in the regular season and again in the semi-final play-off, a game they could, and maybe would, have won if I had not stopped Matt Banahan a metre or two away from our try line. Now Banners takes some stopping, especially when he can smell the opposition line, so I was especially pleased to have made such a vital contribution on what would be my last appearance at Welford Road in the green, red and white of Leicester. Afterwards, I walked around the pitch holding Dylan in my arms and waved to the fans. Despite me leaving the club to join Bath, who for many years were seen as the big enemy until Wasps came on to the scene, I was treated with a great deal of respect and support by the Leicester faithful, as indeed I had been throughout my time there. But I was not emotional that night. We still had one more game to play before the end of the season, and that turned out to be the best Premiership final ever, against Saracens at Twickenham.

The lead continually changed sides until, with three minutes remaining, Glenn Jackson's penalty put Saracens ahead, 27–26. I was off the pitch by then, having been replaced by Craig Newby in the 68th minute, and could only watch helplessly as the game appeared to have slipped away. Yet, as every other team in England and Europe knows, write the Tigers off at your peril. In an amazing climax to the game, Scott Hamilton caught the restart and off-loaded to Danny Hipkiss. Danny, who had come on from the bench and was determined to make his own mark after an injury-ravaged season, was high tackled, which meant a penalty for Toby Flood to win the game. The Saracens players stopped in their tracks but, before the referee could blow his whistle, Danny continued to run, scoring close enough to the posts to make Flood's conversion a formality. Saracens had barely enough time to restart before the final whistle blew and Leicester had successfully defended their Premiership title, winning 33–27.

I sank to my knees on the pitch for a minute or two while all around me my teammates celebrated. Some people thought I was overcome by emotion, but the truth is I was not that emotional, just keen to take it all in. It had been a sensational game and a sensational way to end my time at the Leicester Tigers. I spent forty-five minutes walking around the pitch, much of it with the trophy in my hand, and Dylan cradled in my other arm. I climbed over the advertising hoardings to offer Tigers fans the chance to hold the cup themselves and have photos taken with it and with me. It was the very least I could do for the most remarkable rugby fans in England. Sam Vesty, Brett Deacon, Aaron Mauger and my World Cup-winning colleague Ben Kay were also leaving the club that day, and although they did not feature in the final, at least could enjoy the post-game walkabout on the Twickenham turf. Worst of all I knew this was the very last time I would be playing alongside my mate Geordan. That, more than anything, got to me the most.

It really was the end of an era. The following September I would be running out in the blue, black and white of Bath Rugby. But before all that I had to focus my mind on playing for England. Quite a lot had changed since Brian Ashton had left his post in 2008. Johnno was in charge now, and I knew something potentially special was brewing.

11

JOHNNO'S ENGLAND

England, 2007–10

Nobody was more surprised than I was when I heard the news that Martin Johnson, for me always my captain, had suddenly become the new England team manager. It was after the 2008 Six Nations. Whenever I had spoken to Johnno, he had given me the impression that he was enjoying his post-rugby life too much to abandon it. There was always talk about him returning to Leicester in some coaching or managerial capacity but he was happy with his after-dinner speaking and property interests.

My other emotion was one of great excitement. He had, after all, been my leader for twelve seasons and I just knew that he would be awesome. Why? Well, it wasn't because of his coaching experience. He had none. That was the one aspect of his appointment that I found a little strange. But he had played at the highest level for a long time under various top coaches, and towards the end of his Test career, and most definitely his club career, he more or less coached the teams in any case. His word tended to be final. Yet Johnno possessed something you cannot teach. He knew how to win. That alone made him the obvious choice.

I had to reconsider my relationship with him, however. I told Johnno when I first saw him after his appointment, 'I guess I can't give you as many plum shots any more.' It's always a little awkward at first to have a former teammate become your boss, although I had grown used to it with Deano and Wellsy at the Tigers and England. It didn't mean we couldn't still have some banter, of course, but I was wary about it. Now there was a line, and I was very aware that he still had to select me. The last thing I wanted to do was undermine him in any way in front of the players.

Anyone who has ever played with Johnno has a huge amount of respect for the man, and knows that he would never have taken on this role unless he believed he would do it justice. He's not bothered about his reputation, but he is desperate for England to fare well. I was equally desperate to play well for him and for England to be successful, because Johnno was the very pinnacle of rugby. I also knew, however, that it would take time. Successful teams do not materialise overnight. People kept forgetting how the 2003 World Cup-winning team lost three Grand Slam matches and a World Cup quarter-final before we came good in Australia.

I missed the two-Test summer tour of New Zealand in 2008 through injury. Johnno, wisely as it turned out, also opted out on the basis that he had only just secured the role and had existing commitments, leaving Rob Andrew in charge. England crashed twice to the All Blacks, and some players endured horrendous and unfounded allegations of rape.

There was hope that I would be fit enough to play in the autumn Tests, which is why I was named in the squad at the start of the 2008–09 season. This was my first taste of Johnno, the team manager, and it was a little strange. He was very laid back, trying to feel his way into the post. One of the first areas for discussion was to ensure that all the controversy that occurred on the New Zealand tour never happened again. A former tabloid newspaper editor was brought in to explain the nature of the more scurrilous aspects of journalism, which made us all more aware and nervous. Then we broke off into small groups in order to prepare presentations on roles, standards and what is and is not acceptable within a team environment. Most of us were fairly light-hearted about this, suggesting, among other things, no prostitutes or lady-boys in the hotel after 10pm, but Josh

Lewsey produced a whole flip chart with diagrams and boxes. It remains the only time I have ever seen a rugby player do this at a team meeting and, love him as I do, it was typical Josh.

This was also the first time I came across Danny Cipriani. He had already made his mark by being dropped by Brian Ashton before the Calcutta Cup during the previous Six Nations, after being spotted in a nightclub, and then producing an impressive performance at stand off against Ireland. Ashton had decided to drop Wilko in favour of the young Wasp. .

I am an open-minded kind of guy but it is fair to say that the first impression was not a good one and this was down to one reason. Cipriani decided to turn up to Johnno's first England camp in a Ferrari.

Maybe there's a bit of old school about me, maybe even a touch of the Leicester mute, but when a young man comes into a new squad, I think he needs to keep his head down and get on with it. You stand out because you are a great player dedicated to training and playing. You don't stand out because you turn up in a Ferrari. To me, it was an insight into what made Danny tick. Everyone was talking him up as the next best thing, but the key word here is next. If you've earned the right to turn up in a Ferrari for your first England camp under the stewardship of a legend such as Martin Johnson, then fair play. If you have done the business, your attitude is spot on, you've proved yourself and you have the respect of your peers, I have absolutely no problem with whatever car you choose to drive. But to do this at age 19 seemed to me to be starting off his relationship with Johnno on the wrong foot. If he knew anything about Johnno at all, he'd have known the last thing he should have done was breeze into the England camp in that car.

One of my biggest bugbears in sport, and life, is people with, frankly, more talent than I'll ever possess, who don't have the desire or the understanding of what it takes to be the best, or to be part of a team. People work damn hard for their place in a team. Some don't possess much talent but they are selected because they work to their optimum. Others believe they have a God-given right to be included, but these people can be like a bad apple. The wrong player with the wrong mentality can contaminate a team. I'd love to have Cipriani's talent because I know I would maximise it. My biggest fear has always been not giving it my best shot. Ironically, my biggest regret is that I gave it too much, hence the long list of injuries I've had to endure. At least I won't die wondering about whether I would have been more successful if I'd tried harder.

I just missed out on the 2008 autumn internationals, which, in hindsight, was a blessing in disguise, and not just because England were beaten by record scores at Twickenham by New Zealand, Australia and South Africa. The truth was, although I had just started to turn out again for the Tigers, I was not ready for international rugby and it would have been wrong to pick me. It was not, long, however, before I was back to my best form. As November turned into December and then January, I was enjoying some of best-ever games in a Tigers jersey and this prompted Johnno and Wellsy to call me to say how excited they were by my form, and how much they were looking forward to having me back in the fold. They told me to stay fit – ironic, as it turned out. I replied how determined I was to be part of the new Johnno revolution and how I excited I was, too. Within a week I was back on the phone to Johnno, less than a fortnight before the start of the 2009 Six Nations.

'Bad news, mate,' I told him. 'I've just broken my ankle.' There was a pause.

'You're kidding!'

I could feel his disappointment for me, but at the same time Johnno had to move on. There is little room for sentiment in sport. You're either in or you're out, and when you're injured, you're out!

181

England delivered a decidedly average Six Nations, in which one of the main points discussed within the media was how animated Johnno became in the stands. Certainly, at Croke Park – where I would dearly love to have played – Johnno was seen smashing his fists down in anger. Players are not intimidated by this. In fact, they love to see their coaches become involved and emotional because it shows they care as deeply as we do. I've always liked that in any coach I've worked under. I want them to be as passionate as I am.

I managed to return to the Leicester side, albeit on the bench, for the tailend of the season and this was enough for me to be selected for the England team to play the Barbarians at Twickenham. We lost, I was ineffective and felt as if I lacked match fitness. I've never actually liked playing against the Baa-Baas, as much as the public likes to see them in action. The games are not proper Test matches for starters in terms of winning caps, and you can't analyse the opposition since the guys tend to be on the piss all week and then rock up to play random rugby. Of course everyone loves to watch the Barbarians play rugby because of the club's fantastic ethos that places style above substance. Arguably still the greatest try ever was Gareth Edwards's epic in a Baa-Baas jersey against New Zealand back in 1973, a try every rugby player has seen numerously since. The camaraderie amongst the players is also legendary, with different nationalities coming together to shed any national rivalries and embrace the mantra of free flowing rugby, and the old traditions of clubhouse rugby, hence my hope that before my time is over I finally get to don the famous black and white. Playing against them, however, can sometimes be a nightmare. I had a chance back in 1998 against South Africa, but had to withdraw with a neck injury.

Over the next two weeks, England were due to play Argentina, home and away, first at Old Trafford, the Theatre of Dreams and home to Manchester United, and then in Salta, in the foothills of the Andes. On the Tuesday of the first week, I was weight training, and still fuming over the Barbarians performance, when I saw Johnno lurking in the corner. Eventually, he came over and I could tell by his expression that he was hating this moment.

'Er, you're not in the twenty-two for this Test match,' he told me, adding, 'You all right?'

All I could muster was a 'yeah' before turning round and carrying on with my weights. I appreciated that he found this awkward but still felt sick with rage and disappointment. It was the first time I had ever been part of an England squad and not been selected for the Test match 22 since the Tour of Hell back in 1998. Of course, I had no option but to take it on the chin, but it left me wondering where exactly I went from here.

England went on to win the first Test, with Cuets grabbing the chance to play at his beloved United, and Matt Banahan marking his debut with a couple of trademark tries. The only other high-light for me was to see Whitey win his 50th cap, albeit from the bench. It was a classic performance from the prop. Two minutes after ambling on to the pitch, he received a yellow card for ending someone in a ruck, and with less than ten minutes remaining in the game that was that. I was still chuffed for him, because I knew the half century was a big goal for him, but I couldn't help laugh-ing at his cameo performance.

I was told the same bad news the following Tuesday, just before we left for Argentina. Even though I would be flying to South America, I would not be involved in the Test 22. Wellsy explained that I wasn't match fit but the coaches appreciated my attitude over the past week or so. I was desperate to play for Johnno and this was hardly the start I had envisaged under his management.

At least Salta was a beautiful place to discover. It's pretty much the last city in the country before you hit the mountains, and a fasci-nating place to wander around. I'm a great lover of history and I'd seen a documentary on the Discovery Channel all about the Inca mummies, children who'd been sacrificed to the gods and subsequently found frozen and preserved. Thommo, Whitey and I decided to take a look at them displayed in a museum in Salta, although I'm not convinced the others got as much out of it as I did. Still, it was rare to be on a tour and actually see something of the place.

Twenty minutes into the game, Thommo, also out of the 22, decided that we should have pizza. We were sitting behind a glass window and Thommo entertained himself by banging on it for eighty minutes to make a local policewoman turn round. Somehow, as we laughed at Thommo's antics and munched away at our pizza, watching an England team lose to Argentina, it felt wrong.

Missing the British and Irish Lions tour to South Africa, while deeply disappointing, was not surprising, and it gave me the chance to enjoy a full pre-season and to hit the 2009–10 season running. So being on the bench for Leicester's first game felt like a snub, and I was hit hard by the news that I had been selected for the Saxons, the second team, in Johnno's latest squad. It rounded off a crap eighteen months for me, riddled by injury and illness, put down by Leicester on my return and now being dropped from the senior England squad. The explanation given to me was that I needed some games under my belt. I was furious at first, and very despondent. Where was my career going?

I remember being back at Oakham School just before the trip to Argentina for a testimonial dinner and being asked about my career. I talked about how delighted I was at what I'd achieved and said that if it all ended with England, it had still been an awesome experience. Then I got hit by a series of low blows and all my philosophical musings went out of the window. I was massively fucked off and wanted to ram everyone's views back down their throat. In hindsight, it was exactly what I needed. Suddenly, all my motivation returned in spades. I was 29 years old but felt like I was having to prove myself all over again. And that's exactly what I did. My form was so good for the Tigers that England had little option but to reinstate me for the senior squad in time for the autumn Tests.

It was at this point that Gerard Murphy came into our lives. Johnno felt the presence of a sports psychologist would add to our collective sum, and he was correct, although it did not seem that way at first. During our first meeting with him, for example, Gerard asked Worzel what he felt about the session, and Joe replied, 'I was bored.' We all saw it as a bit of a joke at first. One of our problems was that we all got on well, and there were no real dickheads in the squad. It made honesty sessions, where we had to talk about each other's strengths and limitations, difficult. Gerard reported back to the England management saying that, in terms of interaction and the creation of a group environment, this was the worst bunch of individuals he had ever worked with.

We lost the first autumn Test, 9–18, to Australia. The result was disappointing but I was delighted with my own performance. Wilko was back after his latest injury and again played as if he had never been away. Next up was Argentina, and the build-up was enlivened by a moment of farce. Gerard had asked Mikey, the England analyst, to cobble together some clips of all the positive aspects of the last game. When we sat down as a team to watch it, the film centred almost wholly on Wilko and me. As flattering as this may seem, it was, in truth, agony to watch. The idea was to help build a team environment but, instead, the film concentrated on two players. I recall asking Jonny afterwards how he felt about it. 'A bit weird, mate,' was his reply. I said to Johnno, 'Please don't do that again.' I was actually rocking in my chair with embarrassment as the film played out. Johnno and Wig loved it at the time, but the rest of the lads just found it hilarious.

We beat the Pumas 16–9 at Twickenham. It wasn't the greatest performance by an England team, but a win is a win against the side that finished third in the World Cup two years earlier. Although the collective display was far from perfect, I was again happy with my own performance, especially as it was my pass that put Banners away for the game's only try. I felt for Wilko because at times he was totally exposed. People forget that in 2003 he had great players, such as Matt Dawson and Will Greenwood, on either side of him, both leaders and vocal to boot. The expectation heaped on Jonny by the public and the media, and even within the camp, was huge and unfair.

The other point about this display was that we were too afraid to explore a Plan B. Brian Smith, the attack coach, had told us to kick the leather off the ball because it was raining and the conditions were not conducive to running rugby. As it turned out, we had endless opportunities to attack but never took them. It was poor stuff. We should have said, this is not working, let's change our tactics and start taking all these chances coming our way. But we didn't do that. We didn't possess any rhythm or direction, and although we gave the All Blacks a decent game the following week, losing 6–19, we were still second best by far.

On the eve of the All Blacks Test, we had a second video disaster. This time, Gerard had asked Mikey to cobble together clips of the whole team mixed in with scenes from the movie '300', which tells the story of the three hundred Spartans who held out against the Persian army at the Battle of Thermopylae. It was the film I watched the night before the 2007 World Cup final. These kind of motivational films can often do the job. Tony Biscombe at the RFU used to provide similar films under Clive Woodward in the run-up to the 2003 World Cup. The best film incorporated Eminem's 'Lose Yourself', with the words 'If you had one shot or one opportunity to seize everything you ever wanted in one moment would you capture it or just let it slip?' which has to be one of the best motivational lines of all time.

Unfortunately, the idea didn't quite have the same effect six years later. For a start, Mikey spent five minutes setting it up after a rather impatient Johnno had asked him if we were ready to go. Then we watched with dropping jaws as our play was intermingled with Persians being decapitated, and just as the film was reaching a rousing finale, it shut down. Johnno, one of his huge scowls on his face, told a sweating Mikey to get it going again. I felt for Mikey. He had clearly been given a talking to after the previous week's debacle and now this. Eventually, the film came up on screen again to deliver literally one line, and then finished. Within seconds of the coaches leaving the room, James Haskell let out a huge laugh and soon the whole room was full of the sound of guffaws. I had no problem with Hask, of course. It was a ridiculous moment and quite farcical. But I was also fuming that on the night before facing the All Blacks we had been subjected to what turned out to be a bloody joke.

The 2010 Six Nations began well enough for us. We beat Wales 30–17, Hask scored two tries and another faultless kicking display from Wilko meant that we had won the all-important opening game of the tournament. Next up was Italy in Rome and, although we won, it was a nervous, error-strewn display, except for Matt Tait's well-taken try. We scraped home 17–12 but at no point did we get our attacking play going.

The wheels were loose, but the following week they fell off completely when we lost 16–20 to Ireland at Twickenham. Tommy Bowe's late try gave the Irish the match-winning lead. This was Bowe's second try of the afternoon. He skipped past me early into the game.

Wilko received more criticism from the media for failing to get his backs line going, but only one man was dropped for the next international, the Calcutta Cup in Edinburgh, and that was me. The reason given was that they wanted Worzel for his defensive qualities, although it had been a tough decision. Since I wasn't even on the pitch when Ireland snatched victory from the jaws of defeat with Bowe's second try, I found that hard to take. I was devastated. I'd gone from being man of the series in the autumn to feeling like the scapegoat for the entire team. I told Johnno and the management how disappointed I was with their decision. The bottom line was that if England had gone well at Murrayfield, I could have been out of the reckoning for a very long time.

As it turned out, England regressed even more. The 15–15 draw was one of the worst displays I've ever seen from an England team, and since I was brought on for the last twenty minutes, I have to include myself in this observation. Ben Youngs had been crapping himself all week because he had been named as the reserve scrum half, although he made his England debut off the bench on the wing, and Wilko was replaced by Toby Flood. We didn't know it at the time, but a changing of the guard was taking place at number ten.

Afterwards, the dressing room was deathly quiet. We had not actually lost, but it felt like a huge defeat. I sat there fearful of where both England and my career were going. Yet within a few days, my life would change forever, and England's rock-bottom fortunes would begin to turn.

12

CAPTAIN, MY CAPTAIN

On the Sunday night back at the Pennyhill Park Hotel in Bagshot, I had something of an epiphany. England had been just dreadful the day before up at Murrayfield, and had received a roasting in the media for their efforts. I was sitting in my room, sipping a hot chocolate, when I suddenly realised how stupid it was to spend my life being so frustrated. I was still very much part of the England rugby team, as I had been for over ten years, and even if things were not going completely my, or England's, way, these were still the best years of my life. You are a long time retired and I knew I'd look back on these days and realise just what an amazing time I was having. I resolved to start enjoying myself a great deal more when I was with England. After all, I was at the pinnacle of my profession. If you can't enjoy that, then what, frankly, was the point?

The next morning I sat through the team debrief and started to feel my emotions welling up inside, which is always a dangerous moment for me. All I kept hearing during the meeting was the accusation that there was a lack of urgency about our performances. After the umpteenth time I heard this, I just flipped.

'This is bullshit,' I shouted, which seemed to shut everyone else up. I'd started so, as they say on 'Mastermind', I thought I may as well finish what I had to say. Over the next five to ten minutes, I delivered an angry soliloquy the main point of which was this: 'We're playing for England, for God's sake. We should never, ever be accused of lacking urgency. That is a given.' I then went on to talk about my own little epiphany the night before. I told them how these were the best days of all our lives, how we'd never be able to get them back and how we'd never forgive ourselves when we were retired if we hadn't given it our best shot. All this was said in front of a silent Johnno, the rest of the management and all the players. I ended by stating that we were an exceptional group of players but we weren't reproducing our club form in an England shirt. It just wasn't happening for us and I'd had enough. I apologised for coming over as a grumpy old git but I couldn't accept being part of a team that wasn't giving its all.

Considering the fact that I hadn't even started two days earlier against Scotland, it was, in hindsight, quite a feat to stand up and spout all this, but it was how I felt and I let my emotions win the day. Gerard listened and, once I'd finally sat down, he stood up and went off on one, too, revealing just how passionate he felt about the England team. It was good to see. He was not part of the coaching staff. His role was to enhance team leadership and development skills, but the players appreciated how much he cared for us and how much he wanted us to be successful.

After the meeting, Wilko, Thommo, Steve Borthwick and I stayed behind and started to talk among ourselves. We discussed what we felt was missing. The general consensus was that we were not being hard enough on ourselves, and neither were the coaches. We needed to be far more accountable for our actions. Borthers agreed to set up a meeting with the management team, and the four of us sat down in front of Johnno and the others to say our piece. Wilko made a particularly good point when he pointed out how defensively we were accountable but offensively we were not. One of the strong features behind our 2003 success was that every Monday morning we'd be subjected to a video, pointing out where we went right, and where we went wrong. No one was spared the spotlight if they had failed in any sense. This isn't to say we wanted to create an atmosphere of fear. What we found then was that it concentrated the mind on doing the job.

The bottom line was that we had to start singling out players to remind them of the very high standards expected of them. We all felt too many were just going through the motions of a box-ticking exercise. We weren't there to tick boxes and say we played for England. We were there to be a successful rugby team. Thommo was the most vocal out of the four of us in front of the coaches, and the next day, during the team meeting and in front of the management staff, he took it upon himself to deliver a twenty-minute rant directed at his teammates. The gist of his impassioned and deeply impressive speech was that the acceptance of mediocrity had to stop right now, and if anyone didn't buy into this, then, to quote Thommo, 'they can just fuck off.' He went on to say that he didn't want any player who failed to buy into this in his team. He just didn't want that man around him.

I looked at my old friend with admiration. This was a man who had defied the medics by returning from a neck injury, which seemed to have ended his career. This was a man who had won the World Cup. Yet it still meant this much to him. I'm not sure Borthers could have delivered such a speech, nor Wilko. Thommo was the right man at the right time in the right place. It was exactly what we needed. This, together with the four of us having belief in the squad and knowing we were better than this and having the balls to say it, galvanised everything. Here's the irony of it all. If Borthers had not been injured that week and had captained the team against France, I'm convinced we would have played just as well. This is not false modesty on my part. The reason why we played so much better in Paris that Saturday night was because the events of Monday and Tuesday changed everyone's attitude, not that England sported a new captain. On the Tuesday afternoon following Thommo's speech, the whole squad trained like men possessed. A very evident change had just taken place. It would prove to be a turning point.

That evening, Johnno came up to Nick Easter, known to us all as 'Minty', and me. We were about to go out for the traditional Tuesday evening team meal, taking the opportunity to pillage, as always, the RFU credit card. He told us that Borthers had gone for a scan on his knee and asked if the two of us could take a lead in training. He added that the next day he would know if Borthers would be fit or not, so he would make a call on the captaincy then.

This, to say the least, had come from practically nowhere. Three days earlier I was not deemed good enough to start against Scotland. Earlier that day I had been reinstated into the starting XV on the openside and now Johnno had basically said that either Minty or I would captain England if Borthers failed to come through. I had never harboured ambitions about the England captaincy, nor believed that it would ever come my way. Apart from at Oakham School and the Midlands, and three, random games at Leicester, I'd never captained any other side in my whole career, and now, suddenly, the armband was perilously close to being placed on me. Such a prospect had been mooted briefly in the media after the autumn Tests but I never took such thoughts seriously. It made me nervous even to think about it, although, at the same time, I still believed Borthers would lead out the team that Saturday night. After all, he never mentioned his injury to anyone when we had our gang of four meeting, so I assumed it was not too serious.

My nerves were heightened when Johnno found me just before I left for home and told me that if Borthers failed to recover, I would be captain. He would call me the following day, he said. We always have Wednesdays off in a Test match week. When I told Annie the news, she was excited, but I reminded her that I still did not expect it to happen.

The following day, I was bouncing up and down on the trampoline in the back garden with Dylan when my mobile phone rang. It was Johnno. I looked at it ringing for quite a while and left it. This was quality time with my little boy and, frankly, I wasn't entirely sure I wanted to answer it. Half an hour later I heard Annie's voice from the house. 'Hello, Molly,' she said. Johnno lumbered across the garden with his young daughter, Molly. He lived three miles away from me in South Leicestershire and, having failed to grab me on the telephone, decided to take the short trip over. Molly climbed up on to the trampoline and we watched our kids bouncing up and down for a while in silence. It was one of those awkward dad moments. We both knew what was coming.

'So, you all right to do the job at the weekend then?' he asked, eventually.

'Er, yep,' I replied.

We stood there in silence again as our kids giggled and bounced.

'How do you feel about it?'

I told him I felt pretty nervous and he gave me the best advice I could possibly hear.

'Don't worry about it,' Johnno said. 'Just be yourself. Don't do anything differently.'

That was the end of it. We talked about the kids for a while and then he left with Molly. I dashed for the telephone. The first person I wanted to tell was my dad. It was a nice moment for a son to tell his dad that he'd just been made captain of England. Late that evening I returned to the team hotel ready for the leaders' meeting on the Thursday morning. This was a meet we staged every week, involving the more senior players, such as Cuets, Minty, Wilko, me and normally the scrum half as well. On the way to the meet I bumped into Borthers. He congratulated me, wished me luck and went on his way. Neither of us knew it at the time, but he had, to date, played his last game for England.

For some reason, Borthers was not everyone's cup of tea, not as a player nor as a captain. Maybe it was because he kept himself to himself quite a bit, and was an intense individual. I have nothing but the deepest respect for the man and felt, in my hour of triumph, extremely sorry for him. As I have said, the pendulum swing with England was not down to me, but down to the change in approach and attitudes. Borthers was just unlucky. That is sport. It can be extremely harsh when it wants to be.

He captained England on many occasions and, rather like Cozza, failed to receive the plaudits because it was a primarily losing team. Yet he set the highest professional standards both on and off the field as captain, he spoke well, he worked extremely hard and in many ways was a natural leader. Certainly, at Bath, where he captained the club for so many years, they have nothing but praise for him, and it is no coincidence that he lifted the 2011 Aviva Premiership trophy after leading Saracens to victory over Leicester in the final.

The England team to face a France side aiming for another Grand Slam had a new look about it. Toby Flood had replaced Wilko at ten. Jonny was beginning what would become a long stint on the bench. Ben Youngs was making his first start at scrum half, Ben Foden was doing the same at full-back and the exciting Chris Ashton was making his debut on the wing. Ashy was an interesting character. Although a lot quieter than he is now, he was still full of beans, joking around and raring to go. I'd been watching him scoring tries for fun all season and was looking forward to seeing him in action on my side.

Before the kick-off I gathered the team into a huddle and delivered a pep talk. The problem was I could feel myself welling up inside with emotion and, fearful of breaking down into a sobbing mess in front of my teammates, brought the speech to an abrupt end. I asked Tins for his thoughts as one of our most senior and respected players, but once he had finished all I really wanted to do was get out on to that pitch and have a go at the French.

Early into the game, Fodes scored a superb try in the corner to counter a French drop goal. Finding himself in the winger's position, he finished off a move thanks to a scoring pass from Ashy. Unfortunately, France led 12–7 at half-time with three further penalties. During the second half, Ashy had a fantastic opportunity to score. I remember thinking he wouldn't fail because chances like this one are meat and drink to such a high-quality finisher as he is. Inexplicably, he chipped the ball instead of running at the defender and the moment had gone. This was a classic, first Test moment. It happens to us all. You just need to get the anxiety out of your system. He's never repeated such an error and gone on to become a supremely confident and lethal Test rugby winger.

Wilko managed to grab some of the action late on and, with a difficult penalty, reduced the arrears to just two points, but from that moment onwards, the French were adept enough to keep us, and especially Wilko, too far away from their line to strike. I felt sorry for Wilko. He seemed to shoulder the burden of all the problems in the backs line during the autumn and previous Six Nations games because of who he is. We did not play better because Wilko was not in the starting XV.

In the end, we ran out of time and lost 12–10. People expected us to be cannon fodder for an impressive French side. Instead, we could and maybe should have won the game. Emotions were mixed afterwards. No player ever feels good about losing any game, no matter what the circumstances may be and no matter how narrow the margin. Yet I felt a sense of pride that we had run the French so close and defied those – and there were many – who assumed we would just roll over. Deep down, I knew I could captain my country and now I felt I had proved it.

Perhaps the most humbling experience for me took place during the post-match function. I had to deliver a quick speech, thanking the hosts, congratulating them, and saying well done to my team, too. As my name was announced and I made my way up on to the stage, the England boys began a chant: 'Moodos, Moodos.' I had no inkling this would happen but it was extremely touching, nonetheless, to have your own teammates singing your nickname.

At that point I wished I was 25 and had just been handed the captaincy. I think I now understood what to do, and what an honour it had been to lead my country. I also regretted the fact that the Six Nations had just ended. I wanted to start all over again, with this team and with this new attitude. I had a feeling something special was about to happen with this England team.

As I ventured into the Parisian night, I still believed that I had been nothing more than caretaker captain, keeping the jersey warm for Borthers. Ashy was midway through having a drink with each one of his teammates, the gruelling tradition that all newbees go through, and I was asked to pose for pictures with Franck Leboeuf, the former Chelsea and France footballer, in return for being looked after for the night. It was a surreal end to a Six Nations tournament that had ended positively in defeat and to what I assumed was my short spell as England captain.

My assumption was wrong. The next time England played, I would still be wearing the captain's armband but no longer as a Tiger. By the summer tour to Australia, I had signed for their oldest and biggest rivals, Bath.

13

FAREWELL TIGERS, HELLO BATH

My contract was up at the end of the 2009–10 season and by the time I sat down with the Tigers in December to discuss renewing it, my mindset had changed from the start of the season. Back in September, I was certain this would be my last season at Welford Road. I felt I needed a change of scenery and was keen to ensure some financial stability for my family, which a move to France would provide. I didn't want to join another English club because I couldn't see myself ever playing against Leicester, so I was close to being adamant that the following season I would ply my trade in the Top 14, preferably in the south of France, near to the coast.

Yet as the season wore on, so my love for Leicester was rekindled. In hindsight, my yearning to leave had little to do with the Tigers and more to do with the fact that I had been out injured for so long and was generally fed up with my lot. I felt I needed a new environment.

By December, much had changed. I was enjoying myself again and playing well. Really well. The autumn Tests had gone better than I had hoped, from a personal viewpoint, and I had returned to Leicester as England captain to continue my good form. Yet when the terms came in for a renewed contract just before Christmas, Leicester were offering me less money than my existing contract.

I had already developed a gut feeling about the coaches, and especially Matt O'Connor, the Australian backs coach, who had been with Leicester for just one season but already was playing a more dominant role within the club's set-up. He appeared to have Richard Cockerill's ear. I mentioned to Geordan at the start of the season that something felt wrong. There was something I didn't trust about the coaches. I added that I had a nagging feeling that one or two people at the club – and I was referring mainly to Cockers and especially O'Connor – were out to get me over the forthcoming season. The events of the next few months did nothing to quell those concerns.

The week before the start of the 2010 Six Nations, Mark Spoors and I were summoned to the club for a contract meeting. Mark and I had known each from university days in Leicester. He subsequently went on to launch Big Red Management, which has now become rugby's leading client management agency, and has been a good friend of mine for over a decade and my agent for the past eight years. Present at the meeting were Simon Cohen, Head of Rugby Operations, who dealt with all contracts, Cockers and, strangely, O'Connor. I say strangely because he was, after all, the backs coach. He had little to do with me or my game, and yet he was not only present at the meeting, but firing off most of the questions. They wanted to know what my demands were. I replied that I wanted to stay at Leicester but to receive an offer that meant there was no way I would leave for France. We wanted my market value which the club agreed. We were not holding a gun to their heads.

O'Connor then asked me if I was intending to retire from Test rugby after the 2011 World Cup. It may seem like a fair question, although why a man who had been at Leicester for one season was asking it of a player who had given his body and soul to the club for fourteen seasons seemed a little odd. It annoyed me because I felt he and the club were more or less telling me to retire after the World Cup, whereas the decision was for me and me alone.

The discussions went on for an hour and, at the end, I reiterated my stance. I wanted to play for Leicester until I was physically unable to do so. I wanted to keep running out at Welford Road and end my playing days as a Leicester man, the club I'd played for all my life. I said that I was thinking about France at the start of the season, but this was more to do with my own state of mind than any problems with Leicester. Now the fire in my belly had been rekindled. The meeting ended with a promise from the three-man Leicester contingent that a renewed contract would be offered the very next week.

To be honest, I was still fuming about the reduced offer Leicester had made the previous month. The deal on the table amounted to a 20 per cent reduction in my wage. The club were notorious for making crap offers to players and being tight with their money because they felt, being the biggest and best club in the country, they could do it. They also banked on player loyalty. After all, it was a big call to leave a club like Leicester, and few players have gone on to prosper better elsewhere.

I translated the last offer as a complete piss-take. How would any employer expect an employee, in any profession, to react to being offered a pay cut, especially when they are excelling in their work? Simon Cohen's explanation at the time was that I couldn't expect to keep on being paid more. Why not? There is such a thing as inflation, and I was enjoying some of the best form of my life at the time.

What also irritated me about the way Leicester handled their contract negotiations was that they always made out they were doing you a favour when making any kind of offer. I'd grown used to it by now, dealing first with Deano and then Wellsy in conjunction with Cohen. It was always a painful process, but this time it was a complete joke.

The 'next month' came and went and it became apparent that Leicester were dragging their heels. Mark Spoors suggested we should take a look at an English club or two as well, just to add to the interest being shown in me by Toulouse, Clermont Auvergne and Racing Metro in France.

I had not given a thought to playing for another English club prior to this. As I've said, I didn't want to play against Leicester, and if I was going to move anywhere, it would be to France, with a different culture, different teams, different stadia and a whole new chapter for Annie and me. Mark felt it was a good idea, though, so we discussed it, ruling out all but three of the Premiership clubs – Bath, Northampton and Harlequins. Ironically, the first two are big competitors of Leicester's. The intense rivalry between Bath and Leicester arose in the 1980s and the first half of the 1990s, when they were the two best teams in the country, and the rivalry with Northampton is due to our East Midlands vicinity and the fact that the Saints have grown into a major force in their own right. Bath was my preferred choice because I had a few mates at the club, Annie's best friend was Danny Grewcock's partner, Natasha, and it is, of course, a beautiful part of the world.

I still wanted to stay at Welford Road. All it would have taken was an improved offer. Deep down, I knew it would not be forthcoming. I was bracing myself for a lesser offer or, incredibly, no offer at all, although I didn't really believe that was in fact an option.

Mark made contact with Bath. Their reaction was effusive. He relayed this to me as I drove away from the England team hotel after training. I'm sure Bath felt at the time that we were making enquiries purely to bump up my offer at Leicester. Nothing could have been further from the truth. We were now into the week of the Ireland game, which we lost and I was subsequently dropped for the Calcutta Cup. Mark and I went to Bath to meet the club's CEO Nick Blofeld and the then Director of Rugby, Steve Meehan, and to discuss my possible move to the West Country.

Within a few days, I received a call from Cockers. Could I come in to Oval Park the following morning to meet him for a chat? This was unheard of. Cockers never telephoned me, let alone requested a meeting with me face to face.

It was the team's day off, so all was relatively quiet at the training ground. Cockers appeared nervous and fidgety. He started to fiddle with stuff on his desk.

'We're not going to make you an offer,' he blurted out almost immediately. As he said this, he was trembling. I couldn't quite believe what I was hearing. I knew that this outcome was a possibility, but I could never quite get around to believing Leicester would actually go through with it and behave like this towards a man who had served them so well for fourteen years. I'd thought about contacting the board to ask just what the hell everyone was playing at before meeting with Cockers. It is probably just as well I did not.

'I've spoken to the board and they're OK with this, but it's my decision,' he added. Cockers went on to explain that it was nothing personal, but purely a business decision based on the fact that there was every chance I'd be away for the autumn Tests and the Six Nations and then for the first part of the following season due to the World Cup. I pointed out that so, too, would Ben Youngs, Dan Cole, Toby Flood, Geordan, Louis Deacon, Martin Castrogiovanni and quite a few others, but for some reason I was a different case.

In hindsight, I realised that this was on the cards. Of the three senior players at the club whose contracts were up at the end of the season, both Geordan and Louis Deacon had already received renewed offers. I, on the other hand, appeared to be left out in the cold. It was because I was older, Cockers tried to explain, which of course was nonsense. Geordan and I are the same age, and Deacs is not far behind.

When a club says after fourteen years of service that they are not going to make you an offer, I can tell you that it is very painful. Yes, I had considered leaving the club at the start of the season, and yes I had spoken to Bath and French clubs when it became apparent I was being mucked about, but when the moment finally came, and the cold reality hit me, it hurt like hell.

A few days later, I confided all this to Johnno because I also wanted to explain how my head was spinning and that I may not have appeared to be fully focused. He was astounded by the news.

'Fucking hell,' he responded. 'That's ridiculous.'

My colitis reared its unwelcome head again, brought on by a combination of Six Nations ups and downs, the sudden news that Annie was pregnant with our second child which was very exciting but obviously very stressful, and the realisation that Leicester were, to all intents and purposes, throwing me out. I had to return to the doctor and receive more steroid treatment to control the disorder. For nearly two weeks, I was without a club. For any rugby player, this is not an ideal scenario.

Simply from a pride point of view it would have been better to have received any offer than none at all. Maybe they felt a derisory offer would have been more hurtful than no offer. Besides, as Cockers pointed out, it gave me the chance to explore other offers that were coming in. He argued that Leicester couldn't and wouldn't compete with rival offers.

The only thing I said of substance at the end of the meeting with Cockers was that I didn't want this decision to affect the eight-game final run-in to the end of the season. Cozza and, that same season, Ben Kay had been frozen out of the club towards the very end of their contracts and I didn't want the same thing to happen to me. I offered my hand – something he clearly wasn't expecting – and walked out saying, 'Business is business.'

Of course I was bitterly upset and angry. I phoned Geordan to tell him the news. He was seething. His first reaction was, as club captain, to go straight to the board. I told him that, as much as I loved him as a friend, and as respected as he was as the club captain, the decision had been made and there was nothing he could do about it. Time would pass and Geordan is as professional as they come, but I know for a while there was a sour taste in his mouth over the way I had been treated. Deacs, Whitey and the rest of the boys expressed their anger, too, and shock. Annie was possibly even more upset than I was. It took all my powers of persuasion to prevent her from marching into Welford Road. But the die was cast.

My mood was hardly helped by being dropped for the Scotland game by Johnno, although by then I had just signed the contract to join Bath. It was a little random that, the day after Johnno told me I'd be on the bench for the Calcutta Cup, I attended his 40th birthday celebrations in his local village pub. I was greeted by a host of former Tigers, with whom I'd played in my formative years. To Stuart Potter, Steve Hackney, Wig, Garf, Matt Poole, Backy, Derek Jelley and the others, Bath were still the enemy, and I was on the receiving end of a heap of abuse. Eventually, it subsided and the players took turns to express their dismay that Leicester had not come up with any kind of offer at all.

I spoke to others linked to the club, too, notably Peter Wheeler and Dosser Smith. Wheeler sighed and shrugged his shoulders and basically pattered out the same argument about it being not good business to have someone costing as much as I did who would be away on Test match duty so much. Dosser, on the other hand, was brilliant. He told me it was the best thing to happen, and that I now had a fantastic opportunity with Bath. It was precisely what I needed to hear. He was Leicester through and through, and even he was saying that transferring to Bath, of all clubs, was a good move. Dosser was my coach at Oakham. He still is my coach, even though we're fourteen years on!

To be fair to Leicester, I started all of the remaining fixtures. True, I tended to be substituted with twenty minutes to go but this was the norm and my replacement, usually Craig Newby, is a fine player. I cannot say I ever got along with Cockers throughout my time at Leicester, and it was barely amicable for those last eight games, but at least he played me, and I have to recognise that he has done well as head coach at Welford Road.

At the end, when we collected the Premiership trophy at Twickenham and then held a function for all departing players in a marquee, I was still struggling to believe it, even though I was soon to be a Bath player.

My emotions were mixed. On the one hand I was genuinely excited to be joining Bath. Deep down I knew I needed a change, and the prospect of lending my experience to a new club, and achieving new goals in a totally different environment which I hoped would lead to silverware. Everything about the move was right in terms of meeting friends on and off the pitch and moving to a beautiful part of the country. Best of all, my timing had been impeccable, if fortuitous. Bruce Craig had just bought the club and the multi-millionaire was in the process of moving training facilities and the club headquarters to the magnificent Farleigh House. Things were definitely on the up down at the Recreation Ground, and soon more good news would be delivered in the shape of Sir Ian McGeechan, who would be joining the management team.

On the other hand, leaving Leicester felt like a family bereavement. After so many years, I harboured a deep feeling of betrayal. The way they had handled me, as indeed they handled other loyal servants, such as Ben Kay, was incredibly cut-throat. Part of me wanted to be a one-club man, in common with all the Leicester legends who still worked or hung around the club, men such as John Duggan and Dave Matthew and, of course, Dosser. I'm not sure there will be too many one-club men any more in today's professional game, but that had been my dream at one time.

The fans at Welford Road were, predictably, fantastic. I never heard one dissenting voice, or received one dissenting email or letter. I was cheered by them after the Bath news broke, and I even received a standing ovation for my last game at home, the semi-final

The tackle that resulted in a red card for me during England's win over Samoa at Twickenham in November 2005. Samoa's (and Leicester's) Alex Tuilagi upends Mark Cueto (*above left*). I lose it and throw punches at Alex (*above right*) ... with the inevitable result that referee Mark Lawrence sends me off for fighting (*below*). I am still the only England player to be dismissed at headquarters.

Visiting the Salvation Army school in the Kibera slum in Kenya, on behalf of the Hope HIV charity, was a life-changing experience.

I lead out England against France in Paris in March 2010. This was my first game as captain. We lost 12–10 to the Grand Slam champions, but regained our pride.

Ben Youngs scores England's first try *en route* to a famous win over Australia in Sydney, June 2010.

Afterwards, I console the magnificent Jonny Wilkinson.

Good times: Thommo and I in the Sydney dressing room after our epic defeat of the Wallabies.

Above: That's my boy! Our second son, Ethan, wins our smiling competition!

Left: The next rugby-playing Moody? My son Dylan with his first rugby ball.

Below: At home with Annie, Dylan and baby Ethan – the best team in the world!

play-off win against Bath. This was the second time I'd faced Bath in a matter of a few weeks, and I was determined to play out of my skin to show my new employers what they had bought, and my old employers what they had decided to discard. Afterwards, all the mail I received from Leicester fans wished me luck and thanked me for my years of service to the club.

It would take me six months to get over the shock of leaving Leicester, and the manner in which I left, even though by then I was well into the new season with Bath. After so many years, that club never quite leaves you. There will always be a bit of green, red and white inside me and, of course, the Leicester Tigers continue to be the best and biggest club in the country, despite losing the Aviva Premiership final to Saracens in May 2011. Their standards and ethos remain impeccable and this is passed through the ranks from senior to junior. There is no rocket science about the Tigers. They simply work very, very hard in everything they do.

Leicester bought a Kiwi, Thomas Waldrom, as a direct replacement for me. Thomas went on to have a good 2010–11 season for the Tigers but, ironically, declared himself to be English during the spring and made it known that he wanted to fight for a place in the England World Cup squad. It was hardly what Cockers and the Tigers had envisaged when they signed him up.

Within three weeks of signing for Bath I was made England captain. Bath saw this as a major bonus for the club. As for Leicester, well, you'll have to ask them.

14

STUNNING THE WALLABIES

June tour, 2010

Nine days before Leicester played Saracens in the end of season final at Twickenham Johnno called. 'Are you OK to captain the tour?' was the simple, straight to the point question. He went on to explain that Borthers, who would have a twenty-minute cameo during the final the following week, needed more time to recover from his injury and would therefore not be travelling down under for the two-Test, five-game tour. My reply was effusive.

'Of course, I'd love to.'

Within the space of a few weeks I had gone from being deemed not good enough to start against Scotland to caretaker captain against France and now captain of a full England tour to Australia. It was both bizarre and brilliant, and typical of what sport can do to you. One moment you are in a deep trough, the next on the summit of a mountain. It was difficult to take it all in.

The last game in the Six Nations had given me a tremendous amount of belief in myself as a captain. I realised that, in many ways, captaining your country is easier than captaining any other team, because you are surrounded by leaders on your own side. I wasn't entirely sure I could carry it off but the experience at the Stade de France convinced me I could.

Before the start of the tour, I spent some time with Phil Wall, my friend who founded Hope HIV. He happens to be a motivational coach and he helps teams and individual leaders in all walks of life. We talked a great deal about leadership. One of the aspects

Phil taught me was that it was important for the captain to talk. I always thought it was right to speak when I felt I needed to but Phil explained how, when it's going wrong, the fourteen other members of the team look to the captain. I'd thought about it from my point of view, but not the others in the team. We also spoke about the role of England captain, a role far bigger than any individual. It meant setting an example in all areas, on and off the pitch. Phil's input was of great use to me as a captain and as a person, and it continues to be so to this day.

That said, I got it all wrong at first on tour. It was one thing being in charge of the England team for one week. It was another altogether to be captain of a tour with a forty-man squad. I took it upon myself to be responsible for everything and everyone. I found myself geeing up players, checking out the medics, having conversations with the coaches, and generally building up unnecessary pressure on myself.

During the first week on tour, I picked up a small tweak in my calf. It meant I barely trained. The midweek boys managed to draw our first game against an Australia 'A' side, which featured many of the Test team we would run out against four days later in Perth. But as the days and hours ticked away towards the first Test, so the nerves collectively began to grow. The final training session, the captain's run on the Friday, went poorly. It sometimes happens and it does not always correlate with the next day's performance, but on this occasion it did.

I felt incredibly nervous about the occasion. Despite the high of giving France such a good game, we had subsequently not been together as a team until this week. We were a very new team, including many young players who would be facing one of the Southern Hemisphere big guns away from home for the first time. As I surveyed the scene in the dressing room at the Subiaco Oval, and took in the atmosphere, I could sense that something was wrong.

My fears proved to be correct. We lost 27–17 but that score fails to tell the full story. In truth, we should have annihilated the Wallabies because our pack, and especially our front five boys, totally dominated their counterparts, so much so that we were awarded two penalty tries after the Australians failed to hold us off. That's 14 points gifted to us. The most amazing platform to build on had been provided by the front five, but still we failed to win. It would have been only the third time we had won in Australia in the long history of the fixture. In no time, we had found ourselves 14–0 down but, with ten minutes remaining, had clawed ourselves back to just a three-point deficit with the momentum very much in our favour. Yet we could not capitalise on all the possession and the old, early Six Nations frustrations began to creep in again.

If I am to single out one player for particular criticism, it would be me. I had an absolute shocker, and on my 32nd birthday as well.

As a team we missed thirty tackles, which is incredible, and I missed six of them. If I miss one tackle in a game, it eats away at me. To miss six was beyond my comprehension. I have no idea why this happened, except possibly that the captaincy got to me because I took so much on my own shoulders. From a defensive point of view, it was my worst game in my memory. The fact that I was replaced after 66 minutes by James Haskell only compounded my misery. I felt the defeat was all down to me, and that night was both long and sleepless.

The next day we took the flight across Australia from Perth on the west coast to Sydney on the south-eastern coast. I sat close to the back in purgatory. The defeat, and especially my own performance, was tearing me apart. How could I possibly be picked again as a player, let alone as captain? Mike Ford, the England defence coach, sat next to me for a while and I told him how unacceptable my defensive display was.

'Yeah, six missed tackles,' he said, reinforcing the point. I told him it would never happen again. I spoke to Wellsy, too.

'Don't worry about it, you'll get it right in Sydney,' was his response, which cheered me up a little.

The Monday morning debrief was painful for the team. It should have been excruciating for me personally but, for some reason, the management seemed to gloss over my missed tackles. At one point, they honed in on something immediately after I'd missed another crucial tackle and I had to stop them in full flow, stand up and speak.

'That tackle was unacceptable,' I announced to the team. 'It's not going to happen again.'

I felt uncomfortable seeing my poor play being ignored. We were in it together and it was important to hold up my hand.

Immediately after the debrief we got together with Gerard, the team psychologist, and split up into groups of six to discuss each other's strengths and weaknesses in one of our many honesty sessions. I admitted that I needed to improve on my defence because my display in Perth was atrocious. At this point Jonny Wilkinson interjected.

'Mate, that's a ridiculous thing to say,' he said. 'You've been doing it week in, week out for fourteen years. You don't have to improve at all.'

Up to that point I had grown so stressed over my performance that I was beginning to wonder if I had forgotten how to defend completely, but to hear that from one of the best defenders in world rugby in the past ten years went a long way to alleviating all my anxieties. I hold Jonny in the highest esteem. If you wanted to model yourself on one player in terms of approach to the game and mentality, it would be Wilko. Whether it is his defence, his application or the way he is with people, he is the perfect athlete. To receive such effusive support from him meant everything to me. It was as if a heavy burden had suddenly been lifted from my aching shoulders.

That week I still took extra time after the end of each training sessions to practise my defence, either with Mike Ford or Hask, who would happily try and run over me time and time again. Hask was a big help that week as well in terms of talking about technique. Sometimes you need to reinforce the basics in rugby, and that's what I returned to.

What also helped our cause was seeing the midweek boys beat Australia 'A' in the return fixture. In cold, wet and windy conditions up the coast in Gosford, the England team notched up the tour's first win and it set us up nicely for the Saturday Test match, to be played in the same venue where, of course, we won the World Cup seven years before. There was an element of not wanting to let the midweek boys down. Chris Robshaw, Matt Banahan, Dave Attwood and the others had performed heroics and now it was time for us to back this up.

Despite our numbing defeat seven days earlier, the fact that we knew we should have won, coupled with our collective anger at letting ourselves down, seemed to galvanise us. Our confidence – mine aided by Jonny's praise – was far from knocked. We had complete belief that if we played better than we did in Perth (and we could not possibly be any worse), we would win. Just before we ran out into the Sydney night at the Olympic stadium I asked Wig to have a word with the forwards. We went into a separate room in the away changing room and Wig tore into us saying that he did not expect any of us to come out second best against our Wallaby counterparts. It seemed to do the trick. All eight members of the pack were pumped up to their eyeballs as the whistle blew.

Although we would lose and regain the lead on three separate occasions during the ensuing eighty minutes, I was never in any doubt that we would win the second Test from the moment Benny Youngs darted over in trademark, sniping fashion to score his first try for England. It was what he had been doing all season for

Leicester and now we could see the birth of a potentially long Test career with a try that eased all the nerves. Then Chris Ashton got in on the act, finishing off a move in superb style when, in truth, he still had plenty of work to do. The Northampton winger again showed why he had been selected in the first place. On that night, Ashy, Youngs and Courtney Lawes in the second row came of age.

All around me, the England players produced their optimum. Dan Cole simply refused to quit despite a nasty head wound, Tom Croft was back to his Lions best and Courtney proved immense. I was a little concerned about Courtney because of his laid-back, care-free demeanour, but that's his way and out on the pitch you could not have asked for more from him. Then there was Steve Thompson. Thommo provided me with the abiding image of the night when, at one stage, he held two Wallaby props in both hands and simply laughed at them. Thommo was at his brutish best that night and it was very good to see.

It was perhaps fitting that Wilko came off the bench and kicked what proved to be the winning penalty. He missed with a later, diffi-cult chance, which we may have needed if Matt Giteau had not inex-plicably missed with a kick straight in front of the posts, but in the end it did not matter, except for Wilko, who was beating himself up. That's typical Wilko. Win or lose, if he misses a kick, he punishes himself.

Just imagine how the opposition must feel when after an hour they see Wilko running on to the pitch. For a start, they will realise that any penalty conceded inside their own half will probably result in three points. But, if I was in the opposition, the bigger fear would be that one of my team was going to be ended by a pumped-up Jonny producing a massive hit and desperate to do as much as he can in those last twenty minutes. The man still has an aura about him and he is someone you always want playing for you, and not against you.

Towards the end we were counting down the clock, producing little pop passes to each other and taking the ball into rucks to while away the seconds. Minty and I found ourselves lying at the bottom of a ruck, screaming at Danny Care, who had replaced Youngs, to kick the ball out of the stadium to end the game. We won 21–20. After that, it was just sheer elation.

I hugged Ashy and Benny, neither of whom would ever forget the day they scored their first international tries, and then made a point of hugging all the coaches as well. They, I suspected, had been under enormous pressure. Johnno's position was relatively safe, but would another defeat have signified changes in the coaching staff? Possibly, but not after winning for only the third time in Australia, and with a young team. They bore no comparison with the 2003 England team that beat the Wallabies twice in that year.

As we were still celebrating on the pitch, I was summoned up on to the makeshift stage to answer a few questions into a microphone. If you watched this on TV, or live in the stadium, you would have witnessed a peculiar display from an England captain, flinching every other second. This was because behind me some of the players, led by George Chuter, were throwing plastic bottles at my back. Later that night we went out and saluted out victory as a squad. We'd come a long way in a short period of time and every player had played their part.

The next day we went our separate ways. Some of us headed home, while others moved on to New Zealand where an England team were to take on the New Zealand Maoris in our final tour game. I thought it was a little strange to be sent home, considering that I was the tour captain, but, at the same time, it was the end of what had been a very long and tiring season. In my absence, the boys went down bravely to a physical Maoris side.

This was the first time it really hit home that I was no longer a Leicester Tiger. Instead of saying 'see you in pre-season' to the

Tigers contingent in the England squad, it was now a case of 'see you when I see you'. I made a point of hugging Youngs and Chuter, and even Dan Cole, not the cuddliest of individuals, said a fond farewell.

The flight home was split into two – Sydney to Singapore, then Singapore to London. On the first leg, we discovered a bar at the back of the plane, so Toby Flood, Tom Croft and I agreed that we would have a couple of drinks and then, after an hour or so, sleep. In the end, we sat at the bar for the whole ten-hour flight and knocked back vodka and limes.

On the second leg, to London, I had time to reflect. I'd never lost confidence in myself as a captain, but I had, until Jonny said his bit, as a player. As a captain, however, I had learnt one valuable lesson. It is not my job to take everything on to my shoulders. It is my job to lead from the front on the field, and to rely heavily on the senior players around me.

It would be five months before we played again as a unit. Already I could not wait for the autumn internationals to begin, even if the first Test would be against the formidable All Blacks. If we had won the first Test, and then lost in Sydney – especially in the manner in which we went down in Perth – my mood, and the whole England team's demeanour, might have been different.

As it was, I felt, on that sleepy flight back home, that we now had the ability to beat anyone. A predominantly young team had just earned its Test spurs.

For me, there was the small matter of joining a new club after fourteen years in the East Midlands. For the next few months Bath and only Bath would be at the forefront of my mind. Deep down, however, I knew we were a little over a year away from the World Cup and, in the space of a couple of months, England had suddenly become contenders.

15

NEW KID AT SCHOOL

Bath, 2010–11

While I was captaining England in Australia, Annie single-handedly sorted out our big move from Leicester to Bath. I left these shores as a Leicester Tiger and returned as a Bath player. I guess it really struck home when, collecting my car at Heathrow Airport, I headed west down the M4 and not north up the M1.

Once again, Annie took everything upon her shoulders and made a potentially traumatic event appear relatively simple. House moving in any circumstance is hard work, but doing it on your own, with a toddler in hand and heavily pregnant, is a huge ask for anyone. She is incredibly laid back and has a calming influence on my more manic personality. The thing about Annie is that she rarely if ever complains. She just gets on with it. Life is nice and simple with her. It's not as though she's not driven. After all, she set up her own design company and worked very hard at it, but Annie has no desire to conquer the world. She wants to be a good wife and a good mother and have a happy home.

One of the aspects I appreciate most about her is how she looks after me. Even though she often manages just four hours' sleep a night due to Dylan and, later, our second son Ethan, she still insists that everything is in place for me to do my work to the best of my ability. If that means me sleeping in the spare room to ensure good rest, so be it. When I have had my downs – and there have been a few of them – she has been my rock. When I was appointed England captain, she immediately made herself available to all the other players' wives and girlfriends in terms of advice or just a shoulder to lean on, something she learnt from Kay Johnson, Johnno's wife. And there is no doubt that Annie is fiercely loyal towards me. It makes me feel cared for and loved very much. Once she gave Stuart Barnes, the former England stand off turned Sky Sports rugby pundit, a fearful tongue lashing after he had criticised me. He introduced himself to some of the wives during the 2007 World Cup and was then subjected to Annie venting her spleen before departing with his tail between his legs. That's typical Annie. It is a classic example of her loyalty. She will defend me to the hilt.

There were a couple of weeks before I officially started my time at my new club. One of the new-found perks of being England rugby captain was being invited to sit in the Royal Box at Wimbledon, where Annie and I watched Andy Murray beat his opponent, and Roger Federer kill his. Mr and Mrs Jason Leonard were there, too, as was Bobby Charlton, Glenn Hoddle, Sachin Tendulkar and winter Olympic gold medallist Amy Williams. We latched on to Amy quickly because she lived in Bath. The only formality was to stand up and wave to the centre court crowd when introduced before the start of play. It meant having to wear a suit and sit in what turned out to be a hot spot on a scorching summer's day. Whenever I could, I darted inside to cool off and talk to the security boys.

Quite a few of my Bath teammates were in the England squad in Australia, and it was good to start getting a feel for my new club by chatting to David Flatman, Matt Banahan, Olly Barkley, Shontayne Hape, Lee Mears and Davy Wilson. It made me determined to hit the ground running when I reported for my first day's training.

By then, I had packed in two weeks' hard training by myself. I'd bought some Bath kit from the club shop on Pulteney Bridge to wear in the university gym, and it felt extremely strange to be in Bath colours for the first time, even though I was working by myself. However, when we performed our training drills on our first day, I came out as fittest among the forwards after an exercise not dissimilar to the bleep test.

That first day reminded me of my first day at Oakham School – so many new faces, so many new names to learn. I've never been good at names at the best of times. Fortunately, I already knew ten of the players, but I had to remember the names of the rest of the squad, the backroom boys, the masseurs, chefs and so on. Suffice to say it took some time. Still, I was genuinely excited when I received my new kitbag and discovered all the goodies inside. At least it was different from the same old bag handed to me every year at Leicester.

For a while, it was small talk, even with those I knew fairly well or had played with in an England shirt, because I was seeing them in a different environment, their environment. Also I was wary of how I would come across. I wanted to be appreciated for how I went about my business and how passionate I was about both rugby and the club I played for. I would have hated to come across as some big time Charlie, having made the big, summer move from the champions of England. So I kept my head down for a while and threw everything into my training, so much so that quite a few of the players asked Sam Vesty, who had also transferred from Welford Road to the Rec, if I was always like this. 'He'll get a lot worse,' Sam told them.

Humour still had a place, however, such as an accidental plum shot I made on David Barnes, the esteemed players union chairman in his last season as a prop for Bath. A ball-skills session required us to run holding a ball in one hand while trying to knock balls out of other players' hands. Predictably, in attempting to karate chop the ball out of Barnesy's hand, my hand instead careered into his privates. He was down and out for an alarmingly long time.

There was a noticeable difference in training between Leicester and Bath. My new club focused more on ball skills, which meant every player got to touch the ball much more than they did at

Leicester. This suited me down to the ground, since I particularly wanted to improve in that area. At the same time, it was important not to forget the basics. At Leicester, far more emphasis was placed on rucking and mauling, and I imparted this information, when asked, as I was constantly, about how Leicester went about their business. After fourteen years at the greatest club in the professional era, I had something to offer Bath, and the management appeared keen to glean as much information as possible.

Slowly, I was growing into my life in Bath. Olly Barkley was a particular help to me, walking up and down the pitch at the Rec, teaching me all the new moves and calls. On the short pre-season tour to Aix-en-Provence I met the new club owner, Bruce Craig, who lives in this beautiful part of the world. Bruce played the game and is passionate about rugby and Bath, but he's not too overpowering, as some owners could be. It may be his ball, but he lets others play with it.

My debut was at Ulster in a pre-season friendly, which we won comfortably. It felt extremely weird running out of the tunnel and on to the pitch in a blue shirt behind Grewy and Flats, but I was pleased with my performance and another hurdle was cleared. We won our first Aviva Premiership fixture, away at Leeds, and then beat London Irish at the Rec to make it a good start to the season.

It is fair to say the Rec is not Welford Road. An open site, it lacks the noise and numbers of the Tigers stadium, and the changing rooms are probably the smallest in the Premiership. We used to warm up on the field beside the pitch at the back of the stand, but the players decided it would pump up the crowd a little if we trained on the pitch and completed our manoeuvres with a jog around the perimeter, as Gloucester do to some effect at Kingsholm. This has proved to be a great success and there is a discernible difference in the atmosphere when we emerge from our changing rooms. As for the actual position of the stadium – well, there is no finer place to play rugby than in the centre of one of the most beautiful cities in the world, with surrounding hills on all sides.

Northampton smashed us in the next game, not helped by Phil Dowson successfully selling me a dummy, and although we came back to beat Sale, we were then undone by Gloucester at home. In that game, I contracted an injury that was unique, scary and permanent.

At half-time we had already conceded three tries and, with the anger of the coaches still ringing in my ears, I was fired up and pissed off. Charlie Sharples was in possession of the ball and began to take the telltale small steps in readiness to kick it out of his own 22. I made fast yards and attempted to charge him down but as I did so his kicking foot smacked against my arm, which, in turn, forced my knuckle straight into my left eye.

I lay on the floor punching the ground with my fists in absolute agony. The medics rushed on and I assumed the pain would ease off and my sight would return. I was wrong on both counts. When the docs shone a torch into my eye, I could not see a single thing. An eye specialist, who happened to be in the crowd, watching the game, came to have a look at me, and he insisted I go straight to hospital. Helen, the club masseuse, escorted me there, and I was told that I would need to spend the next ten days at home, sitting on a couch doing nothing, because my retina was scarred and I couldn't afford to have any more pressure or blood in my eye.

This was the same weekend that Gavin Quinnell lost the sight in his left eye after playing for the Scarlets against Cross Keys. It turned out that I was lucky not to be in the same, unfortunate position as Gavin. During the evening, I began to discern a faint shadow with that eye, and by the morning my vision was up to 10 per cent – not great, but at least there was an improvement. To this day, I have some scar tissue in my retina, which means that the sight in my left eye is reduced by 25 per cent. My vision is distorted and there is a permanent white spot in front of this eye. I have to look away from bright sunshine, for example, because it can be uncomfortable, but it might have been much, much worse. Another millimetre, I'm told, and I may have lost my sight in that eye completely, or at least detached my retina, which would have ruled me out for many weeks.

My immediate concern was not my sight, however, but my rugby. I had played a handful of games for my new club. I was so passionate to perform well for them and already I was removed from the fray with the start of the autumn Tests just four weeks away.

Three weeks later I returned to play against Harlequins, having been given special dispensation by the England management to play a game one week before I was due to lead England against New Zealand. I needed some game time under my belt but, in truth, I was just as bothered about doing my bit for Bath as I was about proving to the England management that I was neither rusty nor semi-blind.

One of the other minuses to result from all this was that I missed Bath's Premiership fixture at Welford Road the week before my comeback. We lost, as most do at Leicester, but I was obviously disappointed not to have run out on my old stamping ground. I missed the return fixture at the Rec as well, through another injury. To date, I have yet to play a fixture against the Tigers.

I also needed that game against Quins because my confidence had been affected by the nature of the injury, and my damaged eyesight meant I suddenly had a blind spot, which affected me subconsciously. Both areas needed attention, which is why I practised so hard in the days running up to the fixture, working on my ball skills and movement. During the game, it took time for me to regain my confidence fully. I'd take myself out of ball-handling situations, which I would never do normally. It hardly helped that inside the first minute of what turned out to be a 6–6 draw at the Stoop, I clashed heads with fellow Bath back-rower Simon Taylor and had to leave the field for major repairs on my blood-soaked head. During all this drama, Annie and I had to contend with the birth of our second son, Ethan, in September. I was overjoyed, which only added to my amazing mix of emotions at the time. When Dylan was born, I was hopping around in a surgical boot and soon went under the knife to sort out my hip and shoulder. Within weeks of Ethan's birth I was semi-blinded. At least this time there were no labour dramas as there were with our first-born. In fact, I was able to watch the 'A Team' movie on my laptop during the labour before Ethan came calmly and naturally into this world.

This was typical Ethan. He is so chilled and laid back, and in this sense is like his mother. Dylan, on the other hand, is all over the place. It's hard to put into words the love you feel for your children, especially when they first come into your life. Nothing prepared me for fatherhood. I used to enjoy playing with friends' kids, and wanted to be a father myself at some point, but it was not high on my imme-diate agenda. I spent the first three months of Dylan's life believing that it would soon become a great deal easier. When I discovered during months four and five that this was not the case, I hit the wall a little. It was harder work than I ever imagined. I was forever tired during training but never allowed it to show. Back home it took me a good six months to begin to understand a father's role. Up until then it had mainly been supporting Annie but as Dylan grew older, the more I came into the reckoning. I remember coming back from the Argentina tour in 2008 after being away for a month and being heartbroken when Dylan started to cry because he didn't recognise me. Tours were harder, and it made me realise that time spent with the kids is precious. When you see the rugby boys away on tour, you may think we are all hardened, macho men, who like nothing more than to knock lumps out of each other. Yet those of us who are parents – and many of the England team are – also spend some of their time alone in their rooms, furiously writing messages or making calls to their kids. It preys on all our minds that when our young children cry out 'Daddy', we are not always there for them. I like nothing more than to play with my boys, although it's not all good. Dylan jumping on your head at four in the morning, or indeed knee-dropping you from behind the sofa, can be a little wearing at times, but the fun and joy they bring far outweigh any minor negatives. This is why I didn't answer Johnno's call in the summer, when I knew it was about captaining England. I was having fun with Dylan on the trampoline and that was more important.

Around this time, I got to know Andrew Strauss and Alastair Cook, before they jetted off down under to win that remarkable Ashes series against Australia. Strauss, the captain, scored many runs, including a century, and Cook, the vice-captain, broke all scoring records with his incredible batting displays. Both played a major part in England's stunning success.

The three of us, together with Courtney Lawes, were asked to be ambassadors for Austin Reed's 'Q Club', and this meant a day in London on a photo-shoot. Like most rugby players, I am acutely aware of my shelf life. Unlike most working people, my employment as a professional rugby player ends at 35 or 36 years of age, if I'm lucky, although as I had almost discovered so many times before, it could end at any time and at any age. This is why I encourage commercial assignments, just as long as they do not impact on my rugby, which, of course, always comes first. I leave this to Big Red Management and, in particular, Louise Hewitt, whom I nag on a daily basis.

Strauss was your classic England cricket captain – very straight, shirt tucked in, but very determined. He is considerably shorter than the rest of us but when we were asked to jump in the air for a photo, he repeatedly leapt the highest. It was a continual source of amusement to us all. I sympathised with Cook, who, by his own admission, had spent the summer playing 'like a busted arse'. He was getting it in the neck from the media and we've all been there in our time. I wished them both good luck and spent as much time as

I could watching the Ashes a month later. When Cook scored a huge double hundred in the second innings of the first Test in Brisbane, I was genuinely excited for him. It was an incredible series, and I could not have been happier for him. We exchanged texts during the Ashes, although, on his return, he was feted so much and popped up on TV so often, I texted him to say get off my screen!

After the autumn internationals, I returned to club duty with Bath, although we managed just two games, both defeats by Ulster, during a snow-affected December. I found it hard to get as up for these games as I did for the autumn Tests, which is not uncommon among the England boys after running out against the All Blacks in front of 82,000. Somehow, a wet, cold Friday night in somewhere like Sale did not feel the same.

This is where my friend Phil Wall came back into play. He had given me such useful advice on leadership before the Australia tour in the summer, I sought his guidance again to overcome this motivational problem, and he came up with three techniques. Number one was to recapture the moment when I thought I was playing at my best. For me, this was not during our 2003 World Cup-winning campaign, but in November 2009, when I faced Richie McCaw and the All Blacks in the autumn Test series, and the media voted me man of the series. There were a couple of moments in that game when I beat McCaw, the arch scavenger, to the ball, and once, when we confronted each other, I turned him over. Phil referred to this as a 'world-class moment'.

Secondly, he suggested listening to a piece of music that always got me fired up. The Foo Fighters and 'My Hero' did it for me. I've always loved their work and I've been to a couple of their gigs at the NEC with Sam Vesty, Dan Hipkiss and Ollie Smith, and I've also seen them at the O2.

The third trick was to have something to hold in the dressing room, which was important to me. I chose my great-granddad's, and namesake's, First World War medal. He was awarded it for his spell in the trenches, fighting with the Royal Sussex infantry during the truly terrible First Battle of Ypres in 1914. As part of the expedition-ary force, Lewis Walton Moody was one of the first men to experi-ence the kind of horrors that I and my generation have never been asked to go through, thank goodness. Day in and day out, he and his comrades risked life and limb in one of the bloodiest battles in the whole, brutal war.

My pre-match routine has thus changed radically. Around 45 minutes before kick-off, and before I have changed, I disappear into the toilet and sit there listening to the Foo Fighters on my head-phones. I think about those McCaw moments and clench my grand-dad's medal in my hand, trying to imagine the adversity he faced.

Every player has his own way of building up to kick-off. Martin Corry used to sit with a towel over his head, hiding his face, alone with his thoughts. Steve Borthwick used to wander around the pitch. Jonny Wilkinson used to go out and kick, not just for practice with the boot, but to deal with his nerves and prepare his mind for the task ahead. For me, this three-pronged method continues to do the trick.

Three wins in January meant we started the New Year well, but that third win, a comfortable home victory over Italians Aironi in the Heineken Cup, proved disastrous for me.

Ironically, I was up against a Kiwi stand off who was and is the boyfriend of Annie's sister, Bryony. As an openside, my job was to get into his face, although we won so easily that this never materialised. I know both Annie and Bryony were extremely nervous about the prospect of a husband and a boyfriend tearing into each other, but by the end of the game this was the least of our concerns.

In the very last minute of the game, someone fell on to my knee as the pack drove a ruck forwards close to the Italian line. I knew instantly it was my medial ligament and that the opening Six Nations fixture away to Wales had gone, but I still reckoned on weeks rather than months. This would have been the case if I had succeeded in coming through my comeback game at home to Northampton in the middle of February. The plan was to return for England in the Calcutta Cup game, but the ligament went again at the end of an otherwise pleasing win over the Saints, and that was that. I missed the whole of the Six Nations and returned just for Bath's last four fixtures. In our penultimate game, we thumped Wasps at Twickenham on St George's Day but fell agonisingly short of a play-off place. A victory over Newcastle rounded off the season. Fifth was a decent rather than impressive return for a team as good as Bath, although at least it guaranteed Heineken Cup action for the 2011–12 season.

The end of the season marked the end of Danny Grewcock's career as a rugby player. I'd known and played alongside him in an England shirt for a long time. To see him aged 38 still putting in extra training before his final game as if he was 21 was an uplifting sight, and one that I hope all the other players took on board.

I look back on my first season as a Bath player with frustration. In total, I played fifteen games for my new club, which is not what I, or they, had in mind, and although I was incredibly excited by the prospect of the World Cup, a small part of me was also disappointed that I would not be returning to the club until November, a third of the way into the season. I decided that I'd just have to make up for lost time.

16

FIT FOR THE AUTUMN, OUT OF THE SIX NATIONS

Autumn Tests 2010, Six Nations 2011

Eye injury or no eye injury, I was desperate to play for both Bath and England. I had missed so much rugby over the years through all kinds of injuries, some common, some anything but, and with one year to go before the World Cup, and the team clearly on the up, I was in no mood to relinquish my place, let alone the England captaincy.

Although I was happy with my performance against Harlequins at the Stoop, six days before we took on the All Blacks at Twickenham, I was still anxious that my brain had not yet grown accustomed to my new, slightly distorted vision. The England management were comfortable but I was not. In the days leading up to the first autumn Test, I spent much of my spare time either asking Dave Sylvester – an England physio better known as Tweety – to throw balls over my head from behind as we walked up and down the Twickenham pitch, or working on some laptop eye exercises devised by Sherylle Calder. Sherylle is the vision specialist recruited by Clive to give the players eye exercises for the 2003 World Cup. Clive, in typical fashion befitting his extraordinary attention to detail, thought it would help to improve our eye-to-hand and ball coordination. Sherylle then worked with South Africa during their victorious 2007 World Cup-winning campaign. By luck, she was passing through the team hotel in Bagshot, heard about my predicament and sought me out.

As a result of our meeting, she devised a computer programme designed to improve my reactions.

More help came from Nick Dash, who provides me with my contact lenses. An eye test showed that I required new contact lenses to deal with the change in my vision. Nick gave me a gadget that looked a little like a windscreen wiper, with a moving arm and a set of small lights that shine at different times. My job was to focus on the lights that lit up. This exercise, together with Sherylle's programme, I still work on to this day.

Just before the four-Test series began, Tag Heuer, England's new watch sponsors, presented members of the management and those players in the squad with over 50 caps to their names, with a £3,000 watch in recognition of their services to the game. Thommo, Wilko, Simon Shaw, Worzel and I became new and proud owners of a beautiful timepiece, commemorating membership of the 50-cap gang. The gesture was much appreciated. It reminded me of when I sat next to Gordon Banks at a sports dinner not long before. Banks, the England World Cup-winning goalkeeper from 1966, was wearing a gold watch that had been presented to him in 1978 when he was part of a team that won the Conference in the American soccer league. It was now 32 years old but still Gordon wore it with pride.

My message during the days before the Test match was simple – the All Blacks are just a group of men like us, who fall down when hit hard. The New Zealanders are often the best team in the world, and they always have an aura about them, which can affect players, especially younger ones, who have never faced them before. Only when you play against them do you realise that you can turn them over or send them backwards. I told the younger guys how much I respected them as players, and emphasised that the All Blacks were definitely beatable, but in order to achieve this feat we would need to be at our best. They had lost to Australia the week before in Hong Kong in a thrilling, one-off Test match, and the fact that we had beaten the Wallabies in our previous meeting gave us great hope. However, New Zealand now had a game under their belts to shake off any rustiness, and they were not in the habit of losing back-to-back internationals.

And so it proved. The statistics will tell you that we lost by 16–26, but the truth is that, having conceded 14 points in a 15 minute first half period, when we switched off defensively, we then took the game to the All Blacks and could, and probably should, have won. Hosea Gear scored a try, which the television match official (TMO or video referee) gave, while Shontayne Hape, late on, scored a very similar effort, which the TMO disallowed. Both decisions were about millimetres, but this is how fine the margins can be at this level in sport. By the end, with the All Blacks a man down in the sin bin, and with us pressing hard on their line, you might have thought that we were the world's number-one side, rather than them, but the lesson from the day was that the best teams finish their chances, and also seize them when offered. We would have won in 2003 but seven years later we did not possess the nous to close the deal. Many positives could be taken from the day, but I ended up frustrated with our vain efforts to beat New Zealand, and exasperated by being substituted, despite being captain, with 14 minutes remaining.

I showed a little insubordination at the time of my substitution. Floody was about to kick a penalty to the corner until I instructed him to go for the posts, and while this was going on Brian Smith jogged on to the field and told me the management wanted me to come off now. I told him to stop being so stupid. There were 14 minutes to go and we were in a position to go on and win the game, so no, I wasn't going anywhere. Brian disappeared to be replaced by Wig, who gave it to me straight. 'Think about the team,' he said. It was clear the decision had been made and I had to leave the field to be replaced by Hendre Fourie. In hindsight, it was the right decision.

I had, after all, played just one game of rugby in over a month, but at the time I was gutted.

At the post-match function, Richie McCaw, the New Zealand captain and probably the world's greatest openside, mentioned in his speech how much he enjoyed playing at Twickenham. I already had some notes for my speech, prepared for me by Richard Smith, the England lawyer, but I made an additional note on hearing Richie's comment. When it was my turn, I began by stating how the last thing I wanted the New Zealand captain to say was how much fun it was playing at the home of English rugby. I wanted him, and every other visiting captain, to hate having to play at headquarters.

It was all friendly banter, of course, even though I wanted to make the point, and afterwards Richie and I caught up for a chat. People sometimes wonder what makes him such a world-class player in a position that isn't always obvious to the eye. Richie, rather like Backy in his pomp, is good at getting away with things on the rugby pitch. When others are penalised, he is not, and you have to give him credit for that. On top of this, he is a master at stealing the ball in the breakdown, and is deceptively big and strong both in the rucks and with ball in hand. He left the function the happier of the two captains. I left knowing that we probably should have beaten Australia and New Zealand in successive Tests.

Since the Wallabies were next up at Twickenham one week later, the pressure was now on. Not only did we want to prove that our win in Sydney the previous June was no fluke, but we also realised that defeat by Australia, with Samoa and then world champions South Africa to come, would make it a long, hard autumn series. I'd be under pressure as captain, the players for their positions and the management could be back to square one. A lot was riding on this game.

On the eve of the match, we were honoured and privileged to

be addressed by Captain Harry Parker, who visited us from the Headley Court services hospital and rehabilitation centre. He had recently lost both legs as a result of a roadside bomb explosion while on foot patrol with the 4th Battalion Rifles in Helmand in Afghanistan.

Johnno asked me if I felt this would be a good idea and my response was effusive. Normally, the Friday night before a Test match is the worst time for the mind to play tricks, but not on this occasion. Instead, we were spellbound by Harry's story, his reaction to such enormous adversity and his message. You could hear a pin drop in the team room as Harry addressed us, apart from when he admitted that the first thing he did after the bomb had exploded was check that his crown jewels were still intact. The laughter from the boys broke what was otherwise a respectful silence. His job, although a million times more important and dangerous, depended on the same fuel as ours – teamwork. That was the gist of his message. Each of us was only as good as the men around us. Rely on your training and your teammates and all will be fine.

We appreciated his correlation between the rugby field and the battle field, even though all of us understood the vast difference between the two, and we appreciated his sense of perspective. Harry insisted that he was one of the luckier ones. In Headley Court, he explained, there are triple amputees, paraplegics and hideously burnt colleagues. How some of them even survived was amazing. I sensed a different mood around the camp that night. The England boys had been given plenty of food for thought and, from a rugby perspective, it proved to be a huge success. I was deeply moved and inspired by meeting Harry, as were we all, and the respect I have for him and his colleagues has no bounds.

How much effect all this had on the next day is hard to quantify but England, wearing grey, produced the best performance I have played in for ten years, and yes, that includes the World Cup-winning team.

The reason why we won 35–18 was that everything clicked on the day, and everything we tried came off. All departments were covered, from our defence, to our repeated success in turning the ball over, to our attack and to our kicking. Floody kicked nine out of nine to score 25 points.

Ben Youngs was deservedly the man of the match, but the man who made all the headlines was Ashy. If his first-half try was well-taken, his second-half effort will go down as one of the great tries, one of the best witnessed anywhere, let alone at Twickenham. It came from three pieces of sublime skill, although Youngsy's initial dummy probably arose because he saw big Courtney outside him and didn't fancy the lock forward kicking the ball to clear. As it turned out, he need not have worried. Courtney simply drew his man and unleashed Ashy, and the rest, over 85 metres, is sporting history. The two overriding memories of Ashy's run, for me, was first thinking he had cut inside too early, which he hadn't, and my half-hearted attempt to chase after him in case he needed to offload. By the time I had made it to the halfway line, Ashy was launching into his swallow dive and I knew that I had just witnessed the best try scored by an England player in a very, very long time.

The point about Ashy's wonder try was not just how good it was, but also that it killed off Australia. Despite our dominance, the Wallabies were pressing hard and went for a try when a simple penalty kick at goal might have been the better option. The quick Australian tap resulted in a turnover and suddenly Ashy was away.

Australia being Australia were not entirely finished, though. Kurtley Beale scored two tries to make it 32–18. When Floody was again looking to kick a late penalty to the Australian corner, I had to almost wrench the ball from his hands and tell him to slot over the penalty.

'Let's finish this game now,' I told Floody. By finding his target, Toby put us three scores up.

In the dying seconds, I had to grab Danny Care by the collar just as he was about to tap and go. 'Mate, just kick that fucker out of the ground,' was what I instructed him, which Danny duly did. Even though we had won the match, I didn't want Australia to have the final say with a late score. Of course, I have no problem with Toby or Danny wanting to be inventive or continue the pressure, but there are times when you just need to draw breath and consider the right option.

Understandably, the scenes in the England dressing room were euphoric, especially as we also had the massive glass Cook Cup in our hands. It was the only trophy I had ever lifted as a captain of any rugby team, and as I was presented with it on the Twickenham pitch, I was mindful of breaking the top of the Heineken Cup a decade earlier. I therefore made sure the bottom of the trophy was tight, and that the lid was secure, before lifting it high above my head and showing it to my elated teammates.

Typically, it did not end smoothly. The resulting sprayed champagne from the boys ended up in my eyes, which stung like fury. That's one celebratory tradition I have never understood or enjoyed. I want to drink the stuff, not rinse it out of my stinging eyes.

On the Monday, both Tins and I were told that we would be rested against Samoa. I told Wellsy I wanted to play but, once again, the management were probably right in their assessment. Tins and I were not getting any younger, the 2010–11 season would be a long campaign – although, as it turned out, not as long as I hoped it would be – and it gave one or two other players the chance to play a Test match. After all, a successful World Cup campaign would need all thirty players in the England squad to come to the party.

If Ashy was expecting a happy video review of the win over Australia, he was disappointed. The way the England management addressed him was as if he had endured a poor game. Two silly penalties were highlighted, as was his swallow dive, which had been christened the 'Ash Splash' by the media. By all means celebrate, he was told, but after the ball has been touched down. It was a minor issue that would soon become bigger.

Minty was made team captain and I made sure not to step on his toes too much during the week. I held the pads, worked on my conditioning, and threw in my shilling's worth when required, but I did sense an air of light-heartedness and over-confidence during the week, and therein lay the problem. Everyone expected us to beat Samoa, including us, and that can make it hard sometimes.

The 26–13 win was comfortable enough but three tries were rightly disallowed and the boys forgot about all the hard work that goes into making those try-scoring opportunities in the first place. Instead of working hard and being patient, they tried to create try-scoring chances from nothing. I hated watching the game from the stands, especially as I was perfectly fit to play, although it was interesting to watch the England management team at work, and gave me a better understanding of the task they face on match days.

Despite the average display, some of the England boys still appeared a little over-confident at the beginning of the week of the last match in the series, against South Africa. The Springboks had lost against Scotland at Murrayfield over the weekend, and some felt that if Scotland could beat South Africa, then we definitely would. I saw it very differently. To me, the Scottish win was a bad result for us because there is nothing more dangerous than a wounded Springbok. I spent all week telling the less experienced players what to expect – South Africa are a special team in world rugby, they know just one way to play, and that is with sheer, physical brutality.

During one training session, I mistakenly believed that prop Paul Doran-Jones had elbowed me in the face. I reacted by throwing a couple of punches until Dos wrapped his arms around my head and held me in a headlock. I aimed another punch at his head and then Hask came in to defend his old Wellington College schoolmate. It all blew over very quickly but was an insight into the growing tension I felt as the game drew nearer.

I was right to feel the tension, because on the day we had no answer to South Africa's brutality. We knew what was coming, or at least most of us did, but still we could not find a way through or around the Springbok grip. It hardly helped losing three key players. Floody left the field after just 34 minutes, dazed, and with Wilko injured, Charlie Hodgson, who had not played Test match rugby for a while, entered the fray. Tom Croft lasted 22 minutes before he damaged his shoulder, an injury that forced him to miss all but the last of England's Six Nations games. To lose a player of Crofty's talent so early was a big blow, especially as he is an integral part of the lineout, which, traditionally, is always one of South Africa's strengths. To all intents and purposes, we lost Ashy for most of the game, too, even if he was on the pitch. A blow to the head in tackling Victor Matfield left him a peripheral figure for the rest of the game.

The 11–21 scoreline suggests it was a close game. It was not. Fodes's late try placed a little gloss on the score, but that's all. We were well beaten and the most disappointing aspect for me was how I was unable to do much to avert the inevitable. To be honest, some of the younger guys looked a little shell-shocked when I gathered the team under the goalposts and tried to convince them that we could still win this game. We had moved away from our game plan and were punished for doing so. The inevitability of that happening is something every Test match player learns when first facing the Springboks. We were all disappointed afterwards, especially those who had expected to win, but I knew South Africa had meted out an invaluable lesson. Better then, I reckoned, than in the World Cup.

The autumn Tests ended with us winning two out of four, which was a reasonable rather than impressive return. We were a good team, our potential was incredibly exciting, but it was also clear we would need every one of the eight Test matches before the World Cup to develop still further.

If the Six Nations had started the following week, I would have been happy. I was that desperate to put right the wrongs of South Africa. Instead, England had to wait ten weeks before taking on Wales in Cardiff in the opening game, and by then I was out injured again.

I knew the medial ligament injury sustained playing for Bath against Aironi would rule me out for the first two Six Nations games, in Cardiff and then at home to Italy, but I targeted the third match at Twickenham against France for my return. I tried everything in my power to achieve this aim. During the first two fixtures, I joined England and instructed Tweety and Dan Lewindon, another of the England physios, to flog me to death in order to work on my knee and my overall fitness. This they duly did, to the point when it was common for me to feel physically sick after each session. On one piece of equipment, similar to a rowing machine, I missed my target by a metre twice on the last round of repetitions. I was furious, Tweety suggested I had two more attempts and, having reached the target, I finished exhausted but much happier with my work. In the week of the Wales game, I focused on punishing, conditioning exercises, using the ski ergometer, boxing, tug of war and weights in each session. After each one, I did an hour with Dan, concentrating purely on my legs. In 18 days I had just one day off. The rest of the time was sheer purgatory, designed to bring me back to full fitness in time for France.

As if this was not enough, I was also spending an hour each day in the cryogenic chamber at Fulham FC's training ground at Motspur Park in south-west London. England team doctor Mike Bundy knew the Fulham physio, Martin O'Connell, and he very kindly offered to help. A cryogenic chamber is designed to speed up the healing process, especially in ligaments and bones. You lie in a pressurised cylinder shaped like a sausage, wear an oxygen mask and inhale 100 per cent pure oxygen. I took the 40 minute drive from Bagshot to Motspur Park each day, and back again, because I wanted to leave no stone unturned in my recovery process.

The day before the Wales game I overslept and was late for my fitness session at Twickenham. This was unheard of and suggested that I had been overdoing it somewhat. During the session, my leg buckled and as I fell I squashed my damaged knee. I let out a yelp of pain and immediately thought I had injured it again. Tweety decided to end the session immediately, adding that my being late was evidence enough that I had probably overcooked myself. Instead, I jogged around the pitch a few times to run off the pain and to curse my ill luck.

The following evening, England beat Wales 19–26 at the Millennium Stadium in front of the usual passionate Welsh crowd. An impressive performance was capped by two more tries from Ashy, and two more swallow dives. Any win in Cardiff is a good win, especially one to kick off a Six Nations tournament in which momentum counts for so much. Tom Wood, who came in for me, did well on his debut and it was a decent night at the office for England, especially after our experience against South Africa in our last game.

Ashy, or rather his swallow dives, predictably became the story. After his autumn swallow dive, the coaches had shown the team a video of Juan Leguizamon, the London Irish and Argentinian back row forward, dropping the ball while unnecessarily in mid-air during the throes of scoring a try. The ball, which the Puma held one handed, slipped from his grasp and the Exiles missed out on a possible seven points. The message to Ashy was supposed to be kept within the camp but it slipped out into the media and suddenly a minor issue became a very big deal. When Ashy proceeded to finish off both his tries in Wales with yet more swallow dives, it appeared to the press that the winger was sticking up two fingers at Johnno's authority. The truth is nobody was unduly concerned. If Ashy is going to carry on and score many tries for England, he can swallow dive for as long as he likes. I guess one day he will drop the ball. That, probably, will be the last time he swallow dives, but nobody in the England camp took particular issue with him at all.

This was just as well because the following week he did it again – twice – as he scored four tries and England put Italy to the sword at Twickenham. The 59–13 victory was pleasing because we achieved what we failed to do against Samoa, and were ruthless in our finishing. Italy went on to play better than they did against England. Indeed, they ended the tournament by defeating France, but we did all that could be asked of us on the day.

My comeback game for Bath against Northampton came in between the games against Italy and France, and that was when I injured the same ligament again. At the beginning of the week, I did not know the full extent of the damage. The England management suggested I wait for the results of the scan later that week but I withdrew from the team to play France in any case, because, deep down, I knew I would not make it. It would have been unfair both on me and on Tom Wood, my replacement, to have withdrawn on the Thursday or Friday before the Saturday Test. As it turned out, I was right to do so. The scan confirmed that my Six Nations was over.

Once again, I was devastated by an injury. I had half-killed myself to regain fitness to no avail. It was utterly soul-destroying but I had to ensure my despondency was not too evident. In the England camp, the first thoughts of a Grand Slam were beginning to appear. Up until the injury, I had been a vocal, non-playing captain, even though Tins was wearing the armband for the matches. I had checked with my old friend beforehand if he wanted me to play any part, and when he replied that he would be delighted if I did so, I was more than happy to try to make an impact. Once I knew my tournament was over, however, I took more of a back seat.

In my absence, England despatched a physical French team 17–9 at Twickenham, and then slightly stuttered to a Calcutta Cup win at headquarters over Scotland by 22–16. Any win over France is good, and although we lacked the free-flowing finesse of our performance against Italy, we proved that we had learnt from the South African game and fronted up pleasingly well against a team selected to push us around. The Scottish win was fraught with nerves as we edged closer to a stab at the Grand Slam. Scotland produced their best performance of the tournament – as is so often the way when teams face England in the Six Nations – and we lost Tins with an injury during the game, so we gladly took the victory with the attitude that a win is a win. But as we entered the final week, we were not quite in the best shape for the enormous challenge that awaited us – a tilt at a first Slam since 2003 against Ireland in Dublin.

Tins spent the week training with me in rehab. I felt desperately frustrated for him and could see the pain and hurt in his eyes as he began the slow process back to fitness. At the same time, I was pleased that at least I had a training partner. He also became my travel agent for the trip over to Dublin, courtesy of Zara, his then partner and future wife, whose friends organised a private jet to take us over the Irish Sea. It is, I have to admit, some way to travel, and even though I faced a training session over in Ireland that morning, I treated myself to a glass of champagne and a few strawberries *en route*. In Dublin, Tins and I took part in a question and answer session at 'Tigers Events' with my best rugby buddy Geordan, who was also out injured. Soon, though, we settled down to watch the drama unfold.

I have to admit I had grown increasingly worried about this final match, a concern born once again out of experience. Ireland had been much criticised for their tournament up to this point, even though the margins between them winning and losing had been fine. A win over England, led by Minty on this occasion, would put right all the ills of the world. Moreover, a glance at the two team sheets showed that we smacked of inexperience. Ireland, in contrast, had the excellent Brian O'Driscoll and Paul O'Connell, making his return from injury, and would be overflowing with confidence.

At half-time Ireland, who had battered us for much of the first half, led by 17–3. Minutes after the break they extended their lead to 21 points. It was game over, although England calmed down after that, stopped chasing the match so much and played much better for the rest of the game. I sat alongside Tins and, midway through the first half, apologised to the couple sitting in front of us for my continual swearing. They took it very well and told me they had heard far worse.

Despite a generally positive Six Nations campaign, the defeat in Dublin showed how much Tins and I were missed. Any player who says he wants his replacement to play well is lying. Yes, you want your team to win, but you don't want the man challenging you to shine. Tom Wood didn't do anything especially wrong, and there is little doubt in my mind that he has a long international career ahead of him. Tom had a superb season and was rightly named Player of the Season at the Aviva Premiership awards. He took the step up from club to country incredibly well and he's clearly going to be around the Test set-up for years to come. It was just that this game was crying out for experience. We knew how hard the Irish would hit us but there was nothing the players seemed able to do about it out on the pitch, and certainly nothing Tins or I could do about it sitting high up in the Aviva Stadium stands.

Tins and I decided it would be best not to hang around for too long afterwards. We went down to the dressing room and consoled the lads. There were a few tears on show because we had been well beaten, and the realisation that a Grand Slam had just been battered out of our hands was sinking in. Later, all of us reconciled ourselves with the thought that we did at least win the Six Nations title for the first time since 2003, an overall result that we would have grabbed at the start of the tournament, but on that Saturday night in Dublin, nobody felt like celebrating.

We joined up with the boys again after the official post-match function, and had the pleasure of meeting Rory McIlroy in the bar. Rory, of course, went on to contest the US Masters the following month, and then obliterated the field at the US Open in June. He is a big Irish rugby fan, and, in particular, Ulster, although how much he enjoyed being dragged around the bar by Thommo is open to question. Later, Thommo persuaded security staff to allow former England scrum half turned broadcaster Matt Dawson to stay when they were about to throw him out. Ashy had jumped on Daws while he was sitting on a sofa, not the other way round, as had been assumed.

In the cold light of the next morning, it was clear that England had taken some positive steps forward, learnt from previous lessons and also been handed another lesson or two. It was all good preparation for the World Cup, but I reckoned that this was the last time we could use the excuse of inexperience. Even our newest players had featured in some big Test matches by now, as well as played many high-profile games in European club rugby. We would be re-assembling in Bagshot in July for our World Cup camp and for the three August warm-up Test matches. Right now, we were in a good position. A lot of hard work, three good displays in the summer and an agonising selection choice, and we may just be in the right shape to give the World Cup a seriously good go.

Before all this, though, came a couple of weeks of high and totally unforeseen tension for me and my family, which began during a week's holiday at our apartment in Puerto Banus in

Spain. Annie and I took the kids and travelled with a few friends down to the Spanish coast for some sun, rest, relaxation and, for me, some light training. My mood had improved greatly after my four appearances for Bath at the end of the season and I was, finally, fully fit again. One night, we decided to make it a lads only occasion. We were walking through the town when a guy came up to me and accused me of being abusive to a woman in the street. Obviously, I told him I had no idea what he was talking about. The conversation escalated and he threatened me with what he said 'would happen next.

That, so I thought, was the end of it. We enjoyed the rest of the week, returned home and as I was packing on a Sunday night to travel to Twickenham for a pre-World Cup mini-camp – an optional training session for those who were not on holiday – Matt Powell, the Commercial Director at Bath, telephoned me. A complaint had been made about my conduct in Spain. Matt explained that this guy was demanding an apology. Matt added that the bloke seemed like an honest enough rugby fan and maybe this was the best course of action.

I told Matt that I wasn't going to apologise for something I did not do. I recalled the incident and also the fact that a couple of girls had tried to latch on to us for pretty much the whole evening. They came out of nowhere and wanted to have their photos taken with me. I was very aware of my position both as England captain and a very happily married man and refused. Now all this had blown up. I spoke to my agent, Mark Spoors, and to my lawyers, who made it very clear that if I apologised it would seem like an admission of guilt even though I had done nothing wrong. They contacted the man, who insisted he required an apology from me. I told my lawyers that I would apologise if he felt I was a little drunk or noisy, but not for being abusive towards anyone. The man replied that he would not hold further discussions with us.

My mini-camp was pretty much ruined. Most of it was spent in a state of high anxiety or in meetings with Mark Spoors, Phil Wall or the RFU, all of whom were extremely helpful.

The guy then sent us an ultimatum. If he had not heard anything by the Tuesday of the mini-camp, he would go to the Spanish authorities and to a British national newspaper with the story. Obviously, there was no story to tell, although that hasn't always stopped some of the newspapers in the past. He also claimed he had a video with the evidence. This was not true, although I was rather hoping he did possess a tape, which would, of course, have exonerated me.

We decided to lie low. Let him go to the papers if he wanted. My lawyers were ready. The deadline came and went. He emailed us again to say how sorry he was about my refusal to apologise and that, as a result, he had gone both to the Spanish authorities and also to the now defunct *News of the World*. We ignored him and we have heard nothing from him since.

On the face of it, all this may seem like a ridiculous and far-fetched distraction, but it was much more serious than that. I have never endured an experience like it before and never want to again. Annie and I had many sleepless nights, it stressed me out to the eyeballs – although there was no vicious attack of colitis, thank goodness – and it ruined my World Cup mini-camp.

What I learnt from the horrible experience was twofold. Johnno, Mark Spoors and the RFU management and communications team handled the whole affair superbly and gave me much-needed support. But it was a stark reminder that, unfortunately, the captain of the England rugby team, especially in World Cup year, was seen as fair game by some.

By the time we all assembled in Bagshot at the end of June, I was ready and very willing to focus my mind totally on the crucial and final build-up to my third World Cup campaign.

At long last I had no injuries and no threats from chancers to contend with, simply the small matter of leading England to a World Cup in New Zealand. Expectations for a successful tournament were immense.

17

ENGLAND'S WORLD CUP CAMP AND WARM-UP GAMES

All forty-five players in the provisional World Cup training squad assembled at Pennyhill Park for the start of what would be a gruelling four weeks in camp. There was a mixed air of excitement, anticipation and foreboding about what lay ahead. In reality, Johnno already knew twenty-three to twenty-five of his players for the eventual thirty-man squad to fly to the World Cup, so a maximum of seven places were up for grabs between seventeen players. Competition would be intense because every player believed he stood a chance of making it to New Zealand, and this is just how the England management wanted it to be.

This was outlined on the first evening in camp when a squad meeting took place. Johnno laid out exactly what he expected from us all and, it is fair to say, he ensured nobody misunderstood the message. He demanded 100 per cent from every player in every training session on every day, and nothing less. Then the team doc, Mike Bundy, announced that lateness for any appointments with the medics would not be tolerated, and Calvin Morris, England's head conditioning coach, went through the various fitness and weights sessions looming. Each player was presented with focus points to work on during training before Johnno ended the proceedings with a final rallying call. He was as fired up as I had seen him for a very long time. As he finished he turned to me and asked if I had anything to add. He'd said it all but this action alone was enough to suggest that he was sticking with me as captain.

We hit the ground running, or rather wrestling. For the next three, shattering weeks, the boys would be subjected to three-hour fitness sessions in the morning, followed by another two-hour session in the afternoon, or vice versa. These sessions included weights, fitness, skills and . . . wrestling! They were devised by Paul 'Bobby' Stridgeon, one of our fitness coaches, who has a background in wrestling. Special ankle boots were provided, as was a dojo (a martial arts court), which was placed on the training pitch at the team hotel. Each day, two 'King of the Ring' contests were staged with the backs and the forwards. The winner of the first bout took on another player, and another until he was beaten and that player stayed in the ring taking on challengers until he was beaten, and so on, while everyone else surrounded the dojo and cheered. I managed to win a couple of bouts but the best forwards were Thommo, Simon Shaw – because he simply picked people up and walked around the ring with them – and Matt 'Sos' Stevens, who, during his two-year ban for taking cocaine, became a wrestler to keep himself fit. Among the backs, Banners, through his sheer size, proved to be useful, but the outright king was undoubtedly Manu Tuilagi, the youngest of the Samoan Tuilagi brothers.

In the past season, Manu had broken into the Leicester Tigers first team and had made such an impact that he was now catapulted into the extended England squad. I had played alongside four of his brothers – Freddie, Henry, Alex (who accidentally broke my ankle and also received a red card with me after our fight when England beat Samoa in 2005) and Andy – all at Welford Road, and now Manu, qualified for England through residency rights, was the coming man. He announced his World Cup intentions at the first available opportunity by throwing Tins out of the ring. Tins is a big man but

Manu treated him like a rag doll. As if this was not enough, Manu lifted heavier weights than anyone else in the squad, and yes, that includes all the forwards. He managed to bench press 80kg 40 times. The next best was 27! It is fair to say that the 20 year old centre made an instant impression.

The increasingly popular King of the Ring might have been staged for the whole camp had Benny Youngs not hurt his knee cartilage during a bout. The injury kept him out of all three warm-up Tests, although he flew to New Zealand very close to being fully recovered. After that mishap, the wrestling was abandoned in favour of exercises to aid us in specific areas, such as clearing out rucks.

I was feeling very fit, very fresh and very quick by now, and the speed element of this was down to some sessions under the expert tutelage of Darren Campbell, the former Olympic silver medallist in the 200 metres, gold medallist in the sprint relay and serial medallist and champion at the Europeans and Commonwealths. As I used to be a half-decent athlete at school I have always followed the sport and knew all about Darren's huge success as an athlete. So after Cuets used him to improve his speed work on the wing, I thought it could work for me. Clashes of schedules and my injuries meant that our first meeting, planned for before the Six Nations, finally took place in May at the University of Bath's indoor track, but the benefits were instant.

Darren is one of those guys who makes you feel good about yourself. His glass is always half full and this rubs off on you. I was impressed with his planning, too. He researched the work an openside has to get through in a game, and prepared his drills accordingly. His attention to detail was meticulous. In no time he made me realise how speed comes as much from the arms and shoulders as it does from the legs, and after four ninety-minute sessions, I believed I had regained my best speed.

In sport, belief is always half the battle. Unfortunately, your body needs to back you up and at the World Cup camp mine, temporarily, failed to do so. At the end of week one, a back spasm forced me to withdraw from training and when a day's rest failed to do the trick, an epidural in Chelsea and a scan that revealed damage to a disc meant that, although I could still train, it had to be on the medics' terms and not out on the pitch with the squad. This was hugely frustrating for me, especially the first two days, which were spent in bed. At least it was just a minor setback, and during the ensuing weeks I still lifted weights and worked on rehab and drills.

I also had time to take part in two TV commercials, both for O2, to be aired in the run-up and during the World Cup. In the first one, I had to pore over video analysis, while Ashy stared at the camera with intent. The second was designed to encourage punters to wake up, get out of bed and enjoy a pie while watching our games on TV. The ad was shot in someone's house on a Camberley estate, just down the road from the team hotel. It was supposed to be a secret shoot, but when we arrived, hundreds of kids had got wind of it and were hanging around for a glimpse of the action.

Everyone was squeezed into a caravan while waiting to be called in front of the camera, and we were told to cover up the new, all-white England World Cup jerseys, because they were due to be revealed in the second warm-up game in Cardiff. As I feature first in the advert – hauling a half-naked man out of bed and telling his wife to be quiet – I left the boys in the caravan and went off to shoot my part. Others featuring include Ashy, again, in the kitchen, Jonny, Hask and Worzel, producing a pie for the man, and Johnno, handing over the TV remote. An hour later, when I returned to the 7 by 7 foot caravan, mayhem had descended, which is what you'd expect if you leave a group of rugby players alone in such a confined space for that length of time. There were chocolate wrappers everywhere, and Coke cans, while Hask's face had been painted like a transvestite.

During that first week in camp, we held a major media awareness session in which the RFU's media team outlined the heightened interest in us as a World Cup squad. I stood up and relayed the story of the chancer who made false allegations against me after we met in Puerto Banus. I also mentioned my stage diving antics in Paris during the 2007 tournament the night after South Africa humiliated us in the pool stages, something that came to light after the World Cup was over, for which I was duly thankful.

We were also constantly tested on our plays and moves, having been handed an England playbook on the first night. It was one thing showing our knowledge on the field, quite another using a whiteboard and a felt-tipped pen. None of us got too badly caught out, although Ashy and Manu had their moments.

Thommo seemed to be targeted more than anyone else by the fitness boys. I don't know why this was but the boys brutalised him. Each night my good friend was shattered. Once he was lying on his bed naked – he spent half his time in our shared, two-bedroomed apartment with no clothes on – when someone from housekeeping knocked on the door. Unaware of Thommo's state of undress, I asked the lady to come in, but fortunately spotted the error in time and asked her to wait just a few seconds while I told Thommo to cover up.

'No,' he shouted. All he had to do was pull the duvet over himself. 'No, fuck off!' And that was that. He was so tired he could not even muster the energy to grab the duvet.

When he was feeling livelier – and after four weeks he had lost weight and body fat and come through everything the conditioning boys had thrown at him – Thommo had an annoying habit of switching off all the lights in our room when he heard me walking down the corridor, and then jumping out at me shouting his head off. It worked every time. I was a nervous wreck after a few of these experiences.

Still, it was fair enough because I had been pulling off similar 'danger' antics for many years in the England camp, and still managed to succeed with Hask. When I noticed his door was ajar, I crawled along the floor commando style, and waited until he had settled in bed with his computer. Hask is a big man but he screamed like a baby when I leapt up shouting, 'Danger.' If you think all this is rather puerile, you would be right, but it underlines the things players do to alleviate the boredom of camp.

During the second week, poor Annie had to move house again without my services. She did it when we moved from Leicester to Bath while I was away on tour in Australia, and she did it again when we moved from the small village of Rode to Bradford-upon-Avon while I was tied down in the England camp. The previous summer she was heavily pregnant with Ethan. This time she had to cope with the energetic Dylan and ten-month-old Ethan.

At the end of the fourth week, the squad were given a week off. At that time, five players were supposed to be cut from the forty-five-man squad, but Johnno felt that everyone had worked so hard the least he could do was give them a chance to shine when games against each other were staged at the end of week five. By that time, I was back training with the squad out on the pitch.

Johnno arranged a full-on series of twenty-minute games at the Stoop, Harlequins' ground in Twickenham. This included changing in separate rooms to try to create some kind of enmity between opponents, an exercise that proved difficult because by now we had been transformed into a club rather than a country team. Wayne Barnes officiated, and since Tins was preparing for his wedding that weekend, Minty and I were opposing captains. After twenty minutes, this mini series did not seem such a good idea. Courtney had been stretchered off with what appeared to be a serious neck injury, although, thank goodness, it turned out to be a bang and nothing more. Then David Strettle was carried off, leaving us wondering who would be next. Luckily, we managed to get through the rest of the games unharmed, which was a good way to end the week. We had enjoyed our first competitive rugby of sorts since May.

Afterwards Tom Croft, or 'Yog' as he is known, played a trick on me. I always spray a substance called Stickum on my legs, which is an adhesive that helps the lifters at lineouts. It takes ages to get it off, although the use of Stickum Remover speeds up the process. So in the dressing room I asked if anyone had the remover, and Yog very helpfully threw me his. It was only after I had sprayed my legs completely that I realised I had re-applied a second dose of Stickum while the rest of the squad looked on and giggled. I promised Yog that retribution, when it came, would be severe.

This was the point when we lost our first five players. My old friend Worzel failed to make the cut, having been held back by injury, and my former Tigers teammate George Chuter didn't make it, either. Strettle's injury confirmed his absence, the luckless James Simpson-Daniel missed out again and an injury to Thomas Waldrom prevented him from playing in the practice match, which ended his chances. The remaining forty were sorry to see them go, but breathed a collective sigh of relief that at least it wasn't any of them.

For the next few days the focus switched completely for those invited to the royal wedding of Mr Mike Tindall and his lovely bride Miss Zara Phillips or, in other words, my old mate Tins and Zara, whom I'd got to know reasonably well over the years. Not everyone from the squad was invited – after all, Tins had all his former Bath and current Gloucester teammates to think about, plus the retired 2003 World Cup friends – but a good contingent of the World Cup squad headed north to Edinburgh for a quite stunning weekend.

Annie and I flew to Scotland on the Friday afternoon with the Grewcocks, the Flatmans and the rest of the Bath contingent. At our hotel, we were met by police issuing various pieces of security information, which included not taking mobile phones to the wedding and being able to produce a checkable form of ID. We needed to show this next day as we boarded the bus to take us to Canongate Kirk in the Royal Mile.

In the church, the men all dressed up in morning suits, were Woody, Shaggy, Lol, Johnno, the Bath and Gloucester boys, Paul Sampson and Kirsty Gallagher, Jackie Stewart, Amy Williams and, of course, the small matter of the royal family, who all sat at the front. Some of the congregation had been to a function the night before on the royal yacht *Britannia*. Annie and I had had dinner with Leon and Lisa Lloyd, and also the Grindals (James was a former Tigers teammate) before making the most of a night without the kids to grab some much-needed sleep before the big day, and Annie's ridiculously early appointment at the hairdresser's.

The wedding was very beautiful, and very royal. Zara, incidentally, looked stunning. Afterwards the bus took us through the crowds of well-wishers and on to Holyrood Palace where the reception took place. If the wedding was formal, the reception was anything but. The Queen left sharpish but the rest of the royal family – Prince Philip, Princess Anne, Prince William and Kate, and Prince Harry – stayed to enjoy best man Iain Balshaw's speech. Balsh (who now plays for Biarritz and was on the pitch with me when England won the 2003 World Cup) is a cheeky chappie but he was crapping himself at the thought of striking the right balance with his best man's speech. How could he make his audience laugh while keeping it clean? In the end, Balsh pulled it off triumphantly. One gag was close to the knuckle, but for the rest of the time, Princess Anne and Prince Philip laughed long and loud. Afterwards you could see relief etched all over Balsh's face.

During all this I was seated next to Kate, and Annie was opposite next to William. I knew William slightly through his love and support of rugby, but this was the first time I'd met Kate, just weeks after the whole nation, including Annie and me, had been mesmerised by their own royal wedding. I have to report that William and Kate are two of the nicest people you would ever wish to meet and no, this is not a public attempt to receive a knighthood in years to come. They were delightful, down-to-earth company, so much so that Annie, who always grabs the chance to show a few shapes on the dance floor, persuaded Kate to join her for a bop.

I stayed rooted to my seat, adopting my traditional stance of not venturing anywhere near a dance floor. Besides, for all the fun, on this occasion I never quite let my hair down. Always in the back of mind was the fast-approaching World Cup. I would have liked to have had a chat with Princess Anne and, in particular, Prince Philip, who seemed to be enjoying himself no end. His fitness and health is incredible for a man who had just celebrated his 90th birthday.

Towards the end of the evening, Prince Harry ambled over to say hello and soon got to reminiscing with Annie about that night, nine years previously, when he pulled over in his car to see if she needed help, since she was crying, and she jumped on him in the streets of Twickenham after we had beaten New Zealand and I had been injured. When William heard the story, he looked at Harry, remarking, 'A young blonde in distress, eh? Hmm!' Harry laughed.

'Imagine,' he said to Annie, a big grin on his face, 'you could have ended up with me. Instead, you're with him!'

It was a fun way to end what had been a memorable day for us, and an even more memorable day for Tins, who, the next day, would be travelling back to Bagshot and World Cup camp.

On the plane on the way home I thought about the journey Tins has taken. We pretty much started our Test careers together, becoming regular members of the England team just before the 2003 World Cup. It was there, of course, in Australia, that he met Zara, and nobody could have handled the extra pressures a high-profile relationship with a member of the royal family creates better than the Yorkshireman. Tins is, without doubt, one of the most laid-back individuals I have ever met, and thank goodness for that, but I was focusing on his career as a rugby player.

Like me, he has endured his fair share of misery due to injuries. He missed out on both the 2005 Lions tour and the 2007 World Cup so, in those terms, I have been luckier than he has been. If I'm not England captain – as I wasn't during the Six Nations – then Tins is the player I'd have as captain instead, hands down. I believe we have a kindred spirit on the pitch. Whenever I've been captain, I've always asked him for his thoughts, or to deliver a few words to the boys. Now the man who had played alongside me, off and on, for so many years, had just married his girl, who just happened to be the Queen's granddaughter.

This had been a second wedding in a fortnight. The weekend before, Annie and I had travelled to a small town near Shannon in Ireland to attend the wedding of an old Oakham school friend of mine, JD. In a local bar, I was catching up and swapping old school tales when a local drunk started to bother me. He was horrifically drunk, actually, and he wouldn't go away. He was right in my face and kept prodding me. I was concerned he was looking for a fight. In a perfect world it would have been nice to eject him from the pub personally, but as England captain I couldn't be seen to be reacting. A new degree of responsibility and awareness of my role were changes in my life that I had to adhere to. It was definitely not befitting an England rugby captain to be seen ejecting someone from a pub or becoming involved in a bar-room brawl. Happily, the landlord had already given him a last warning and it wasn't too much longer before he was thrown out.

Back in camp we prepared for our first warm-up game, against Wales at Twickenham. I was tremendously excited because it would be my first international since the previous November, and I was back as captain, but the weeks leading up to warm-up games are very different from those leading up to the autumn or Six Nations Test matches. We continued to train our guts out as if it was pre-season. The forwards endured two-hour sessions twice a day in which we basically beat the crap out of each other. Whenever I glanced up at the backs on the other side of the pitch, they'd be yipping and squealing and playing kiss chase. It never quite seemed to tally but that's probably my fault for becoming a forward.

One happy distraction could have been meeting Johnny Depp and Tim Burton who, we discovered, were spending a couple of nights at Pennyhill Park while shooting some scenes for their latest film – a vampire movie – nearby. I say 'could' because I never got to see them, save for a fleeting glimpse of Burton as he walked through the lobby. I am a huge admirer of Depp's quirky films and Burton's genius of a mind, and would happily have chatted away to either or both of them given half the chance. Gerard Murphy, the team psychologist, managed to buttonhole them, however, and the next thing I heard the whole of the England management spent some time with the actor and director, which resulted in Depp and Burton receiving two tickets for the game, and the pair cheering England on against Wales.

The team selection was interesting mainly because Manu would be making his Test debut at outside centre, Sos would be making his first start since he received his ban, and I would be winning my 67th cap, which meant I overhauled Backy as the most capped England flanker of all time. I wouldn't say that milestone was at the forefront of my mind. Being in charge of my country again after so long out, with the World Cup just around the corner, occupied most of my thoughts, but it was nice to achieve the accolade, and even better to have done so by passing such a great player as Backy in the process.

I was pleased for Sos, too. I remember speaking to him during his ban. Sos told me how much he'd fucked up his career, and how desperate he was to get back on track. I told him what was done was done and it was best if he put his head down, which is precisely what he did. After half a season with Saracens, culminating with a Premiership victory over Leicester, he had held his hand up and now found himself back in an England jersey.

Two days before the game, Darren Campbell popped over to stage a speed session with Cuets, Wiggy (scrum half Richard Wigglesworth) and myself. Afterwards, the management team roped him in to play a game of football. Darren had 'bigged' himself up about his football skills, having temporarily turned his back on athletics to try out his luck as a semi-professional footballer with Plymouth Argyle and Newport County, but I think he was a little surprised by the roughhouse tactics adopted by Johnno, Wellsy and company.

Game day could not come quickly enough for me. I was so psyched up that I almost forgot to take the young female mascot out with me as I ran on to the Twickenham pitch, sporting our new second kit, which was all black. Tom Palmer had to shout to me moments before I sprinted out of the players' tunnel. The game went rather well, too, or at least it did for an hour. Manu began his Test career with a try just before half-time and this followed a pick-up-and-go try for Hask after great work from Sos in the front row. Jonny bagged 13 points, including two drop goals, but the game changed after 50 minutes when the Welsh full-back, Morgan Stoddart, was stretchered off the pitch on oxygen, having broken his leg. After an eight-minute delay we never regained our dominance, and allowed Wales in to score a couple of soft tries, which, despite losing, gave them confidence before the return fixture in Cardiff the following weekend. Still, I was pleased to take a 23–19 win.

Not long after Stoddart's removal, I followed, believing that my World Cup was over before it had even started. Tom Palmer fell on to my knee, the same one that had kept me out of the Six Nations after two previous injuries. I knew immediately that I was in trouble.

This is why I was punching the Twickenham turf and shouting. It was not pain, but sheer anguish. The medics wanted to stretcher me off but I refused point blank. I never intend to leave the field of play like that and this was no exception. Instead, they helped me to hobble off the pitch and into the medical room where Stoddart was lying on a bed with an oxygen mask strapped to his face. On the TV the game was showing, and I sat there, drained.

Eventually, I limped over to poor Morgan. There were tears on his face. I shook his hand, wished him luck and said sorry that he had been injured so badly. The Welshman nodded his head under the mask. There are few more traumatic places to be than the Twickenham medical room on an occasion such as this. I was facing the end of my dream to lead my country in what would be my third World Cup. It would have been a sad end to my World Cup career – there was no way I'd be able to last until the 2015 tournament. I'd put in so much work to get back to where I was after so many injuries and my illness over the last four years, but now I realised that I may have played my last game at headquarters. After all, who is to say I would still be captain, or even selected for my country, after the World Cup? At least I had experienced two tournaments, though. Stoddart's dreams were shattered into tiny pieces and, even in my own time of high anxiety, I felt deeply for the man.

As the day passed into evening and then night, my knee did not react too badly and I felt the first shoots of optimism. On the Sunday morning, after a night interrupted by icing of the knee on a two-hourly basis, little to no swelling had taken place and my mood brightened considerably. It just didn't feel anywhere near as bad as before but much would depend on the results of the scan on the Monday after my now familiar visit to the hospital.

The initial report was soul-destroying – a complete rupture of the MCL (medial collateral ligament). That, without any doubt, would rule me out of the World Cup. This did not seem correct at all, and the doctor felt the same. When we passed on to him the scans taken from my previous two injuries to the right knee, it all became much clearer. I did not possess a normal medial ligament in the first place, hence the distortion.

Andy Williams, probably the country's foremost knee specialist, kindly saw me at his home after what had undoubtedly been a long day's work for him. He'd also seen me in the dressing room at Bath after I'd injured myself in my comeback game against Northampton. After a great deal of manipulation, Andy concluded that I had contracted a low-grade strain or tear of my MCL and that there was no reason why I should not be ready, or at least very nearly ready, for England's first World Cup pool game against Argentina five weeks later. This, quite obviously, was excellent news. I was advised to rest completely for a fortnight, which is the exact opposite of what I had done with my previous injury, and to wear a protective brace for the next two weeks. I also had an injection of a sugar solution that has been proven to have a tightening effect on animal ligaments. This process was to be repeated on the day I left for New Zealand, and again during the tournament.

The medics refused me permission to travel with the boys to Cardiff for the re-match. Instead, I had to rest – again – and watch Wales v England from home. It was, to say the least, a frustrating experience. We managed to lose 19–9 and it took some doing. We had plenty of penalties but kicked for the corners, we should have had a penalty try awarded, and with the large amount of territory and possession we enjoyed, we should have won at a canter. But, somehow, we lost and took that frustration into our last warm-up game in Dublin.

The final England World Cup squad of thirty was announced nine days later on the Monday before the Ireland fixture, but the players were all told seven days before then. Ten of our number were told thanks, but not this time. Professional sport can be brutal, and here was another example of it. Good players, and good people too, including Ugo Monye and Charlie Hodgson, Paul Doran-Jones and Riki Flutey, had suffered all of the summer's pain but would now experience none of the World Cup glory. That morning, Johnno told Danny Care the good news that he was in the squad. It was never in doubt. By the afternoon the scrum half had withdrawn after discovering the dreadful news that he had broken a toe during the Welsh defeat. I phoned Danny when I heard of his shattering setback but there really wasn't much I could say. He was a big loss, though, because his form had been terrific and, as a lively character, Danny was also a good tourist.

At least I didn't have to suffer the night of uncertainty that I'd endured before the 2003 and 2007 World Cup squads were announced. Wellsy had left a message on my phone after the Welsh defeat, saying that we should discuss the game the following week. It was his way of saying that I was in. You might think it was a given as I was squad captain, but it was still a relief to receive the green light.

The bottom line is that any one of those forty players who heard the news, good or bad, that Monday could have done a job at the World Cup. Certainly, mixed emotions were to the fore once more, even if we were all away from the hotel at the start of our week off. Danny would have felt for Ugo, and then vice versa when Danny's injury became evident. Hask would have been upset for his best mate and school friend Paul Doran-Jones, and so it went on.

For the rest of us, the start line for the World Cup was edging closer and closer, a point hammered home by the official sponsors' World Cup send-off dinner. This was held at Twickenham on the evening of the day the final squad of thirty players was announced. We all assembled in a holding room and awaited our turn to be called up one by one on to the stage by the compere of the night, the very tall Martin Bayfield, who played for Northampton and England back in the early 1990s. This was to take place in alphabetical order, with myself as captain and Johnno as manager the last to make an entrance. Tom Stokes, who was in charge of all administrative and organisational duties for us, had only started his new job in March. This meant the players wanted to test his mettle. Just before each player's name was about to be called out they would tell Stokesey that they would refuse to walk out like a catwalk model. This, predictably, sent him into a wild panic. Equally predictably, when the name was called out went the player. By nature of the alphabet Tom Wood and then Ben Youngs were last to walk out before me, which is why I saw how Lenny grabbed Woody's tie and performed a 'peanut'. Remember at school how people would yank your tie so hard it would end up an inch long and ending just below your neck? Unfortunately Woody had no time to put it right and thus entered the stage still trying to put on his tie. If this looked odd then Bayfield was quick to jump on the unfortunate Woody who was then publicly admonished for not even bothering to have got himself dressed. Later that night Johnno and I conducted a question and answer session which, I was told, would not be going out on TV. I was not told, however, that it would be streamed live on the internet, which is why I received a text from a friend pointing out that it might not be such a good thing to openly call Bayfield a 'knob' which, of course, I had just done. By the time Madness appeared as the evening's main act, we were long gone, heading back to the hotel in readiness for the next morning's training.

The following night, our new social events committee, comprising Lee Mears, Chris Ashton and Matt Stevens, hired one of the theatres at the Camberley Vue cinema complex for a special screening of the hit film of the summer, 'The Inbetweeners Movie'. Some of the senior players decided that this trio would make the perfect social committee because Mearsy is a born organiser, Sos is a very sociable chap and Ashy needed some kind of sedation. A ragtag collection of thirty players, medical and conditioning staff spent a couple of hours laughing, drinking Fanta and hurling popcorn and Maltesers at each other. Reliving our own teenage rites of passage via the film helped to ease the pressure from the last few days of squad selections, and of the looming final warm-up Test against Ireland.

Unusually with a game just forty-eight hours away, the boys staged a full-on training session on the Thursday, and since there were one or two absences, Johnno decided to play an active role. He may have retired from rugby in 2005, but there is still a bit of life in the old dog, and within seconds he became very involved. As he lay at the bottom of a ruck, Thommo raked him with his boots to try to get the England manager's huge body out of the way. Johnno responded by grabbing Thommo in a headlock and, for a split second, I feared a fight was on the cards. Instead, Thommo flipped his boss over on to his back, showing great strength, leaving Johnno panting and floundering on the turf. It all happened in a flash but I managed to catch it and it made me laugh. Johnno saw the funny side as well. Understandably, he's not as fit as he once was, but he seemed to appreciate the moment as much as I did.

Afterwards, the boys set off for Dublin. Once again I was not permitted to travel. The medics were leaving nothing to chance. My rehab was going well and they wanted no setback. It was frustrating not to be able to be there in person to support the lads, but at least I had the injured Woody and Shape (Shontayne Hape) with me back at base for company. Before they left, Tins, Minty and I discussed showing another video to the team before the Ireland game. Minty suggested that it should be played on the Saturday morning instead of the Friday night. Previous video showings have, as I have outlined, not always gone to plan, but this time a tape revealing the boys at their best, accompanied by music, played its small part in what was to ensue that afternoon in Dublin.

England's 20–9 win was just what we needed forty-eight hours before boarding the plane and taking the long flight to New Zealand.

Two wins out of three, especially as two of the games were away from home, was a decent return from the warm-up Tests, and we all knew we should have beaten Wales in Cardiff as well. Better still was the performance. Some areas still needed improvement, of course, notably our discipline in the breakdown, but the pluses were many. Our defence was resolute, and in fielding Tins at twelve and Manu at thirteen our midfield was impressive. Manu scored again, his second try in his second Test, and he continued to excite, but I was particularly pleased for Tins, again standing in as captain, who produced a tremendous display at inside centre, including a deft grub kick that gave Delon Armitage the chance to score and settle the issue.

Strangely, I was also pleased for one Irishman. Geordan missed out on 2003 after a last-minute injury. Eight years on and his participation in the World Cup was looking doubtful, but an injury to Felix Jones in Ireland's previous warm-up Test gave Geordan a belated opportunity. It was not the way Geordan would have wanted it, but fate tends to even things up, and 2011 makes up for 2003. At one point in the game, Manu broke clean through and ran most of the length of the pitch. Only one man could stop him and that was Geordan at full-back. As an England player, I wanted Manu to score. As Geordan's close friend, I was delighted to see the Irishman bring Manu down.

Once the boys returned to Bagshot, some of us went to Legoland for the Sunday with our families. Mearsy and Shawsy joined Annie, myself and the kids for an enjoyable few hours. Obviously, Shawsy's huge frame contrasted somewhat with the Legoland figures, Mearsy not so much! That evening, our last night in England for many a week, we had a barbecue for all the players, management and families. Manu continued to make his mark on the squad, this time performing the traditional England first timer's song and playing his guitar at the same time. Out of all the players forced to sing on debut in front of the squad over many years, Manu was the first I had ever seen accompany himself on guitar. However, once Matt Stevens had witnessed this event, he couldn't help himself, and the rest of the evening featured Sos delivering his repertoire.

The festivities ended the way they often do in the company of Thommo. Someone lobbed half a lime in his direction, the lime collided with a glass and the drink spilled all over his lap. I was next to him, holding a tray of drinks, which, after he kicked out with violent intent, showered me with alcohol of various kinds while half a dozen glasses shattered on the floor. One way or another, something like this often happens when I'm with Thommo. I recalled the time when I nudged him and his head banged into a doorframe during the 2003 World Cup, resulting in masses of blood and faked injuries. I felt my temper beginning to well up in the pit of my stomach, had an anger management moment by myself, and decided this was as good a time as any to call it a night.

The morning proved to be hectic. I had treatment and rehab, media duties, farewells to my family, whom I would not be seeing for four weeks into the World Cup – and this included a difficult goodbye to an unhappy Dylan – and thanks delivered to the staff at Pennyhill Park, which included various gifts of team kit. It all went in a flash. Suddenly, we were on the team bus *en route* to Heathrow. In the air was a buzz of nervous excitement. Many of us had been here before. Many of us had not. The usual japes and tricks went on at the airport. Ashy had his passport purposefully stolen for a while, which produced an understandable panic attack, and then we found our seats on the plane set for New Zealand.

I sat back in my seat and gazed out of the window. The waiting was over. The World Cup was upon us. Previous years had taught me that I should expect nothing, and prepare for everything. Were we ready to do ourselves justice? Well, we weren't in the shape of 2003, but considerably better than 2007. All I knew was that we had a chance, and if we could produce the kind of form we showed against Australia home and away, in parts of the Six Nations, and against Ireland forty-eight hours earlier, then it would take a good team to beat us. Time, as always, would soon tell. I made a vow to myself as the 747's wheels left the Heathrow tarmac. I would do everything that was possible, both mentally and physically, to give this my very best shot.

18

PROBLEMS, PROBLEMS – BUT WINNING PROBLEMS

The 2011 World Cup pool games

A s we took off from Heathrow, with the prospect of a long flight ahead, I looked around the business-class cabin at my England colleagues. Some were embarking on a wonderful adventure for the first time while others, including my old, battling colleagues Steve Thompson, Jonny Wilkinson and Mike Tindall, had been there and seen it all before. None of us had any real idea how the next eight weeks would pan out. I knew we had a chance, and I knew that we would have to overcome some tough times ahead. We would be required to dig deep, mentally and physically, to overcome the inevitable barriers placed in our way, but after that it was anyone's guess. In 2003, we were favourites to win but succeeded only after a series of close games, injuries, calls to have us banned and a desperately dramatic denouement. In 2007, we very nearly snatched the most unlikely of victories, having stared down into the deepest depths of defeat and humiliation. What, then, would befall us in 2011? And what would befall me? Already the thought had occurred to me that I could have left Pennyhill Park for the last time as an England player. What was not in doubt was that this would be my final World Cup experience. I sat back and concentrated on planning the half dozen films I would devour during the ensuing twenty-four hours spent at 36,000 feet in the air.

Even though it was 4.30 in the morning, and raining, when we arrived in Auckland, a few hundred people had gathered at the terminal to greet us, including quite a few New Zealanders. One group of schoolkids treated us to an immediate haka – an early indication of just how much rugby means to this nation.

The next few days were low key, with a little light training to blow the cobwebs away while we acclimatised to the huge time difference. We also went sailing in Auckland Harbour, which, of course, is spectacular; and rugby boys being rugby boys, the day was not without a few moments of farce. Players and management were split into two mixed teams, and each team was assigned one of New Zealand's former America's Cup boats. Before we got going, we were told how to blow up life jackets manually, although we were not to do this unless it was necessary. Within moments someone had pulled Hask's toggle, his jacket inflated and he spent the rest of the day with it sticking in his face.

Early on in the race, my boat had built up a lead of at least 800 metres, and we were all looking forward to aiming the obvious banter at the other crew when our skipper decided to ease up to give the other boat a chance. Unfortunately, they not only caught us but shot straight past and we were unable to catch them. All we could do was throw fruit at them as they sailed past, and when we realised the race was lost, our attention returned to the life jackets. Cuets blew mine up, Lenny (Ben Youngs) had his inflated and then Sheri (Andrew Sheridan) grew especially irritated when someone had the temerity to blow his up. He took it off and flatly refused to wear it again!

That was the fun side of our time in Auckland. The next day, reality came crashing back into my life. I had always known that participation in the opening group game of the World Cup, against Argentina in Dunedin, would be a 50–50 call for me and my recovering knee, but I still harboured great hopes that, as captain, I could lead out my men. On the Friday, however, I still felt a fair degree of pain in the damaged area. This was the day when the team to face the Pumas was selected, even though it was not officially announced until a few days later, and at that point I was withdrawn.

This was a very, very difficult moment for me. For a while I thought my World Cup could be over before it had even begun. If this had been the case, I would have seen it as an utter, and extremely personal, humiliation. To be named as England captain despite carrying a knee injury, and then have to pull out due to that injury without playing a minute's action, would have suggested that the injury was worse than diagnosed. Moreover, after a span of thirteen years playing for England, this was not the way I would have wanted it, at least potentially, to have ended.

But I had to remain upbeat for the squad. I was their captain, and the worst thing any player can do is spread his own bad vibes or misery, like a bad apple in a barrel full of fruit. I was concerned enough about my depressed demeanour to check with Gerard, our psychologist, but he insisted I was still coming over well. Watching the in-flight safety instructions *en route* from Auckland to Dunedin on the Sunday cheered me up a little, as delivered by All Blacks coach Graham Henry and some of the players, including Richie McCaw, who posed as an Air New Zealand pilot in the cockpit. It was a bit bizarre, verging on ridiculous, but it was also funny. I drank my tea out of a special Dan Carter emblazoned mug provided by the stewards, which served to remind me just how big a deal this tournament is in a country where the sport really is deemed to be a religion.

That night in Dunedin we attended an official, World Cup cap-awarding ceremony in the town hall. The place was packed to the rafters, which created a vibrant atmosphere, and we were treated to a full Maori reception. All the players had to perform a 'hongi', the traditional Maori greeting, involving a handshake and the touching of foreheads and noses. As there were twenty officials and thirty players plus management, this took quite some time. Each player went up on stage to receive his cap, named in alphabetical order. Predictably, Jonny got the loudest cheer. Finally, I was called upon to deliver a short thank-you speech, quite daunting on my first day in Dunedin, in which I apologised if I had accidentally head-butted some of the dignitaries by mistake. Our Maori guide began to sing 'Swing Low' in response to a song delivered to us, and we all, somewhat reluctantly, joined in. Again, this merely presented another reminder that we were in a country where rugby means more than it does anywhere else.

While the rest of the troops involved in the forthcoming Argentina game got down to serious pre-match training, I continued my rehab and also took the chance, along with Johnno, Lee Mears, Davy Wilson, Shontayne Hape and Alex Corbisiero, to visit the earthquake-hit city of Christchurch. This was going to be our World Cup base and venue for the first three pool games until the quake, eight months earlier, destroyed large areas of the city and wrecked the recently improved AMI Stadium. After two school visits, we went to the stadium. As we approached, it appeared to be unaffected by the quake. Inside, however, it was a different story. The stadium was full of rubble and the pitch undulated dramatically. Much worse was the city centre. Jamie Hamilton, my old Tigers teammate who is now coaching with Canterbury, took me there to show me. The central area is still out of bounds due to the danger of unstable buildings, including the city's tallest structure, which now tilts at an obvious lean. The out-of-bounds section has decreased in size over the past few months but is still large and resembles a ghost town. Visiting Christchurch was an experience that placed a few things in perspective, and that included my injured state.

The next day, back in Dunedin, my prospects improved significantly when I underwent a full contacts drill and took quite a few of my frustrations out on Tweety, now fitness coach. After twenty minutes of smashing into the guy it was clear that at last, at long last, I was fit again. I returned to my hotel room, turned up the volume for Billy Vision and the Dancers 'Summer Cat' and danced around like a crazed drunk. Four days earlier I had been as low as I had ever been. Now I was euphoric. The emotions of being a rugby player can make you seem almost bipolar at times. That's how much it means to you.

I went down to the team room, surveyed the scene and felt good to be back as a player again. This is the one area in the hotel exclusive to the players, where the public and media cannot enter. There is normally a dartboard – Tins and Thommo were normally the best on the oche – a pool table and a table-tennis table. I beat Banners and Fodes in the two games I played and can proudly announce that I was unbeaten during the World Cup. Then there were laptops for players to study the opposition or review their own performances, plus PlayStations and Xboxes for the likes of Fodes and Floody to perfect their FIFA, as well as masses of food, drinks and supplements. Everyone could see I wore a huge grin on my face but still we had to be cautious.

At a push I could have played against Argentina, but with a long campaign ahead of us, there was no point in risking it. I warmed up with the team before the start of the game, though, and this was a strange experience. I was all fired up and ready to go, but instead had to return to the bench and watch the drama unfold. Some people had likened the magnificent Otago Stadium to a plastic, see-through bag stretched over an overturned shopping trolley, but to me the stadium is a work of art. Better still, its fixed roof and natural grass make it the perfect venue for rugby, unaffected by the elements.

The game went as I expected, although I did not think we would make it quite as hard for ourselves as we did. In the last ten years, England has not had a single easy game against the Pumas, and in most of them the difference has been a score or two. We were never going to win by a large margin against such a hardened, experienced bunch of players, and so it proved to be. As the game lurched towards the hour mark, I was growing increasingly concerned. Not only were we losing but, worse, we were failing to create any meaningful opportunities. Jonny was missing a few kicks as well, which hardly helped matters. I sat there marvelling at how he refused to let this unfamiliar setback affect any other aspect of his game, but also frustrated because I knew how much he would be beating himself up over missing even one kick. Luckily, we had the armoury to get over the line, which Lenny revealed when he emerged from the bench and added some immediate tempo to our game. On the front foot we can play fast, attacking rugby. On the back foot it's ugly rugby. Lenny's impudent try and Jonny's later penalty proved enough to win the day, 14–9, but it was clear much improvement was necessary. Afterwards the feeling in the changing room was one of melancholic relief. We knew we had to win this game if our designs to win the pool, let alone venture deep into the tournament, were to bear fruit, and to that extent it was job done, but none of the players were performing cartwheels.

The next morning we travelled to Queenstown, the extreme-sports capital of the world. We saw it as a good opportunity to get away for a few days, since we would be ensconced in Dunedin for quite some time to come. The apartments, each one for three, came complete with gas-powered log fires. My roomies were Mearsy and Fodes and after a wet training session we'd sit in front of the fire drinking tea and eating chocolate, invariably supplied by Fodes who, despite being the leanest and most ripped player in the whole squad, has a massive chocolate addiction. Hask somehow managed to obtain some all-weather jackets for the whole squad, while Shawsy pulled off a similar feat with gloves and scarves for everyone, but the most popular blagger turned out to be Tom Croft. Through a

Farewell Welford Road. In my last home appearance for Leicester, in May 2010, we beat Bath in a play-off semi to reach the Premiership final. Afterwards, Dylan and I salute the crowd.

My last few moments as a Leicester player – leaving the pitch having been substituted during our winning Premiership final against Saracens at Twickenham. May 2010.

It's all over. My Leicester career ends with another Premiership trophy. Geordan and I hold it aloft at headquarters.

Bath's new owner Bruce Craig (*left*) stands alongside Director of Rugby Sir Ian McGeechan. October 2010.

Olly Barkley kicks a penalty for Bath in our Heineken Cup win over Aironi at the Recreation Ground in January 2011.

Bloodied but unbowed – leaving the field after clashing heads with teammate Simon Taylor against Harlequins at the Twickenham Stoop, October 2010.

Danny Grewcock marks the end of a long and staggeringly successful career with a lap of honour after his last professional game for Bath at Newcastle. May 2011.

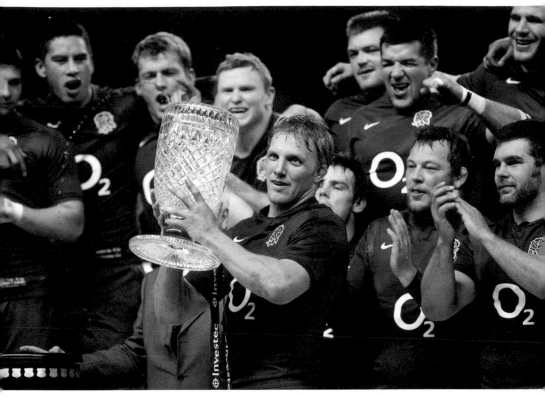

Lifting the Cook Cup after beating Australia at Twickenham with a display as good as any I can recall by England. November 2010.

My 2003 World Cup-winning teammate and Six Nations stand-in captain Mike Tindall and I sit out the defeat in Ireland that cost us the Grand Slam. We were both injured. March 2011.

Left: Dressed to thrill – Annie and I ready for a royal wedding, Mike Tindall and Zara Phillips's big day, Edinburgh, July 2011.

Below: The happy couple – Mike and Zara, having just tied the knot on a memorable day for them and for us all.

Above: The hard yards – running sessions at the team hotel in Bagshot, with Steve Thompson just in front.

Above right: Is my World Cup over? I fear the worst as I'm helped off at Twickenham against Wales with another knee injury. August 2011.

Below right: A star is born – Manu Tuilagi announced his Test match arrival with his first try against Wales, and followed up with his second against Ireland in Dublin on 27 August 2011.

Below: Stuck on the sideline – another rehab session and a heavily protected right knee.

Plain sailing: hard at work on an ex-America's Cup yacht racing England colleagues in Auckland Harbour. September 2011.

Standing on ceremony: with Martin Johnson at the World Cup welcoming ceremony in Dunedin's City Hall.

Georgia on my mind: taking a run at Tedo Zibzibadze and Merab Kvirikashvili in my first game against Georgia at the World Cup.

Ouch! Mike Tindall's knee introduces me to a world of pain as it says hello to my crown jewels against Romania.

Battle scars – a cut face and six stitches, but well worth it in beating Scotland.

Touchdown! Mark Cueto completes an 11-minute hat-trick against Romania.

Better late than never – Chris Ashton wins the game for England against Scotland with this late try at Eden Park.

The comeback begins? Ben Foden scores in the 56th minute of the quarter-final and we dream we can still beat France on 8 October 2011.

Preaching to the converted – Jonny Wilkinson converts Ben Foden's try to give us renewed hope against France.

End of an Era: I watch the quarter-final slip away in the dying minutes from the bench, together with old muckers Jonny Wilkinson (*right*) and Steve Thompson (*far left*) as well as the bearded Dan Cole.

contact, he sorted us out with a ton of chocolates and sweets, much to Fodes' delight and our conditioning staff's dismay. It didn't take long for the chocolate to disappear, only to resurface in the management's room.

During our first day some of us went canyon swinging, which, in my case, was a big mistake. For a man with a fear of heights this proved to be the most terrifying experience of my life. In my naïvety I thought it would be a gentle and completely safe swing. What I had not bargained for was an almost 130 foot, about 40 metre, drop down first, like a bungee jump, before the swinging even began. I decided the best way to do this was by sitting on a chair, but when it came to the moment of release I refused to let go of the bars. While my teammates, led notably by Cuets, found the sight of a jibbering captain hilarious, the man in charge took ten minutes to extricate my hands and send me plummeting. It did nothing to improve my fear of heights. The scary day, however, soon descended in another fashion altogether.

I had been growing concerned about the attitude in the camp, which became apparent pretty much from the moment we arrived in Auckland. We were on the other side of the world, a lot of the guys were young, well-known, wealthy and, as all young men believe, invincible. I remember thinking that some of the lads were not quite in the right mind-set.

I have to take some responsibility here. As captain, it was my watch, after all, and I don't think I helped matters by reintroducing a process that seemed to work well when we were in Australia in June the previous year. We had a series of awards each day, ranging from fact of the day, provided by Sos, and joke of the day, provided by Lenny, to pepper of the day (for the player deemed to have brown-nosed the coaches the most, or peppered them) and dick of the day. Fodes won that last award, for example, when we had our Auckland sailing day because he just sat there eating sweets all the time. Hask, somewhat predictably, also took the esteemed award after a joke he tried to make about Sheri went completely wrong. It was all designed to break any ice and inject some fun but instead it added to the feeling that everything was being taken a little too light-heartedly. After a week I canned the awards.

On the Sunday night in Queenstown the plan was to watch some sport and have a few beers in a bar that turned out to be staging something called a Mad Midget Weekend. For a while, everything was just fine and Mearsy, in particular, fit in nicely. We had a few beers, had photos taken with some punters and watched the TV. The owner looked after us very well and when the sport was over, I decided to make my way back to the hotel.

If I'm honest, the alarm bells had already been ringing, but this was a result of my experience in Puerto Banus and subsequent events. I was acutely aware from the moment I stepped on to New Zealand soil that, as England captain, I needed to be very careful in everything I did, and anywhere I went. We had spoken about this very area time and time again, both at the team hotel in Bagshot before the tournament and when we arrived, and I had reminded the squad of my distress following the false accusations levelled at me back in the early summer. Be sensible was the message. Don't turn anything into an issue. So that night in the Altitude Bar I was on my guard, and growing increasingly worried. Puerto Banus had really burned me. I didn't feel I could go out and have a good drink with anyone except close friends and family, which was a bit sad but a stark reality when you are the captain of an England team at a World Cup. When the drinks really began to flow and the people in the bar began to crowd us, that was my exit sign. I just smelled potential problems looming. Still, although I heard subsequently that some of the guys drank quite a lot, I had no issue with that, just as long as their antics didn't lead to trouble. Even in 2003 the guys enjoyed a drink or two, especially some of the senior players, and nobody's going to question them as rugby players, or their form or contribution in that tournament. As I would shortly discover, it would be a very different case with us.

The following day, some of the guys went bungee jumping on the notorious Nevis jump. As an alternative, Tins had organised a trip into the country to see someone he knew who ran a ranch. The journey involved narrow roads with 300 metre drops on either side, and then a boat trip along old gold-mining routes. We also spent some time with a local guy who lived in the most barren place imaginable, with no running water or electricity. He still mined for gold and sold possum pelts. It was a stunning day out, living the life of Grizzly Adams, but by the next morning our squad troubles had increased.

Before the proverbial hit the fan from Queenstown another problem reared its unwanted head. News came to us of some antics the previous week in Dunedin. The gist was that three of the England players had upset a female hotel employee by making what were seen as inappropriate comments when she went to their room to retrieve a walkie-talkie of hers. Johnno asked to see me to break the news and hear my views on the players – Hask, Ashy and Dylan Hartley. It was, to say the least, and after all the warnings meted out by me, Johnno and the management team, frustrating. It was also totally unacceptable behaviour, and in a squad meeting that Johnno called on the Tuesday, he made it absolutely clear to everyone how he felt. News of this was not made public for another fortnight but it caused unwanted worry for the 'Dunedin Three', as they were subsequently dubbed.

It is fair to say that the three felt humiliated at this meeting. They were completely gutted by what had happened. You could see it in their body language. For a couple of days afterwards their usual chirpy demeanour was notably absent. So now we had a difficult balancing act on our hands. On the one hand they had to know that their behaviour was out of order, but on the other we could not afford to have men down at a World Cup, so we also had to pick them up off the floor.

I am not going to defend what happened – it was indefensible. However much I am convinced that the lads did not mean to be rude, intimidating or offensive, they got it very wrong. Rugby players throughout the world will recognise the scenario – what we term changing room banter in a rugby team can get brutally close to the edge, but the public at large may find it hard to understand. To them, quite rightly, a lot of what we call banter is just plain rude or offensive. It is, in truth, not acceptable in the real world. As stupid as the Dunedin Three's actions were – I don't imagine for a moment it was meant to be personal or offensive, but it backfired big time because it involved a young woman on her own and a group of men.

On the Thursday, the next off-field issue came along. The English tabloids ran with photos of the guys in the Altitude Bar. They included Ashy mucking about with the midgets, and one of me posing, thankfully, with other players and a few fans. Sadly, they also ran photos of Tins getting drunk with a young woman, which could have been deemed incriminating if you did not know the story. This is a fact of life. This doesn't mean to say that Tins wasn't a bit naïve, and he knows it. The fact of being an England rugby player in a country where the spotlight is completely on us, the fact that he had just captained England against Argentina in my injured absence, and, for that matter, the fact that he had married a member of the British royal family just a few weeks earlier, all meant that there was no way he could get away with being the northern lad any more.

Whatever the rights and wrongs of it – and I've been a mate of Tins's for a long time, and more recently of his wife Zara, too – it was not my job to worry about the public's perception of the England squad. My priority had to be protecting the squad and maintaining our designs on winning the Rugby World Cup. Once again, I had to take some of the blame. I was captain, after all, and ultimately the buck stopped with Johnno and me. Of course I was frustrated. It wasn't ideal. It was another issue for Johnno to deal with rather than focus on rugby. Tins coped with the subsequent media flak incredibly well, but he was churning up inside because I imagine he felt he had let a lot of people down. I am no moral arbiter. I did know that Tins had done nothing more than get drunk with an old friend, and that he was a man down at a time when we needed his experience in the squad. I appreciate it made a story back in England, but to have it as one of the first few items on *News at Ten* in between stories of economic downturns, famines and train crashes, was just ridiculous. I hope Tins feels I supported him to the hilt that week and gave him my complete backing, and subsequently, as the story rumbled on.

Still, something had to be done. Having discussed it with Johnno, I called a players meeting. The management did not need to be present. This was a problem we had created and we needed to resolve it ourselves. We had to ensure that we were all singing from the same hymn sheet here. Footballers generally seem to bear the brunt of microscopic media attention, and as rugby players we had been somewhat cocooned, but in New Zealand we were undoubtedly a little too free-spirited and, as a result, got burned. At the meeting, we agreed on a course of action. From now on we'd have just a few beers, be very controlled and look out for each other so that no further trouble would arise. We understood that we had to be squeaky clean.

Another problem had hit us that week – Sheri was going home with an injured shoulder, his tournament over after less than a full game against Argentina. Sheri is a huge player for us in every sense and it was very sad to see him go after he had worked so hard to get to the World Cup following previous injury. Johnno called the whole squad in at the end of a training session to thank Sheri and bid him farewell. He's not really the hugging type, so I shook his hand and wished him well. His absence would be a big blow, not just because of his scrummaging, but also for his extensive knowledge of wine, among other things. There is a great deal more to Sheri than meets the eye, what with his love of fine wines – he is a trainee sommelier – his singing and guitar playing, and his admirable insistence on being his own man. If he didn't want to do something, he didn't do it, rather like Julian White, and I liked him for that. Hask tried to get him to wear a 'dick of the day' hat early on in the tour but Sheri flatly refused and that was that. People may think that wasn't being a team player but I rather took to Sheri's independent streak. He may be a quiet man but he is a character, and a squad must possess all kinds to make it work.

As if all this was not enough, Courtney Lawes received a two-match ban from the citing commissioner following a tackle made on Mario Ledesma during the Argentina game. The big lock's knees rammed against hooker Ledesma as he tried to score a try in the corner. To me it was nothing more than a desperate attempt to save a try but the citing commissioner saw things differently. It was a blow for a young man just back in the team after injury, but he took it surprisingly well. It was also bad for the team's continuity. The games affected were against Georgia and Romania, and at least we had plenty in reserve when it came to the second row.

The only positive thing that went right in the build-up to our second pool game, against Georgia, was that – and I'm taking a personal view here – I was back in the team and as captain, although this didn't stop Dan Cole accidentally gashing my hand in my first full training session. Then in the warm-up, twenty minutes before kick-off, I feared the worst after I twisted my right knee, the one that had caused all the trouble, in a ruck. It put me into an immediate quandary. Should I tell the physios, get hauled off and look like a dick? Or should I battle on and, in a worst case scenario, let the knee go in the game? The physios told me later that they saw me go down during the team run and nearly sprinted on to the pitch to see me, but thought better of it. As soon as the game began the focus set in and for the next fifty-odd minutes I never felt it again. The plan initially was for me to play for just a half, but every extra minute counted in my quest for game time under my belt. It was not, I admit, one of my better games, but this was understandable. I just needed to get it done and to prove that, even when you slightly twist your previously damaged knee in the warm-up, you can get through nearly an hour's Test rugby.

In truth, none of us were too clever that day. You may think a 41–10, six tries to one victory is hardly shabby, but we were poor in so many departments against a team we should have blown away, despite their physicality. Johnno said later that he would rather we had played in the way we wanted to and won by less. We just tried too hard and forced it, instead of keeping it simple and laying the foundations to score big points. I was pleased that Ashy scored twice because I knew his lack of tries since his amazing four against Italy in the Six Nations back in February was bugging him. I was pleased for Shape, too, who also bagged a brace, and for the increasingly impressive Manu, who scored his first World Cup try, but I was annoyed with myself for missing a tackle – an area I pride myself in – which led to Georgia's only try.

On the face of it, we had played two, won two, including a big Test against Argentina, but we were not playing anywhere near as well as we should have been, and that is why the team leaders – Jonny, Tins, Cuets, Thommo, Minty, Floody and me – called for a meeting with Johnno. We asked Johnno and the coaches to come down hard on us from now on, to make the squad meetings harsh and even embarrassing for any offenders. We had to be made accountable for our errors on the field. We also demanded a collective improvement in our standards, which meant everyone wearing the correct training kit and everyone turning up to meetings on time. I'd noticed that these important elements had slipped in the past few weeks and this could not be allowed to continue. Does it matter if someone's not wearing the same training kit, or is a minute late for a team meet? Absolutely. It's all part of the persona. A team that is immaculate in everything it does can portray an image of invincibility.

The following day's squad meeting was the best since we arrived in New Zealand, even if one of the players did turn up late. It would be the last time. Jonny, in particular, spoke well. He is by nature a quiet man, so when he speaks about how much these aspects mean, it always makes a bigger impact, especially with his track record. The day's training was, by some distance, the most clinical and professional of the tournament up to that point.

Much of Wednesday and Thursday were spent with the family. It was Ethan's first birthday and Paolo, the team chef, baked him a cake. Paolo is Italian, based in New Zealand. The England party had met him the previous summer in Napier when we lost narrowly to the New Zealand Maori in our final game of the June tour, by which stage I had returned home. Everyone was so taken with him that the management snapped him up to be our team chef for the World Cup. Annie and I took the boys swimming, drove up the steepest hill in the world in Dunedin, and had tea and cake in a café. On the Wednesday night, Dylan stayed with me in my room. It was awesome to see the boys again. We watched an animated movie called 'Rio' about a blue parrot and cuddled all night.

For all the apparent glamour of being an international rugby player, the absences from home and your loved ones are never easy to deal with. I'd not seen Annie or the boys for four weeks, which, especially in the lifespan of Ethan and even Dylan, is a considerable chunk of time. For the dads in the England squad, this is the toughest part, which is why you grab every opportunity you get to see them. Of course, when you are training or playing, your mind is totally focused on the job in hand, but back in your room at night, far, far away from home and alone with your thoughts, that's when you ache for a cuddle with your kids, and to be with your wife. Having Dylan there meant that it was not the soundest of night's sleep, but I would not have swapped it for the world, and although it was sad to see them off again on the Thursday evening, I felt a great deal happier for spending such priceless, quality time with the most precious people in my life.

All in all, life seemed to be getting a lot better, and this continued into our game against Romania. You can argue about the strength of the opposition, but to score ten unanswered tries and concede none was a decent effort, especially considering the nature of our play. We were all far happier with our performance, and we were certainly happy with the scoreline, 67–3. Cuets, playing again after his back troubles, bagged an 11 minute hat trick, Ashy also scored three tries and Fodes added another one. Any team that produces seven tries from its back three must be doing something right, and Lenny, Crofty and the rampaging Manu scored as well. I was happy with my own display, even though I played for just an hour. My knee felt strong and I was running around all day. However, one moment of drama was reminiscent of what Jason White did to me, or more precisely to my privates, at Twickenham a few years earlier.

Just before half-time Tins and I both jumped for a high ball. Tins used one leg for leverage but, in midair, somehow performed a scissor kick, which resulted in his knee smashing into my crown jewels. I went down as if a sniper had shot me from the Otago Stadium stands, and lay there writhing. Such mishaps are always hilarious, just as long as they do not happen to you. Thommo later insisted that it was purely karma for all the plum shots I had delivered over the years. The physios sprinted on to the pitch, believing my knee had gone again.

'What's up? What's the problem?' shouted Pasky.

'It's my bollocks,' I spluttered, through gritted teeth.

If you study video tape of these moments, you will see that Pasky then starts to laugh before radioing back his report.

'It's OK, guys. It's his bollocks.'

Even in those moments of sheer, excruciating pain, I could see the funny side of it, and would have laughed myself had I not still been in agony. Later, Dan Lewinden, another of our physios, downloaded a picture of the moment of impact as Tins's knee crashed into my groin, and it appeared as a screensaver on all the physios' laptops. That made me feel less guilty when, on the Sunday morning, I had to shave my pubic hairs and have Dan massage an area just a matter of millimetres above my crown jewels. There was, shall we say, substantial bruising!

Despite Tins's assault on my privates, I went out with him after the Romania game, together with Annie and Zara, who had travelled to New Zealand to spend some time with him, plus some other mates, including the people who ran the gold-mine ranch. Predictably, conversation included a fair degree of banter surrounding my battered bollocks.

That Sunday night, Scotland lost narrowly to Argentina, which meant that we still had some work to do to guarantee qualification for the knockout stages. As the Pool B table stood, a losing bonus point against the Scots, just as long as they did not grab a winning bonus point, would be enough for us to go through, although we set out, of course, to win the game. The Pumas would be playing Georgia and were expected to do enough to secure their own passage into the quarter-finals, so it would boil down to a shoot-out between us and our oldest and arguably biggest rivals.

The tension began to build early in the week. On the Wednesday morning we ended up having a particularly feisty training session. Tins and Floody had a few handbags after a disagreement and then I had a bit of a scuffle with Minty, which was made worse when Mearsy, in trying to hold me back, managed to pull my jersey over my head.

This got me even more irate. Minor incidents such as these, if kept in check, tend to be positive in the build-up to a big game, but there's no doubt we felt under pressure that week, and we only had ourselves to blame. We talked too much about the potential for the game to turn into an arm wrestle, something we didn't want to happen. By focusing on this, worrying about the opposition and not concentrating more on our own game, that's exactly what we turned it into.

The other problem was our collective tiredness. That Wednesday, after the feisty training in the morning and then a hard weights session in the afternoon, I felt exhausted enough for it to concern me. I wasn't the only one who was tired. As our subsequent display against the Scots proved, we were lethargic. It had happened in the build-up to the 2003 World Cup quarter-final against Wales, which we scraped through despite being exhausted by our extensive training.

Another controversial problem that blew our way this week concerned the balls that Jonny chose to convert some of our tries in the Romania game. Everyone knew that some kickers were having problems. In practice, Jonny was given eight numbered balls and each of them had their individual nuances. This is where the problem lay. Under the rules you are supposed to convert a try with the ball used to score it. But some of the balls were considered to be defective so instead Jonny used ones selected by kicking coach Dave Alred and our conditioning coach, Paul 'Bobby' Stridgeon. In the grander scheme of things, it really didn't matter too much, but the local media grabbed hold of it and tried to make out we were cheating. At worst, it was a bit naïve of us but in New Zealand it was seen as a heinous crime. The reaction was 2003 all over again, when we mistakenly threw on Dan Luger for 40 seconds at the end of our Samoa game and fielded sixteen players as a result. Back then, there were calls for our suspension from the tournament. This time it did not reach quite such ridiculous heights, but Dave and Bobby were banned not only from the match but from the stadium for the Scotland game, and instead watched the drama unfold from the team hotel. It was almost funny to see just how big a deal some people made it out to be, and I took it as a compliment that so many seemed intent on damaging England.

On the Friday night I wanted to go to the cinema to see 'Planet of the Apes' but Fodes had already seen it. He and I still went to the cinema but just to pick up some sweets and popcorn for the boys assembled in the physios' room to watch the American Football flick 'We are Marshall'. The next day, match day, went slowly, as they always do when we have night-time fixtures – breakfast, a team walk-through at a local rugby club, a long sleep in the afternoon and then off to Eden Park, the country's biggest and most famous rugby stadium where the World Cup final would be staged.

At once you could sense the occasion. The atmosphere was electric, and after three games under the Otago Stadium roof, we were facing the elements. I knew the Scots would be pumped up to their eyeballs, referring to every historical injustice suffered at the hands of the English, and triumph over us, as they invariably do. After 80 minutes one of us would be on our way back to Britain. We were keen to make a good start but it did not pan out that way. Scotland took an early quick tap and immediately went on the front foot, a situation that continued for the first half. Chris Paterson penalties and a drop goal from Dan Parks made it Scotland 9 to England's 3 thanks to a penalty from Jonny. Unfortunately, he had also missed a few again and I have to take some of the blame for this. The thing about Jonny is that he backs himself to succeed with every kick, and when a man of Jonny's stature says he can make it, you tend to throw him the ball, especially when you're keen to see the scoreboard ticking over. In hindsight, I should have told him on at least one occasion in the first half, and again in the second half, to kick for the corner to place the Scots under pressure. I should have taken the decision out of his hands and I failed to do so.

At half-time we were far from out of it – after all, we were only six points down – but our scrum had come off second best, we had been defending for most of the 40 minutes, we were not playing well and Jonny was missing most of his kicks. Johnno, voice raised, spelled out that a repeat performance in the second half would result in us going home prematurely. After that, he proceeded to make a series of tactical points, equally forcefully, while Wellsy did the same with the forwards.

During all this I was having three stitches inserted around my troublesome left eye after an incident that left me believing, for a split second, that my World Cup was over and, even worse, my eyesight was in danger. Fifteen minutes had passed in the first half when, in the midst of rolling away from a tackle, I was accidentally stamped on by Joe Ansbro's wandering boot. Initial impressions suggested his stud had gone straight into my eyeball, and I had visions of my eye hanging out. But as the seconds passed the pain subsided and, to my great relief, I realised I could still see out of it. The stud had caught me across my eyelid and to the side of the eye. The three half-time stitches failed to do the job, though. The wound opened up again in the second half and I was forced to leave the field to have three more stitches inserted and to replace my blood-soaked jersey.

In my absence, another Paterson penalty made the score 12–3, and with a nine-point lead Scotland were, at this moment, in the quarter-finals and we were out. This worrying situation continued for just two minutes, which was the time it took for us to win the re-start and set up a drop goal for Jonny. I returned to the fray sporting a numberless jersey and for the rest of the half we exerted our authority. After a torrid first half, the pack began to take charge. Jonny popped over a penalty and at just three points down, we had one, albeit unsatisfactory, foot in the quarter-finals.

This all changed in the 76th minute. By now Jonny, nursing an injured elbow, had left the field and Floody, who was already on for

Tins, had assumed the kicking duties. We were awarded a penalty from a difficult angle and from a distance. Even though a successful penalty would have drawn the scores level, both Floody and I agreed that he should kick for the corner. Given a choice this is nearly always the option Floody prefers in any case. It is not that he lacks any confidence as a kicker but he always prefers to attack. It proved to be the correct decision. From the lineout and the resulting ruck, Floody spun a long, looping pass that missed out two players and landed in the hands of a grateful Ashy. He still had a bit of a work to do but the man's a natural finisher and his try in the corner gave us the lead for the first time in the match. At this stage we were two points ahead but Floody's conversion, from the right touchline, increased the lead to four, which meant a Scottish penalty or drop goal in the dying seconds would not be enough. As it was, the score, 16–12, remained the same for the final couple of minutes and, once again, we had found a way to win a game of Test match rugby.

The mix of emotions afterwards was strange. While we stood around on the pitch waiting to receive our participation medals from the IRB, something all the teams were given at the end of the pool stages, Floody was keen to talk to me about getting the players together to thrash out why we were falling short of the standards of play we knew we were capable of producing. He was frustrated, and understandably so, having watched much of the action from the bench. Johnno wore a wry smile. He told us we'd forced him to age forty years. We had won, we had done the job, but we were making life very difficult for ourselves. The one, huge positive to come out of it all was that, despite everything, we were still winning World Cup games.

The night after a Test match is always difficult for me, but this night was incredibly hard. After less than two hours' sleep, I headed for the team room where the IT guys, who were up all night, were preparing footage on all the players for the postmortem. I watched the whole game, growing more and more frustrated with both the team's performance and my own. I had been, by the high standards I set for myself, very average, and that was not good enough.

We had just qualified for the World Cup quarter-finals having won all four of our pool games, we had beaten two very good sides in Argentina and Scotland along the way, and showed tremendous character in refusing to accept defeat in either game, but if we were serious about winning the World Cup, or at least staying in New Zealand for another two weeks, then we had to start playing in the way we knew we could.

Next up was France, a written-off France who had just lost to Tonga, but in the crazy, unpredictable manner of French rugby, that made them even more dangerous opponents. Knockout rugby was upon us and as dawn broke over Auckland while I pored over the Scotland video, I was determined that our adventure would not end that week.

19

THE END

I needed two days to recover from the Scotland game. Most of my left arm was purple after a massive haematoma in my bicep spread. I had a torn ligament in a finger, six stitches in my face and a tight hamstring. I felt like the oldest 33 year old in the world. As a rule, flankers are battered more than most because our world is the world of the breakdown, and this means you place your head and body where the ball tends to be. More often than not this ends up with a beating.

The Scotland game was obviously tough but what people may not quite grasp is just how physical the game has become, no matter who the opposition may be. Back in 2003, we destroyed Uruguay in a World Cup pool game and, in all honesty, it was a case of men against boys. Now no game is easy, at least physically. In this sense, the game has changed beyond recognition, even in the past eight years. You may still get to score tries for fun against some of the minnows, but you know all about it the next morning when you try to prise yourself out of your bed.

Dylan (that's my son, not Hartley) stayed with me on the Saturday night. On the Sunday the Moodys went up the Auckland Sky Tower, which, of course, was unbelievable fun for Dylan, and unbelievably uncomfortable for his vertigo-stricken dad, especially when we looked down through the glass floor to the streets hundreds and hundreds of feet below. While I stood frozen to the spot, clutching on to Ethan in my arms, Dylan leant against the glass walls. A zipwire clung taut to the tower, ready for anyone who wanted to accept the challenge of a cable-controlled jump.

'Can I go on it, Daddy, can I go on it?'

Inside my head a voice shouted, 'Hell, no!' I smiled weakly. 'Some other time.'

The following evening, Thommo, Corbs (Alex Corbisiero), Courtney and I went to see the New Zealand versus England netball international, even though I still felt pretty exhausted. I'm not sure Courtney was too bothered about it, but Corbs dragged him along. The Kiwis – or Silver Ferns – won fairly comfortably, but it was good to be supporting another English national sports team, and we quickly said our hellos and our bad lucks afterwards. There are, believe it or not, similarities between netball and rugby in terms of speed, spatial awareness and communication. In my early days at Leicester, a netball coach used to come along to help us improve our coordination. You can just imagine the comedic sight of the coach attempting to explain it to Darren Garforth.

Although the team to face France in the quarter-final was not made public until Thursday, we knew who was in two days earlier. An immediate change was Cuets for Delon, who had been cited for a high tackle on Scotland's Chris Paterson and, after a hearing, banned for one match. He was obviously a bit down about the decision. Having been recalled in place of Cuets for the Scotland game, he had now lost the jersey again. He did not know it at the time – none of us knew it – but Delon's World Cup was over.

The other changes were Toby Flood in for Tins at inside centre, Minty in for Hask at number eight and Tom Palmer in for Courtney who, with Hask, would be on the bench. It was tough on Hask. Arguably, he had been our best forward up to that point, and had dealt with the self-created media attention well. The two-match ban on Courtney after the Argentina game had perhaps slightly blunted his sword against Scotland, hence TP's recall, but the main talking point was the selection of two stand offs at ten and twelve.

I don't know what team Johnno may have selected had Tins been fit, but a dead leg suffered against the Scots meant that he was unable to train until Thursday and Johnno felt this was too late for a game of such magnitude forty-eight hours later. Besides, according to one school of thought, Jonny worked best when he had a good communicator beside him, as was the case when he played along-side Shaggy or Catty. Floody was another good communicator and this was important because the team had been very quiet during the Scotland game.

That night some of the lads took a trip to Spookers – a haunted house filled with men covered in blood, holding axes and cleav-ers, whose sole role was to scare the shit out of those who got their thrills from jumping out of their own skins. I took a rain check on this, since I was still easing my battered body back into shape for the quarter-final, but the stories told by the ashen-faced players when they returned provided plenty of fodder. Delon, for example, saw himself as a bit of a 'gangsta', a boy from the hood, but appar-ently he spent much of his evening running around, screaming like a girl. Ashy was another whose high-pitched squeals filled the night air. Crofty and Dylan hid round a corner, waited for Courtney and then tackled him to the ground, before removing his shoes. This prompted Courtney to leg it back out of the entrance, much to the consternation of those still waiting to go in. If a man the size of Courtney was sprinting for safety, what chance did everyone else have? Courtney was very concerned about going back inside to retrieve his shoes – after all, it was pitch black and there were idiots running around with chain saws.

On the Wednesday, some of us spent the afternoon in the Auckland suburb of Ponsonby, at a house that had been rented by my agents at Big Red Management. Pressure was mounting as the week wore on, and it was good to escape the tension. Fodes, Cuets, Tom Wood and Richard Wigglesworth came along and we spent the afternoon lounging around, drinking Coke (I don't feel I can ever have another beer in my life after all the negative press at the World Cup) and playing what became a highly competitive game of French cricket. It was the most I'd laughed in weeks and weeks, but soon it would be French rugby we'd need to be focusing on.

After speaking with Johnno, we decided to ease back a little in training. We had undoubtedly put in a tired performance against the Scots and we didn't want to repeat this in the quarter-final. I was still concerned, though, as the week went on. Training was OK, nothing more. In truth, the only time I felt we really clicked on the training field was the week of the Romania game, which ended with our best display, and, in all honesty, Romania were the team we least needed to perform against. It just wasn't quite happening for us in training and it was, to say the least, frustrating.

Despite this, I felt confident we had enough in our locker to beat the French. I really did. Of course I knew how dangerous France could be. Of course I knew that they, like us in 2007, were particularly dangerous now because they were wounded animals. And, of course, I knew how motivated they would be after losing to us in the 2007 and 2003 World Cup semis, as well as at Twickenham in the previous Six Nations. But I still believed we had much more to come ourselves, and a clear, Six Nations route to the final had opened up – the winners of our quarter-final would play the winners of the Wales versus Ireland quarter-final in Auckland. Before that, though, we still had a job to do against Les Bleus.

The next couple of days went pretty quickly. A team meal out on the Thursday, a trip to the cinema on Friday with Thommo and Sos to watch the Hugh Jackman film 'Real Steel' and suddenly it was game day. At no time did I feel any sense of what was about to hit us.

I was called into a separate room at Eden Park, close to our dressing rooms, to toss the coin alongside the French captain, Thierry Dusautoir. We exchanged nods and handshakes, maybe a quick hello, but obviously this wasn't a time for too many niceties. He won the toss but decided to choose ends, leaving us to kick off, which is how I wanted it in any case.

Back in the dressing room the mood seemed right. There was anger in the England players. More than ever before I believed this would be our night. Calvin Morris, our fitness coach, stood at the dressing-room door and gave us the countdown. Three minutes to go, then two, then one. In the final seconds we huddled in the dressing room before walking purposefully out into the tunnel to be met by our French counterparts. Sometimes in the tunnel I shouted final comments to the team, designed more to prey on the opposition psyche than to gee up our guys, but on this occasion I felt everything had been said. Sometimes a glance across at the opposition conveys a message. Again, this time I looked behind at my team, and then straight ahead. I liked what I saw, too, in the faces of my players. One or two had a faint smile etched in their expressions. Ben Youngs had a tear rolling down his cheek.

Afterwards, someone told me that a rather large, mainly naked Maori warrior with a staff welcomed our entrance on to the Eden Park by blowing a conch. I can honestly say I never saw him in any of our World Cup games, such was the level of concentration. A slow walk, then a short sprint on to the field and a couple of kick jumps and I was ready for a final huddle to remind the boys we wanted to hit the ground running and, after a couple of rousing national anthems, that's exactly what we did.

I could not have been more pleased with our start. From the very first whistle we attacked and appeared dangerous, and my positive feeling about this game grew. Then, not for the first time, we conceded two stupid penalties and before we knew it we were six points down. Moreover, mistakes began to creep in to our play. In an eight-minute spell, before the half-hour mark, France scored two tries, which suddenly made a difficult task monumental. First, Clerc wriggled his way past four tackles to score in the corner. Then Palisson was tackled in the corner by Fodes but so keen were Ashy and Manu to cover that they all followed the winger, allowing Palisson to flip the ball inside for an unmarked Médard to touch down. It was lucky that Parra missed with both conversions, otherwise we would have found ourselves 20–0 down.

This was a nightmare. We had handed France all 16 points due to conceding silly penalties and then gifting them two simple tries. For two years we had prided ourselves on our defence and now, when we needed it most, we had let ourselves down.

There was an opportunity, though, to make amends in the dying seconds of the half, but Jonny stumbled and sent his pass too high for Ashy to gather well enough, when a clear, try-scoring chance in the corner was on for a finisher of Ashy's quality. If we had scored then, it would have changed the whole momentum of the match. The fact that we failed to do so did not diminish my belief that we could, and probably would, still go on to win the game.

In the half-time dressing room there was no major panic. One or two voices were raised in getting over points but we all knew, especially with what we believed to be a brittle French temperament, that a try by us early on could change everything. Every time I looked at the French they seemed shattered. All we needed was the composure that we lacked in the first half.

Without any question we played much, much better after the break. It took longer than I'd hoped but when Fodes nipped over to score a try in the 56th minute, converted by Jonny, we were nine points down with 24 minutes remaining. One more score, of any type, and we would have been into the French, but the clock ticked on and no score came our way. Desperate to make something happen, the management decided to make changes. Courtney replaced Crofty in the back row, which, I have to admit, surprised me. Matt Banahan came on, Floody moved to stand off and Jonny went off after what could have been his final appearance in an England jersey. Dylan replaced Thommo and, somewhat to my surprise, I was hauled off. I never think it's the best idea to replace your captain unless he is injured, especially as it was my view that I was carrying the belief of the team at that point, but the decision was made and I had to adhere to it.

I sat on the bench alongside Thommo and Wilko, three players who had grown up together and experienced so many of the highs and lows that rugby, especially international rugby, offers. It occurred to me, for a fleeting moment, that this might be the last time any of us played for England, and when Trinh-Duc popped over a drop goal to stretch the French lead to 19–7 with just seven minutes remaining, I knew our glorious opportunity had been extinguished.

Cuets made it interesting in the 77th minute when he managed to score a try, which, ironically, was awarded after long deliberations from the TV match official. I say ironically because it was the TMO, of course, who denied Cuets his try in the 2007 World Cup final, a decision that eats away at my friend to this day. Floody missed the conversion but we were suddenly seven points behind with over two minutes still to go, enough for Thommo to mutter from the bench that if we scored a converted try to make the game level, we would definitely go on to win, probably in extra time. It was a hopeful point made by a passionate man desperate not to see us go out of the World Cup, but I knew, deep down, it was over for us. For some reason, despite our confidence, it was just not supposed to happen.

The dressing room resembled a funeral parlour. I felt no emotion. I was completely numb. A clearly devastated Johnno told us all how proud he was of our second-half performance, which we had won 12–3. I made a small speech aimed mainly at the younger players.

My chance had now gone, as it had for quite a few of the older guard, but they had plenty to look forward to. I told them to remember this feeling and just how much it hurt, and to make sure it never happened again. The silence was almost deafening. I made a point of shaking every member of the squad by the hand. As they glanced up at me several had tears rolling down their cheeks.

Most of all I felt for Johnno. This is a man I idolised, and still do. He did not deserve this, nor the resulting flak he would receive. He was pretty worn out, as we all were, by the emotions of the past few weeks, much of which he spent having to deal with crap off the field, not on it. Clearly, at least some of this was down to his own players. No wonder it prompted him, even in his hour of pain, to remind the boys that before leaving New Zealand we should all be on our best behaviour. Unfortunately, not everyone took heed. Within twenty-four hours Manu had been hauled out of the Auckland harbour waters, having jumped off a ferry. This resulted in him being detained by Auckland police, a pre-charge warning and photos of him standing dripping wet in his underwear, explaining himself to officials. He's a good kid, and has the potential to be a superstar in rugby, but he didn't do himself, or Johnno, any favours then.

My night could not get worse after losing to France, or at least that's what I thought, but the guy who threatened to go to the tabloid newspapers back in May with false accusations about my behaviour in Spain did just that. On Sunday, the *Star* ran an appalling article without giving me any right of reply. After sixteen years of professional rugby, in the dying embers of my international career, a complete fabrication was published, hours after one of the biggest playing lows of my life. I wanted to spend the night in the bosom of my family and friends. Instead, I spent half of it with RFU lawyers and communications people.

You can gloss over it as much as you want but to be an international sportsman means you need to be honest. There had been so much good in my career up to this point, but the 2011 World Cup campaign had been a disaster. What made it even more disappointing was that I knew just how much work had been put into preparing for the tournament, the many weeks in Bagshot and in New Zealand training, the time spent away from home to ensure that no stone had been left unturned. I believed, genuinely, that we were ready to perform to our optimum. To fall so far short of what we are capable of was devastating.

To be knocked out of the tournament in itself was a unique experience for me, having played in the previous two finals. I knew it was possible for us to win. This may seem ambitious when you look back on how we performed, both on and off the pitch, but look again. A team that won the Six Nations, and subsequently beat Ireland in Dublin, were required, in the knockout stages, to beat a France team that had not fired in the tournament so far, and then a very good Welsh team in the semi. A wonderful opportunity to reach the final was there for us, no question, and against a New Zealand team nervous about their record in failing at the World Cup anything was possible. If we had played anywhere near our potential, it might, just might, have happened, but 'if' is a very big word for one spelled with just two letters.

Of course, for many, England's World Cup will be remembered for the off-field incidents. I have had my say on this already. I maintain that they were blown up and taken out of context but, at the same time, I concede that some of the behaviour was at best naïve and at worst totally unacceptable. If I could change one thing about the Rugby World Cup 2011, knowing some of the characters we had in that England squad, it would be to have banned them from going out at all, and so taken any decision out of their hands. It is impossible to say how little or how much of an impact the off-field stories had on our performances, but clearly they didn't help.

I had thought about what would happen at the end of the World Cup before the tournament had even begun. In the back of my mind, win or lose, I thought there was a good chance I would call it a day, at least in Test rugby, and do it on my terms. I sat down with Annie in the hotel coffee shop on the Sunday morning and raised the subject. I'd been off on tours for eleven years with England, way too much for her liking, and now I had two small boys to consider as well.

Moreover, England needed to move on. If they were going to rebuild elements of a young team for a proper crack at the 2015 Rugby World Cup, they needed to appoint a new captain, preferably to be in charge for the four-year period running up to the next tournament. I would be long gone by then. Besides, would I possess the same passion, commitment and desire? The prospect of not doing so scared me. Part of me still felt young and fresh. Even though I'd been playing for England for so long, I felt, at least mentally, that I could play for another eleven years. My body, however, begged to differ, and the way it felt left no room for negotiation.

Then there was Bath. I'd joined them the previous summer and had barely played any games for them due to injury and England commitments. One of my major bugbears at Leicester was how many games I missed for my club for the same reasons. I didn't want the same to happen at Bath. Instead, I fancied a really enjoyable two years in which I committed myself to club rugby, on and off the field, helping Bath to win silverware and playing my part in the development of their younger players, and all within a few miles of my home where I could spend more time with my beautiful family.

I told Annie my thoughts. She had always let these decisions be mine, but it was clear these were words she wanted to hear. That clinched it. For all the arguments, it was still a big decision to end your time playing for your country, the ultimate honour for any sportsman, but I knew it was the right decision to make at the right time. In the hotel lobby I bumped into Phil Pask who asked me if

I wanted him to keep hold of my contact lenses until next time, or return them. I asked for them back.

Although many of the squad would be returning home on the Monday night, some left twenty-four hours earlier and I made a point of shaking their hands and saying goodbye. To most of them it was a case of see you before the Six Nations. For me, even though they did not know this, it really was goodbye.

We were due to spend the following week with Annie's family in Nelson, on the northern tip of South Island, before flying back to Britain, where I would return to the blue and white colours of Bath. Away from virtually everything, it would be the perfect time to reflect and gain some perspective on life. But I had already made up my mind. My England career was over. It was not the way I wanted it to end, but it would be arrogant to try to dictate sport, the greatest leveller life can produce.

As I sat in the hotel, however, and watched the England boys depart, I began to look at the eleven years, and beyond, and not just the past seven weeks. I had played alongside some of the greatest players the sport of rugby has ever witnessed. I had won a World Cup and received an MBE for my efforts. I had played in two World Cup finals, and three World Cup tournaments. I had won 71 caps, two Heineken Cups, seven Premiership titles and many other winner's medals and trinkets.

The problem about being a professional sportsman, and especially a rugby player, is that you have so little time ever to reflect. The next game, or the next training session, is always at the forefront. Strange as it may seem, I had never really considered my career before, at least not the full picture. As I sat in that Auckland hotel, I realised that most of my dreams had come true.

Would I like to have done a Johnno and ended my England career by lifting the World Cup? My God, yes. Would that scrawny kid being battered by Leon Lloyd on the Oval Park training field the first time he turned up as a Tiger cub, or receiving that dead leg from a teenaged Jonny Wilkinson, or receiving a bollocking from Dean Richards while wearing a curry stained T-shirt, have taken the career that panned out for him with both hands? Hell yes!

Maybe the perfect ending did not quite happen for me as a Test match rugby player, but I'll tell you what. To captain your country at a World Cup and to end it all at Eden Park, the home of the New Zealand All Blacks, takes a lot of beating.

I'll settle for that.

CAREER STATISTICS

Lewis Moody's Test Career
for the British/Irish Lions

- **Moody, L W** (*Leicester and England*) 2005 Arg, NZ 2,3
- Three Tests, one draw and two defeats. One try (5 points).

TEST 1: DRAWN 25–25 v ARGENTINA, 23rd May 2005, Millennium Stadium, Cardiff

British/Irish Lions: G E A Murphy; D A Hickie, O J Smith (rep S P Horgan), G W D'Arcy, S M Williams; J P Wilkinson, G J Cooper (rep C P Cusiter); G C Rowntree, J S Byrne (rep S G Thompson), J J Hayes (rep J M White), D P O'Callaghan, D J Grewcock (rep B J Kay), M E Corry, M J Owen (*captain*), L W Moody

Lions Scorers *Try:* Smith　*Conversion:* Wilkinson　*Penalty Goals:* Wilkinson (6)

TEST 2: LOST 18-48 v NEW ZEALAND, 2nd July 2005, Westpac Stadium, Wellington

British/Irish Lions: O J Lewsey; J T Robinson, G Thomas (*captain*), G L Henson (rep S P Horgan), S M Williams; J P Wilkinson (rep S M Jones), D J Peel; G D Jenkins (rep G C Rowntree), S G Thompson (rep J S Byrne), J M White (temp rep G C Rowntree), D P O'Callaghan (rep M E Corry), P J O'Connell, S H Easterby, R P Jones, L W Moody

Lions Scorers *Tries:* Thomas, Easterby *Conversion:* Wilkinson *Penalty Goals:* Wilkinson (2)

TEST 3: LOST 19-38 v NEW ZEALAND, 9th July 2005, Eden Park, Auckland

British/Irish Lions: G E A Murphy (rep R J R O'Gara), M J Cueto, W J H Greenwood, G Thomas (*captain*) (rep S P Horgan), O J Lewsey; S M Jones, D J Peel (rep M J S Dawson); G D Jenkins (rep G C Rowntree),J S Byrne (rep G C Bulloch), J M White, D P O'Callaghan, P J O'Connell, S H Easterby, R P Jones (rep M E Corry), L W Moody (rep M E Williams)

Lions Scorers *Try:* Moody *Conversion:* S M Jones *Penalty Goals:* S M Jones (4)

Lewis Moody's Cap Career
for England

- **Moody, L W** (*Leicester, Bath*) 2001 C 1,2, US, I (R), R, SA (R), 2002 I (R), W, It, Arg, NZ, A, SA, 2003 F 1, W 2, F 2, 3(R), [Gg(R), SA, Sm(R), U, W, F(R), A(R) at RWC], 2004 C, SA, A2, 2005 F, I, It, S, A, NZ, Sm, 2006 W, It, S, F, I, A1, NZ, Arg, SA1(R),2(R),W2(R), 2007 [US(R), SA1(R),Sm(R),Tg,A,F,SA2 at RWC], 2008 W, 2009 A,Arg 3,NZ, 2010 W,It,I,S(R),F,A1,2,NZ1, A3,SA, 2011 W2 [Gg, Rom, S, F at RWC]
- 71 Tests winning 46, drawing one and losing 24. Only Lawrence Dallaglio and Joe Worsley have played more Tests in the England back-row.
- Fifty-six starts for England and 15 appearances as an impact substitute off the bench.
- Scored forty-five points for England comprising nine tries.
- Two RWC Final appearances: 2003 (winner) and 2007 (runner-up)
- Played for England's 2003 Six Nations Grand Slam Championship winning team.
- Succeeded Steve Borthwick as England captain in 2010. In eleven Tests as skipper he has led England to six wins and five defeats.

CAP 1: WON 22-10 v CANADA, 2nd June 2001, Fletcher's Field, Markham, Toronto

England: O J Lewsey; P C Sampson, L D Lloyd, J D Noon, M Stephenson (rep T R G Stimpson); D J H Walder, K P P Bracken (*captain*); G C Rowntree, D E West, J M White, S W Borthwick (rep S D Shaw), B J Kay, M E Corry, J P R Worsley (rep P H Sanderson), L W Moody

England Scorers *Tries:* Lewsey (2), West, Bracken *Conversion:* Walder

CAP 2: WON 59-20 v CANADA, 9th June 2001, Swangard Stadium, Burnaby, Vancouver

England: O J Lewsey; P C Sampson (rep T R G Stimpson), L D Lloyd, J D Noon (rep A D King), M Stephenson; D J H Walder, K P P Bracken (*captain*) (rep M B Wood); G C Rowntree (rep D L Flatman), D E West (rep M P Regan), J M White, S D Shaw, B J Kay (rep S W Borthwick), W R S White-Cooper (temp rep D L Flatman), J P R Worsley (rep P H Sanderson), L W Moody

England Scorers *Tries:* Shaw (2), Walder (2), penalty try, Worsley, Wood, Noon *Conversions:* Walder (5) *Penalty Goals:* Walder (3)

CAP 3: WON 48-19 v UNITED STATES, 16th June 2001, Balboa Park, San Francisco

England: O J Lewsey; L D Lloyd, F H H Waters, J D Noon (rep O J Barkley), M Stephenson; D J H Walder (rep T M D Voyce), K P P Bracken (*captain*) (rep M B Wood); G C Rowntree (rep D L Flatman), D E West (rep A E Long), J M White, S D Shaw, S W Borthwick (rep T P Palmer), W R S White-Cooper (temp rep D L Flatman), J P R Worsley (rep P H Sanderson), L W Moody (temp rep P H Sanderson)

England Scorers *Tries:* Lewsey (2), Lloyd (2), West, Sanderson, Worsley, Moody *Conversions:* Walder (4)

CAP 4: LOST 14-20 v IRELAND, 20th October 2001, Lansdowne Road, Dublin
England: I R Balshaw; D D Luger (rep A S Healey), W J H Greenwood, M J Catt, J T Robinson; J P Wilkinson, M J S Dawson (*captain*) (rep K P P Bracken); J Leonard, P B T Greening (rep D E West), J M White (rep G C Rowntree), S D Shaw, D J Grewcock, M E Corry (rep L W Moody), R A Hill, N A Back
England Scorers *Try:* Healey   *Penalty Goals:* Wilkinson (3)

CAP 5: WON 134-0 v ROMANIA, 17th November 2001, Twickenham
England: J T Robinson; B C Cohen, W J H Greenwood (rep M J Catt), M J Tindall, D D Luger; C C Hodgson, A S Healey (rep K P P Bracken); G C Rowntree (rep J M White), M P Regan, J Leonard, B J Kay (rep D J Grewcock), S W Borthwick, L W Moody, J P R Worsley, N A Back (*captain*) (rep A Sanderson)
England scorers *Tries:* Robinson (4), Cohen (3), Luger (3), Hodgson (2), Moody (2), Tindall (2), Healey, Sanderson, Regan, Worsley *Conversions:* Hodgson (14)   *Penalty Goals:* Hodgson (2)

CAP 6: WON 29-9 v SOUTH AFRICA, 24th November 2001, Twickenham
England: J T Robinson; A S Healey, W J H Greenwood, M J Catt (rep M J Tindall), D D Luger; J P Wilkinson, K P P Bracken; G C Rowntree, D E West, P J Vickery, M O Johnson (*captain*) (rep B J Kay), D J Grewcock, R A Hill (rep L W Moody), J P R Worsley, N A Back
England scorers *Try:* Luger *Penalty Goals:* Wilkinson (7) *Dropped Goal:* Catt

CAP 7: WON 45-11 v IRELAND, 16th February 2002, Twickenham
England: J T Robinson; A S Healey (rep I R Balshaw), W J H Greenwood, M J Tindall, B C Cohen; J P Wilkinson (rep C C

Hodgson), K P P Bracken (rep N S Duncombe); G C Rowntree (rep J Leonard), S G Thompson, P J Vickery, M O Johnson (*captain*) (rep D J Grewcock), B J Kay, R A Hill (rep L W Moody), J P R Worsley, N A Back **England Scorers** *Tries:* Greenwood (2), Wilkinson, Cohen, Worsley, Kay *Conversions:* Wilkinson (6) *Penalty Goal:* Wilkinson

CAP 8: WON 50-10 v WALES, 23rd March 2002, Twickenham

England: A S Healey; D D Luger, W J H Greenwood, M J Tindall (rep T R G Stimpson), B C Cohen; J P Wilkinson, K P P Bracken (rep M J S Dawson); G C Rowntree, S G Thompson (rep D E West), J M White, D J Grewcock, B J Kay (temp rep J P R Worlsey), L W Moody (temp rep M E Corry), R A Hill (rep J P R Worsley), N A Back (*captain*) **England Scorers** *Tries:* Luger (2), Greenwood, Wilkinson, Stimpson *Conversions:* Wilkinson (5) *Penalty Goals:* Wilkinson (4) *Dropped Goal:* Wilkinson

CAP 9: WON 45-9 v ITALY, 7th April 2002, Stadio Flaminio, Rome

England: J T Robinson; D D Luger, W J H Greenwood, M J Tindall (rep C C Hodgson), B C Cohen (rep A S Healey); J P Wilkinson, K P P Bracken (rep M J S Dawson); G C Rowntree (rep J Leonard), S G Thompson (rep D E West), J M White, D J Grewcock (rep M O Johnson), B J Kay, L W Moody, R A Hill, N A Back (*captain*) (rep L B N Dallaglio) **England Scorers** *Tries:* Greenwood (2), Cohen, Robinson, Dallaglio, Healey *Conversions:* Wilkinson (5), Dawson *Penalty Goal:* Wilkinson

CAP 10: WON 26-18 v ARGENTINA, 22nd June 2002, Vélez Sarsfield Stadium, Buenos Aires

England: M J Horak; T R G Stimpson, G N Appleford, J B Johnston, P D Christophers; C C Hodgson, A C T Gomarsall; D L Flatman, S G Thompson, P J Vickery (*captain*), A J Codling, B J Kay, A Sanderson, J P R Worsley, L W Moody

Scorers *Tries:* Kay, Christophers *Conversions:* Hodgson (2) *Penalty Goals:* Hodgson (3), Stimpson

CAP 11: WON 31-28 v NEW ZEALAND, 9th November 2002, Twickenham

England: J T Robinson; J D Simpson-Daniel (rep A S Healey), W J H Greenwood (rep J B Johnston), M J Tindall, B C Cohen; J P Wilkinson, M J S Dawson; T J Woodman, S G Thompson, P J Vickery, M O Johnson (*captain*), D J Grewcock (rep B J Kay), L W Moody, L B N Dallaglio (rep N A Back), R A Hill (temp rep N A Back)
England Scorers *Tries:* Moody, Wilkinson, Cohen *Conversions:* Wilkinson (2) *Penalty Goals:* Wilkinson (3) *Dropped Goal:* Wilkinson

CAP 12: WON 32-31 v AUSTRALIA, 16th November 2002, Twickenham

England: J T Robinson; J D Simpson-Daniel, W J H Greenwood, M J Tindall (rep A S Healey), B C Cohen; J P Wilkinson, M J S Dawson; J Leonard, S G Thompson, P J Vickery, M O Johnson (*captain*), B J Kay, L W Moody, R A Hill (rep L B N Dallaglio), N A Back
England Scorers *Tries:* Cohen (2) *Conversions:* Wilkinson (2) *Penalty Goals:* Wilkinson (6)

CAP 13: WON 53-3 v SOUTH AFRICA, 23rd November 2002, Twickenham

England: J T Robinson; B C Cohen, W J H Greenwood (rep T R G Stimpson), M J Tindall, P D Christophers; J P Wilkinson (rep A S Healey), M J S Dawson (rep A C T Gomarsall); J Leonard, S G Thompson, P J Vickery, M O Johnson (*captain*), B J Kay (rep D J Grewcock), L W Moody (rep L B N Dallaglio), R A Hill, N A Back
England Scorers *Tries:* Greenwood (2), Cohen, Back, Hill, Dallaglio, Christophers (penalty try) *Conversions:* Gomarsall (2), Stimpson (2), Wilkinson, Dawson *Penalty Goals:* Wilkinson (2)

CAP 14: WON 25-17 v FRANCE, 15th February 2003, Twickenham
England: J T Robinson; D D Luger, W J H Greenwood, C C Hodgson, B C Cohen; J P Wilkinson, A C T Gomarsall; J Leonard (rep G C Rowntree – temp rep M P Regan), S G Thompson, J M White, M O Johnson (*captain*), B J Kay (rep D J Grewcock), L W Moody (rep L B N Dallaglio), R A Hill, N A Back
England Scorers *Try:* Robinson   *Conversion:* Wilkinson   *Penalty Goals:* Wilkinson (5) *Dropped Goal:* Wilkinson

CAP 15: WON 43-9 v WALES, 23rd August 2003, Millennium Stadium, Cardiff
England: D G R Scarbrough; D D Luger (rep O J Smith), J D Noon, S R Abbott, J D Simpson-Daniel; A D King (rep D J H Walder), A C T Gomarsall; J Leonard (*captain*), M P Regan (rep D E West), J M White (rep W R Green), D J Grewcock, S D Shaw (temp rep S W Borthwick), M E Corry, J P R Worsley, L W Moody (rep A Sanderson)
England Scorers *Tries:* Moody, Luger, Worsley, Abbott, West *Conversions:* King (2), Walder *Penalty Goals:* King (3) *Dropped Goal:* King

CAP 16: LOST 16-17 v FRANCE, 30th August 2003, Stade Vélodrome, Marseille
England: I R Balshaw (rep J D Noon); O J Lewsey, O J Smith, M J Tindall (rep A C T Gomarsall), B C Cohen (temp rep J D Noon); P J Grayson, A S Healey; G C Rowntree (temp rep J Leonard), D E West (*captain*) (rep S G Thompson), J M White (rep J Leonard), S W Borthwick (rep S D Shaw), D J Grewcock, M E Corry, A Sanderson, L W Moody
England Scorers *Try:* Tindall   *Conversion:* Grayson   *Penalty Goals:* Grayson (3)

CAP 17: WON 45-14 v FRANCE, 6th September 2003, Twickenham

England: J T Robinson; I R Balshaw, W J H Greenwood, S R Abbott (rep O J Lewsey), B C Cohen (temp rep O J Lewsey); J P Wilkinson (rep P J Grayson), K P P Bracken (rep M J S Dawson); T J Woodman, S G Thompson (rep D E West), J M White (rep J Leonard), M O Johnson (*captain*) (rep S D Shaw), B J Kay, R A Hill, M E Corry (rep L W Moody – temp rep D E West), N A Back

England Scorers *Tries:* Cohen (2), Robinson, Balshaw, Lewsey *Conversions:* Wilkinson (3), Grayson *Penalty Goals:* Wilkinson (4)

CAP 18: WON 84-6 v GEORGIA, 12th October 2003, Subiaco Oval, Perth

England: J T Robinson; O J Lewsey, W J H Greenwood, M J Tindall (rep D D Luger), B C Cohen; J P Wilkinson (rep P J Grayson), M J S Dawson (rep A C T Gomarsall); T J Woodman (temp rep J Leonard), S G Thompson (rep M P Regan), P J Vickery (rep J Leonard), M O Johnson (*captain*), B J Kay, R A Hill (rep L W Moody), L B N Dallaglio, N A Back

England Scorers *Tries:* Greenwood (2), Cohen (2), Robinson, Tindall, Dawson, Thompson, Dallaglio, Back, Luger, Regan *Conversions:* Wilkinson (5), Grayson (4) *Penalty Goals:* Wilkinson (2)

CAP 19: WON 25-6 v SOUTH AFRICA, 18th October 2003, Subiaco Oval, Perth

England: J T Robinson; O J Lewsey, W J H Greenwood, M J Tindall (rep D D Luger), B C Cohen; J P Wilkinson, K P P Bracken; T J Woodman (rep J Leonard), S G Thompson, P J Vickery, M O Johnson (*captain*), B J Kay, L W Moody, L B N Dallaglio, N A Back (temp rep J P R Worsley)

England Scorers *Try:* Greenwood *Conversion:* Wilkinson *Penalty Goals:* Wilkinson (4) *Dropped Goals:* Wilkinson (2)

CAP 20: WON 35-22 v SAMOA, 26th October 2003, Telstra Dome, Melbourne

England: J T Robinson; I R Balshaw, S R Abbott (rep M J Catt), M J Tindall, B C Cohen; J P Wilkinson, M J S Dawson; J Leonard, M P Regan (rep S G Thompson), J M White (rep P J Vickery), M O Johnson (*captain*), B J Kay, J P R Worsley (rep L W Moody), L B N Dallaglio, N A Back

England Scorers *Tries*: Back, penalty try, Balshaw, Vickery *Conversions*: Wilkinson (3) *Penalty Goals*: Wilkinson (2) *Dropped Goal*: Wilkinson

CAP 21: WON 111-13 v URUGUAY, 2nd November 2003, Suncorp Stadium, Brisbane

England: O J Lewsey; I R Balshaw (rep J T Robinson), S R Abbott, M J Catt, D D Luger; P J Grayson (rep W J H Greenwood), A C T Gomarsall (rep K P P Bracken); J Leonard, D E West, P J Vickery (*captain*) (rep J M White), M E Corry (rep M O Johnson), D J Grewcock, J P R Worsley, L B N Dallaglio, L W Moody

England Scorers *Tries*: Lewsey (5), Balshaw (2), Robinson (2), Catt (2), Gomarsall (2), Moody, Luger, Abbott, Greenwood *Conversions*: Grayson (11), Catt (2)

CAP 22: WON 28-17 v WALES, 9th November 2003, Suncorp Stadium, Brisbane

England: J T Robinson; D D Luger (rep M J Catt), W J H Greenwood (rep S R Abbott), M J Tindall, B C Cohen; J P Wilkinson, M J S Dawson (rep K P P Bracken); J Leonard (rep T J Woodman), S G Thompson, P J Vickery, M O Johnson (*captain*), B J Kay, L W Moody, L B N Dallaglio, N A Back

England Scorers *Try*: Greenwood *Conversion*: Wilkinson *Penalty Goals*: Wilkinson (6) *Dropped Goal*: Wilkinson

CAP 23: WON 24-7 v FRANCE, 16th November 2003, Telstra Stadium, Sydney

England: O J Lewsey; J T Robinson, W J H Greenwood, M J Catt (rep M J Tindall), B C Cohen; J P Wilkinson, M J S Dawson (rep K P P Bracken); T J Woodman (rep J Leonard), S G Thompson (rep D E West), P J Vickery (temp rep J Leonard), M O Johnson (*captain*), B J Kay, R A Hill (rep L W Moody), L B N Dallaglio, N A Back

England Scorer *Penalty Goals:* Wilkinson (5) *Dropped Goals:* Wilkinson (3)

CAP 24: WON 20-17 v AUSTRALIA, 22nd November 2003, Telstra Stadium, Sydney

England: J T Robinson; O J Lewsey (rep I R Balshaw), W J H Greenwood, M J Tindall (rep M J Catt), B C Cohen; J P Wilkinson, M J S Dawson; T J Woodman, S G Thompson, P J Vickery (rep J Leonard), M O Johnson (*captain*), B J Kay, R A Hill (rep L W Moody), L B N Dallaglio, N A Back

England Scorers *Try:* Robinson *Penalty Goals:* Wilkinson (4) *Dropped Goal:* Wilkinson

CAP 25: WON 70-0 v CANADA, 13th November 2004, Twickenham

England: J T Robinson (*captain*) (rep B C Cohen); M J Cueto, H R Paul, M J Tindall, O J Lewsey; C C Hodgson (rep W J H Greenwood), A C T Gomarsall; G C Rowntree, S G Thompson (rep A J Titterrell), J M White (rep A J Sheridan), D J Grewcock (rep B J Kay), S W Borthwick (rep H D Vyvyan), L W Moody, M E Corry, A R Hazell

England Scorers: *Tries:* Robinson (3), Cueto (2), Lewsey (2), Tindall, Hodgson, Moody, Greenwood, Vyvyan *Conversions:* Paul (3), Hodgson (2)

CAP 26: WON 32-16 v SOUTH AFRICA, 20th November 2004, Twickenham

England: J T Robinson (*captain*); M J Cueto, H R Paul (rep W J H Greenwood), M J Tindall, O J Lewsey; C C Hodgson, A C T Gomarsall (rep H A Ellis); G C Rowntree, S G Thompson, J M White, D J Grewcock, S W Borthwick (rep B J Kay), J P R Worsley (rep A R Hazell), M E Corry, L W Moody (temp rep A R Hazell)
England Scorers: *Tries:* Cueto, Hodgson *Conversions:* Hodgson (2) *Penalty Goals:* Hodgson (5) *Dropped Goal:* Hodgson

CAP 27: LOST 19-21 v AUSTRALIA, 27th November 2004, Twickenham

England: J T Robinson (*captain*); M J Cueto (rep B C Cohen), H R Paul (rep W J H Greenwood), M J Tindall, O J Lewsey; C C Hodgson (rep H A Ellis), A C T Gomarsall; G C Rowntree, S G Thompson, J M White, D J Grewcock, S W Borthwick, J P R Worsley, M E Corry, L W Moody
England Scorers: *Tries:* Cueto, Lewsey, Moody *Conversions:* Tindall (2)

CAP 28: LOST 17-18 v FRANCE, 13th February 2005, Twickenham

England: J T Robinson (*captain*); M J Cueto (rep B C Cohen), J D Noon, O J Barkley, O J Lewsey; C C Hodgson, H A Ellis (rep M J S Dawson); G C Rowntree, S G Thompson, P J Vickery, D J Grewcock, B J Kay, J P R Worsley, M E Corry (temp rep A R Hazell), L W Moody
England Scorers: *Tries:* Barkley, Lewsey *Conversions:* Hodgson (2) *Penalty Goal:* Hodgson

CAP 29: LOST 13-19 v IRELAND, 27th February 2005, Lansdowne Road, Dublin

England: J T Robinson (*captain*); M J Cueto, J D Noon, O J Barkley, O

J Lewsey; C C Hodgson, H A Ellis (rep M J S Dawson); G C Rowntree, S G Thompson, M J H Stevens, D J Grewcock, B J Kay, J P R Worsley, M E Corry, L W Moody

England Scorers: *Try:* Corry *Conversion:* Hodgson *Penalty Goal:* Hodgson *Dropped Goal:* Hodgson

CAP 30: WON 39-7 v ITALY, 12th March 2005, Twickenham

England: I R Balshaw; M J Cueto, J D Noon (rep O J Smith), O J Barkley, O J Lewsey; C C Hodgson (rep A J Goode), H A Ellis (rep M J S Dawson); G C Rowntree (rep D C S Bell), S G Thompson (rep A J Titterrell), M J H Stevens, D J Grewcock (rep S W Borthwick), B J Kay, J P R Worsley (rep A R Hazell), M E Corry (*captain*), L W Moody

England Scorers: *Tries:* Cueto (3), Balshaw, Thompson, Hazell *Conversions:* Hodgson (2), Goode *Penalty Goal:* Hodgson

CAP 31: WON 43-22 v SCOTLAND, 19th March 2005, Twickenham

England: I R Balshaw (rep O J Smith); M J Cueto, J D Noon, O J Barkley, O J Lewsey; C C Hodgson (rep A J Goode), H A Ellis (rep M J S Dawson); M J S Stevens, S G Thompson (rep A J Titterrell), D C S Bell (rep M A Worsley), D J Grewcock, B J Kay (rep S W Borthwick), J P R Worsley, M E Corry (*captain*), L W Moody (rep A R Hazell)

England Scorers: *Tries:* Noon (3), Cueto, Lewsey, Ellis, Worsley *Conversions:* Hodgson (4)

CAP 32: WON 26-16 v AUSTRALIA, 12th November 2005, Twickenham

England: O J Lewsey; M J Cueto (temp rep M C van Gisbergen), J D Noon, M J Tindall, B C Cohen; C C Hodgson (rep O J Barkley), M J S Dawson; A J Sheridan, S G Thompson, P J Vickery, S W Borthwick, D J Grewcock, P H Sanderson, M E Corry (*captain*), L W Moody

England Scorers: *Tries:* Cueto, Cohen *Conversions:* Hodgson, Barkley *Penalty Goals:* Hodgson (2), Barkley *Dropped Goal:* Hodgson

CAP 33: LOST 19-23 v NEW ZEALAND, 19th November 2005, Twickenham
England: O J Lewsey; M J Cueto, J D Noon, M J Tindall, B C Cohen; C C Hodgson, M J S Dawson; A J Sheridan (rep M J H Stevens), S G Thompson, P J Vickery, S W Borthwick, D J Grewcock, P H Sanderson, M E Corry (*captain*), L W Moody
England Scorers: *Try:* Corry *Conversion:* Hodgson *Penalty Goals:* Hodgson (4)

CAP 34: WON 40-3 v SAMOA, 26th November 2005, Twickenham
England: O J Lewsey (rep T W Varndell); M J Cueto, J D Simpson-Daniel (rep O J Barkley), M J Tindall, T M D Voyce; C C Hodgson, H A Ellis; A J Sheridan (rep P T Freshwater), S G Thompson (rep L A Mears), M J H Stevens, S W Borthwick, L P Deacon (rep S D Shaw), P H Sanderson, M E Corry (*captain*) (rep J Forrester), L W Moody
England Scorers: *Tries:* Voyce (2), Hodgson, Ellis, Varndell *Conversions:* Hodgson (3) *Penalty Goals:* Hodgson (3)

CAP 35: WON 47-13 v WALES, 4th February 2006, Twickenham
England: O J Lewsey (rep T M D Voyce); M J Cueto, J D Noon, M J Tindall, B C Cohen; C C Hodgson (rep A J Goode), H A Ellis (rep M J S Dawson); A J Sheridan (rep J M White), S G Thompson (rep L A Mears), M J H Stevens, S W Borthwick, D J Grewcock (rep S D Shaw), J P R Worsley (temp rep L B N Dallaglio), M E Corry (*captain*) (rep L B N Dallaglio), L W Moody
England Scorers *Tries:* Cueto, Moody, Tindall, Dallaglio, Dawson, Voyce *Conversions:* Hodgson (2), Goode (2) *Penalty Goals:* Hodgson (3)

CAP 36: WON 31-16 v ITALY, 11th February 2006, Stadio Flaminio, Rome

England: T M D Voyce; M J Cueto, J D Noon, M J Tindall (rep J D Simpson-Daniel), B C Cohen; C C Hodgson, H A Ellis (rep M J S Dawson); A J Sheridan (rep J M White), S G Thompson (rep L A Mears), M J H Stevens, S W Borthwick, D J Grewcock (rep S D Shaw), J P R Worsley (rep L B N Dallaglio), M E Corry (*captain*), L W Moody
England Scorers *Tries:* Tindall, Hodgson, Cueto, Simpson-Daniel *Conversions:* Hodgson (4) *Penalty Goal:* Hodgson

CAP 37: LOST 12-18 v SCOTLAND, 25th February 2006, Murrayfield

England: O J Lewsey; M J Cueto, J D Noon, M J Tindall, B C Cohen; C C Hodgson, H A Ellis (rep M J S Dawson); A J Sheridan (rep P T Freshwater), S G Thompson, J M White, S W Borthwick, D J Grewcock (rep S D Shaw), J P R Worsley, M E Corry (*captain*) (rep L B N Dallaglio), L W Moody
England Scorer *Penalty Goals:* Hodgson (4)

CAP 38: LOST 6-31 v FRANCE, 12th March 2006, Stade de France, Paris

England: O J Lewsey; M J Cueto, J D Noon, M J Tindall (rep T M D Voyce), B C Cohen; C C Hodgson (rep A J Goode), M J S Dawson (rep H A Ellis); M J H Stevens (rep A J Sheridan), S G Thompson (rep L A Mears), J M White, S W Borthwick, D J Grewcock (rep S D Shaw), J P R Worsley (rep L B N Dallaglio), M E Corry (*captain*), L W Moody
England Scorers *Penalty Goals:* Hodgson, Goode

CAP 39: LOST 24-28 v IRELAND, 18th March 2006, Twickenham

England: T M D Voyce; M J Cueto, J D Noon (rep M J Tindall), S R Abbott, B C Cohen; A J Goode, H A Ellis (rep M J S Dawson); A J Sheridan (rep P T Freshwater), L A Mears (rep S G Thompson), J M

White, S W Borthwick, S D Shaw (rep D J Grewcock), J P R Worsley, M E Corry (*captain*), L W Moody

England Scorers *Tries:* Noon, Borthwick *Conversion:* Goode *Penalty Goals:* Goode (4)

CAP 40: LOST 3-34 v AUSTRALIA, 11th June 2006, Telstra Stadium, Sydney

England: I R Balshaw; T W Varndell, M J M Tait, M J Catt (rep J D Noon), T M D Voyce; O J Barkley (rep A J Goode), P C Richards (rep N P J Walshe); G C Rowntree (rep T A N Payne), L A Mears (rep G S Chuter), J M White, L P Deacon, A T Brown (rep C M Jones), M B Lund (rep J P R Worsley), P H Sanderson (*captain*), L W Moody

England Scorer *Penalty Goal:* Barkley

CAP 41: LOST 20-41 v NEW ZEALAND, 5th November 2006, Twickenham

England: I R Balshaw; P H Sackey, J D Noon, A O Allen, B C Cohen; C C Hodgson, S A Perry (rep P C Richards); A J Sheridan, G S Chuter (rep L A Mears), J M White, D J Grewcock, B J Kay, M E Corry (*captain*), P H Sanderson (rep M B Lund), L W Moody

England Scorers *Tries:* Noon, Cohen, Perry *Conversion:* Hodgson *Penalty Goal:* Hodgson

CAP 42: LOST 18-25 v ARGENTINA, 11th November 2006, Twickenham

England: I R Balshaw; P H Sackey (rep O J Lewsey), J D Noon, A O Allen, B C Cohen; C C Hodgson (rep T G A L Flood), S A Perry (rep P C Richards); P T Freshwater, G S Chuter (rep L A Mears), J M White, D J Grewcock (rep T P Palmer), B J Kay, M E Corry (*captain*), P H Sanderson (rep M B Lund), L W Moody (temp rep M B Lund)

England Scorers *Tries:* Balshaw, Sackey *Conversion:* Hodgson *Penalty Goals:* Hodgson, Flood

CAP 43: WON 23-21 v SOUTH AFRICA, 18th November 2006, Twickenham

England: O J Lewsey; M J Cueto, M J M Tait, J D Noon, B C Cohen; C C Hodgson (rep A J Goode), P C Richards (rep S A Perry); A J Sheridan (rep P J Vickery), G S Chuter (rep L A Mears), J M White, T P Palmer, B J Kay (rep C M Jones), J P R Worsley, M E Corry (*captain*), P H Sanderson (rep L W Moody)

England Scorers *Tries:* Cueto, Vickery *Conversions:* Goode (2) *Penalty Goals:* Hodgson (2), Goode

CAP 44: LOST 14-25 v SOUTH AFRICA, 25th November 2006, Twickenham

England: O J Lewsey; M J Cueto, M J M Tait, J D Noon, B C Cohen; A J Goode (rep T G A L Flood), P C Richards (rep S A Perry); P J Vickery, L A Mears (rep G S Chuter), J M White, T P Palmer (rep B J Kay), C M Jones, J P R Worsley, M E Corry (*captain*), P H Sanderson (rep L W Moody)

England Scorers *Try:* Cueto *Penalty Goals:* Goode (3)

CAP 45: WON 62-5 v WALES, 4th August 2007, Twickenham

England: M J M Tait; D Strettle, D J Hipkiss, A D Farrell (temp rep T G A L Flood), J T Robinson; J P Wilkinson, S A Perry; A J Sheridan, M P Regan (rep G S Chuter), P J Vickery (*captain*) (rep M J H Stevens), S D Shaw, S W Borthwick, M E Corry (rep L W Moody), N J Easter (rep L B N Dallaglio), J P R Worsley

England Scorers *Tries:* Easter (4), Robinson, Tait, Borthwick, Dallaglio, Perry *Conversions:* Wilkinson (7) *Penalty Goal:* Wilkinson

CAP 46: WON 28-10 v UNITED STATES, 8th September 2007, Stade Félix Bollaert, Lens

England: M J Cueto; O J Lewsey, J D Noon, M J Catt (rep A Farrell), J T Robinson (rep M J M Tait); O J Barkley, S A Perry (rep P C Richards);

313

A J Sheridan, M P Regan (rep G S Chuter), P J Vickery (*captain*) (rep M J H Stevens), S D Shaw (rep M E Corry), B J Kay, J P R Worsley (rep L W Moody), L B N Dallaglio, T Rees

England Scorers *Tries*: Robinson, Barkley, Rees *Conversions:* Barkley (2) *Penalty Goals*: Barkley (3)

CAP 47: LOST 0-36 v SOUTH AFRICA, 14th September 2007, Stade de France, Paris

England: J T Robinson (rep M J M Tait); O J Lewsey, J D Noon (rep P C Richards), A D Farrell, P H Sackey; M J Catt, S A Perry (rep A C T Gomarsall); A J Sheridan (rep P T Freshwater), M P Regan (rep G S Chuter), M J H Stevens, S D Shaw (rep S W Borthwick), B J Kay, M E Corry (*captain*), N J Easter, T Rees (rep L W Moody)

CAP 48: WON 44-22 v SAMOA, 22nd September 2007, Stade de la Beaujoire, Nantes

England: O J Lewsey; P H Sackey, M J M Tait (rep D J Hipkiss), O J Barkley, M J Cueto; J P Wilkinson, A C T Gomarsall; A J Sheridan (rep P T Freshwater), G S Chuter, M J H Stevens, S D Shaw (rep S W Borthwick), B J Kay, M E Corry (*captain*), N J Easter, J P R Worsley (rep L W Moody)

England Scorers *Tries*: Corry (2), Sackey (2) *Conversions:* Wilkinson (3) *Penalty Goals*: Wilkinson (4) *Dropped Goals:* Wilkinson (2)

CAP 49: WON 36-20 v TONGA, 28th September 2007, Parc des Princes, Paris

England: O J Lewsey; P H Sackey (rep D J Hipkiss), M J M Tait, O J Barkley (rep A D Farrell), M J Cueto (rep P C Richards); J P Wilkinson, A C T Gomarsall; A J Sheridan, G S Chuter (rep L A Mears), M J H Stevens (rep P J Vickery), S W Borthwick, B J Kay, M E Corry (*captain*) (rep L B N Dallaglio), N J Easter, L W Moody

England Scorers *Tries*: Sackey (2), Tait, Farrell *Conversions:* Wilkinson (2) *Penalty Goals*: Wilkinson (2) *Dropped Goals:* Wilkinson (2)

CAP 50: WON 12-10 v AUSTRALIA, 6th October 2007, Stade Vélodrome, Marseille

England: J T Robinson; P H Sackey, M Tait, M J Catt (rep T Flood), O J Lewsey; J P Wilkinson, A C T Gomarsall (temp rep P C Richards); A J Sheridan, M P Regan (rep G S Chuter), P J Vickery (*captain*) (rep M J H Stevens), S D Shaw, B J Kay, M E Corry, N J Easter (rep L B N Dallaglio), L W Moody (rep J P R Worsley)

England Scorer *Penalty Goals*: Wilkinson (4)

CAP 51: WON 14-9 v FRANCE, 13th October 2007, Stade de France, Paris

England: J T Robinson; P H Sackey, M Tait, M J Catt (rep T Flood), O J Lewsey (rep D Hipkiss); J P Wilkinson, A C T Gomarsall (rep P C Richards); A J Sheridan, M P Regan (rep G S Chuter), P J Vickery (*captain*) (rep M J H Stevens), S D Shaw, B J Kay, M E Corry, N J Easter (rep L B N Dallaglio), L W Moody (rep J P R Worsley)

England Scorers *Try*: Lewsey *Penalty Goals*: Wilkinson (2) *Dropped Goal*: Wilkinson

CAP 52: LOST 6-15 v SOUTH AFRICA, 20th October 2007, Stade de France, Paris

England: J T Robinson (rep D J Hipkiss); P H Sackey, M J M Tait, M J Catt (rep T G A L Flood), M J Cueto; J P Wilkinson, A C T Gomarsall; A J Sheridan, M P Regan (rep G S Chuter), P J Vickery (*captain*) (rep M J H Stevens), S D Shaw, B J Kay, M E Corry, N J Easter (rep L B N Dallaglio), L W Moody (rep J P R Worsley; rep P C Richards)

England Scorer *Penalty Goals*: Wilkinson (2)

CAP 53: LOST 19-26 v WALES, 2nd February 2008, Twickenham

England: I R Balshaw; P H Sackey, M J Tindall (rep D J Cipriani), T G A L Flood, D Strettle (rep L P I Vainikolo); J P Wilkinson, A C T Gomarsall; A J Sheridan, M P Regan (rep L A Mears), P J Vickery

315

(captain) (rep M J H Stevens), S D Shaw, S W Borthwick, J A W Haskell, L J W Narraway, L W Moody (rep T Rees; rep B J Kay)

England Scorers *Try:* Flood *Conversion:* Wilkinson *Penalty Goals:* Wilkinson (3) *Dropped Goal:* Wilkinson

CAP 54: LOST 9-18 v AUSTRALIA, 7th November 2009, Twickenham
England: Y C C Monye; M J Cueto, D J Hipkiss (rep A O Erinle), S J J Geraghty, M A Banahan; J P Wilkinson, D S Care (rep P K Hodgson); T A N Payne, S G Thompson (rep D M Hartley), D G Wilson (rep D S C Bell), L P Deacon (rep C L Lawes), S W Borthwick *(captain)*, T R Croft, J S Crane (rep J A W Haskell), L W Moody

England Scorer *Penalty Goals:* Wilkinson (2) *Dropped Goal:* Wilkinson

CAP 55: WON 16-9 v ARGENTINA, 14th November 2009, Twickenham
England: Y C C Monye; M J Cueto, D J Hipkiss, S J J Geraghty, M A Banahan; J P Wilkinson (rep A J Goode), P K Hodgson (rep D S Care); T A N Payne (rep P P L Doran-Jones), D M Hartley (rep S G Thompson), D S C Bell, L P Deacon, S W Borthwick *(captain)*, T R Croft (rep J P R Worsley), J A W Haskell, L W Moody

England Scorers *Try:* Banahan *Conversion:* Wilkinson *Penalty Goals:* Wilkinson (2) *Dropped Goal:* Wilkinson

CAP 56: LOST 6-19 v NEW ZEALAND, 21st November 2009, Twickenham
England: M J Cueto; M A Banahan (rep M J M Tait), D J Hipkiss, A O Erinle (rep S J J Geraghty), Y C C Monye; J P Wilkinson, P K Hodgson (rep D S Care); T A N Payne (rep D S C Bell), D M Hartley (rep S G Thompson), D S C Bell (rep D G Wilson), S D Shaw (rep L P Deacon), S W Borthwick *(captain)*, J P R Worsley (rep T R Croft), J A W Haskell, L W Moody

England Scorer *Penalty Goals:* Wilkinson (2)

CAP 57: WON 30-17 v WALES, 6th February 2010, Twickenham

England: D A Armitage; M J Cueto, M J M Tait, T G A L Flood (rep D J Hipkiss), Y C C Monye; J P Wilkinson, D S Care (rep P K Hodgson); T A N Payne, D M Hartley (rep S G Thompson), D G Wilson (rep D R Cole), S D Shaw (rep L P Deacon), S W Borthwick (*captain*), J A W Haskell, N J Easter, L W Moody (rep S E Armitage)

England Scorers *Tries:* Haskell (2), Care *Conversions:* Wilkinson (3) *Penalty Goals:* Wilkinson (3)

CAP 58: WON 17-12 v ITALY, 14th February 2010, Stadio Flaminio, Rome

England: D A Armitage; M J Cueto, M J M Tait, R J Flutey, Y C C Monye; J P Wilkinson, D S Care (rep P K Hodgson); T A N Payne (rep M J Mullan), D M Hartley (rep S G Thompson), D R Cole (rep D G Wilson), S D Shaw (rep L P Deacon), S W Borthwick (*captain*), J A W Haskell, N J Easter, L W Moody (rep S E Armitage)

England Scorers *Try:* Tait *Penalty Goals:* Wilkinson (3) *Dropped Goal:* Wilkinson

CAP 59: LOST 16-20 v IRELAND, 27th February 2010, Twickenham

England: D A Armitage (rep B J Foden); M J Cueto, M J M Tait, R J Flutey, Y C C Monye; J P Wilkinson, D S Care (rep P K Hodgson); T A N Payne, D M Hartley (rep L A Mears), D R Cole (rep D G Wilson), S D Shaw (rep L P Deacon), S W Borthwick (*captain*), J A W Haskell, N J Easter, L W Moody (rep J P R Worsley)

England Scorers *Try:* Cole *Conversion:* Wilkinson *Penalty Goals:* Wilkinson (2) *Dropped Goal:* Wilkinson

CAP 60: DRAWN 15-15 v SCOTLAND, 13th March 2010, Murrayfield

England: D A Armitage (rep B J Foden); M J Cueto, M J M Tait, R J Flutey, Y C C Monye (rep B R Youngs); J P Wilkinson (rep T G A L Flood), D S Care; T A N Payne, D M Hartley (rep S G Thompson),

D R Cole (rep D G Wilson), L P Deacon (rep C L Lawes), S W Borthwick (*captain*), J A W Haskell (rep L W Moody), N J Easter, J P R Worsley

England Scorers *Penalty Goals:* Wilkinson (3), Flood (2)

CAP 61: LOST 10-12 v FRANCE, 20th March 2010, Stade de France, Paris

England: B J Foden; M J Cueto, M J Tindall (rep M J M Tait), R J Flutey (rep J P Wilkinson), C J Ashton; T G A L Flood, D S Care; T A N Payne (rep D R Cole), D M Hartley (rep S G Thompson), D R Cole (rep D G Wilson), S D Shaw (rep T P Palmer), L P Deacon, J P R Worsley (rep J A W Haskell), N J Easter, L W Moody (*captain*)

England Scorers *Try:* Foden *Conversion:* Flood *Penalty Goal:* Wilkinson

CAP 62: LOST 17-27 v AUSTRALIA, 12th June 2010, Subiaco Oval, Perth

England: B J Foden; M J Cueto, M J Tindall (rep J P Wilkinson), S E Hape, C J Ashton; T G A L Flood (rep M J M Tait), D S Care (rep B R Youngs); T A N Payne (rep D G Wilson), S G Thompson (rep G S Chuter), D R Cole, S D Shaw (rep C L Lawes), T P Palmer, T R Croft, N J Easter, L W Moody (*captain*) (rep J A W Haskell)

England Scorers *Tries:* penalty (2) *Conversions:* Flood (2) *Penalty Goal:* Flood

CAP 63: WON 21-20 v AUSTRALIA, 19th June 2010, ANZ Stadium, Sydney

England: B J Foden; M J Cueto, M J Tindall (rep D A Armitage), S E Hape, C J Ashton; T G A L Flood (rep J P Wilkinson), B R Youngs (rep D S Care); T A N Payne (rep D G Wilson), S G Thompson (rep G S Chuter), D R Cole (temp rep D G Wilson), C L Lawes (rep S D Shaw), T P Palmer, T R Croft, N J Easter, L W Moody (*captain*)

England Scorers *Tries:* Ashton, Youngs *Conversion:* Flood *Penalty Goals:* Flood (2), Wilkinson

CAP 64: LOST 16-26 v NEW ZEALAND, 6th November 2010, Twickenham

England: B J Foden; C J Ashton, M J Tindall, S E Hape, M J Cueto (rep D A Armitage); T G A L Flood, B R Youngs (rep D S Care); A J Sheridan (rep D G Wilson), S G Thompson (rep D M Hartley), D R Cole, C L Lawes, T P Palmer (rep D M J Attwood), T R Croft, N J Easter, L W Moody (*captain*) (rep C H Fourie)

England Scorers *Try:* Hartley *Conversion:* Flood *Penalty Goals:* Flood (3)

CAP 65: WON 35-18 v AUSTRALIA, 13th November 2010, Twickenham

England: B J Foden; C J Ashton, M J Tindall (rep D A Armitage), S E Hape, M J Cueto; T G A L Flood (rep C C Hodgson), B R Youngs (rep D S Care); A J Sheridan (rep D G Wilson), D M Hartley (rep S G Thompson), D R Cole, C L Lawes, T P Palmer (rep S D Shaw), T R Croft, N J Easter (rep C H Fourie), L W Moody (*captain*)

England Scorers *Tries:* Ashton (2) *Conversions:* Flood (2) *Penalty Goals:* Flood (7)

CAP 66: LOST 11-21 v SOUTH AFRICA, 27th November 2010, Twickenham

England: B J Foden; C J Ashton (rep M A Banahan), M J Tindall, S E Hape, M J Cueto; T G A L Flood (rep C C Hodgson), B R Youngs (rep D S Care); A J Sheridan, D M Hartley (rep S G Thompson), D R Cole (rep D G Wilson), C L Lawes (rep S D Shaw), T P Palmer, T R Croft (rep C H Fourie), N J Easter, L W Moody (*captain*)

England Scorers *Try:* Foden *Penalty Goals:* Flood (2)

CAP 67: WON 23-19 v WALES, 6th August 2011, Twickenham

England: D A Armitage; M A Banahan, E M Tuilagi (rep C D J Sharples), R J Flutey, M J Cueto; J P Wilkinson (rep C C Hodgson), D S Care (rep R E P Wigglesworth); A R Corbisiero (rep M J H Stevens), D M Hartley (rep L A Mears), M J H Stevens (rep D G Wilson), S D Shaw (rep M J Botha), T P Palmer, T R Croft, J A W Haskell, L W Moody (*captain*) (rep T A Wood)

England Scorers *Tries:* Haskell, Tuilagi *Conversions:* Wilkinson (2) *Penalty Goal:* Wilkinson *Dropped Goals:* Wilkinson (2)

CAP 68: WON 41–10 v GEORGIA, 18th September 2011, Otago Stadium, Dunedin

England: B J Foden; C J Ashton, E M Tuilagi (rep M A Banahan), S E Hape, D A Armitage; T G A L Flood, B R Youngs (rep J P M Simpson); M J H Stevens, D M Hartley (rep S G Thompson), D R Cole (rep A R Corbisiero), S D Shaw, T P Palmer, T A Wood, J A W Haskell, L W Moody (captain) (rep T R Croft)

England Scorers *Tries:* Hape (2), Ashton (2), Armitage, Tuilagi Conversions: Flood (4) *Penalty Goal:* Flood

CAP 69: WON 67–3 v ROMANIA, 24th September 2011, Otago Stadium, Dunedin

England: B J Foden (rep D A Armitage); C J Ashton, E M Tuilagi, M J Tindall, M J Cueto; J P Wilkinson (rep T G A L Flood), B R Youngs (rep R E P Wigglesworth); A R Corbisiero, S G Thompson (rep L A Mears), D R Cole (rep D G Wilson), L P Deacon (rep S D Shaw), T P Palmer, T R Croft, J A W Haskell, L W Moody (*captain*) (rep T A Wood)

England Scorers *Tries:* Cueto (3), Ashton (3), Youngs, Foden, Tuilagi, Croft *Conversions:* Flood (4), Wilkinson (3) *Penalty Goal:* Wilkinson

CAP 70: WON 16–12 v SCOTLAND, 1st October 2011, Eden Park, Auckland
England: B J Foden; C J Ashton, E M Tuilagi, M J Tindall (rep T G A L Flood), D A Armitage; J P Wilkinson (rep M A Banahan), B R Youngs (rep R E P Wigglesworth); M J H Stevens (rep A R Corbisiero), S G Thompson (rep D M Hartley), D R Cole, L P Deacon, C L Lawes (rep T P Palmer), T R Croft, J A W Haskell (rep N J Easter), L W Moody (*captain*)
England Scorers *Try:* Ashton *Conversion:* Flood *Penalty Goals:* Wilkinson (2) *Dropped Goal:* Wilkinson

CAP 71: LOST 12–19 v FRANCE, 8th October 2011, Eden Park, Auckland
England: B J Foden; C J Ashton, E M Tuilagi, T G A L Flood, M J Cueto; J P Wilkinson (rep M A Banahan), B R Youngs (rep R E P Wigglesworth); M J H Stevens (rep A R Corbisiero), S G Thompson (rep D M Hartley), D R Cole, L P Deacon (rep S D Shaw), T P Palmer, T R Croft (rep C L Lawes), N J Easter, L W Moody (*captain*) (rep J A W Haskell)
England Scorers *Tries:* Foden, Cueto *Conversion:* Wilkinson

LEWIS MOODY'S CLUB CAREER

- Makes Leicester league debut aged 18 v Orrell in September 1996 playing in the back-row with John Wells and Dean Richards.
- Member of the Leicester Tigers squad that wins the English Premiership 1998-99, 1999-2000, 2000-01, 2001-02, 2006-07, 2008-09 and 2009-10.
- Member of the Leicester Tigers match-day squad for the 2001 Heineken Cup Final 34-30 win against Stade Français as an unused bench replacement. Plays for Leicester Tigers in the 2002 Heineken Cup Final 15-9 win against Munster.
- Joins Bath for the 2010-11 season.

INDEX